MW01679593

The Photographer's Guide to COLOR MANAGEMENT

Professional Techniques for Consistent Results

Phil Nelson

Amherst Media, Inc. ■ Buffalo, NY

Published by:
Amherst Media®
P.O. Box 586
Buffalo, N.Y. 14226
Fax: 716-874-4508
www.AmherstMedia.com

Publisher: Craig Alesse
Senior Editor/Production Manager: Michelle Perkins
Assistant Editor: Barbara A. Lynch-Johnt

ISBN-13: 978-1-58428-204-4
Library of Congress Control Number: 2006937282
Printed in Korea.
10 9 8 7 6 5 4 3 2 1

Table of Contents

Acknowledgments

This book is dedicated to my wife, Diane, who puts up with my obsessive behavior on a daily basis, and who has patiently supported me as I built my imaging business.

Just after leaving my job at Adobe Systems, I had the very good fortune of being introduced to a small company in Akron, OH, run by some very smart people who are dedicated to providing the highest quality support, service, and training to anyone struggling with managing color. I owe a large amount of thanks to Will Holland and Eric Harsh, founders of the Graphic Intelligence Agency (now X-Rite Color Services) for taking me in as a color consultant and entrusting me with many of their national seminars. Equal thanks go to Mark Gundlach, who never ceases to amaze me with his knowledge of color management. Thanks to Marc Aguilera, Nick Wilcox-Brown, and my good friend, Charlie Griswold, for their input.

And thanks to Livia, Ian, and Alex, who have finally accepted the fact that I will forever be taking their picture.

About the Author

Phil Nelson started his career in graphic design and film production at a time when computer graphics technology was very expensive and designers relied on T squares, hot wax, and rapidograph pens as standard tools. Phil understood earlier than most the value of technology to the graphic artist and started experimenting with one of the first Macintosh computers in 1984. After developing some computer expertise, Nelson was asked to provide input on graphic design and computers to Apple Computer. Nelson also provided input to Aldus Corporation on PageMaker, one of the first page-layout applications that helped launch the desktop publishing revolution.

Putting his design career on hold, Nelson was lured away by Apple Computer in 1986 to help communicate with the design community the benefits of computer technology in publishing. After ten years at Apple, he went on to Adobe Systems to manage major corporate clients in the advertising, publishing, and entertainment industries.

In 2004, Phil traded in his corporate suit for a camera bag and tripod and has built a business around photography and digital imaging. Nelson specializes in landscape, travel, and architectural photography. In addition to creating fine art images, Phil has produced images for numerous magazines, as well as corporate and private clients.

Nelson has also teamed up with GretagMacbeth Global Services (now owned by X-Rite), the services arm of one of the premier suppliers of color-management solutions. As a GretagMacbeth Color Expert™, Phil leads seminar, classroom, and on-site color training sessions across the United States and Europe. He often helps photographers transitioning to a digital workflow and serves as a consultant for businesses working out the tricky aspects of digital color management.

Phil lives with his wife, Diane, and three children in southern Connecticut. Phil's fine-art images can be seen at his web site, www.panelson.com.

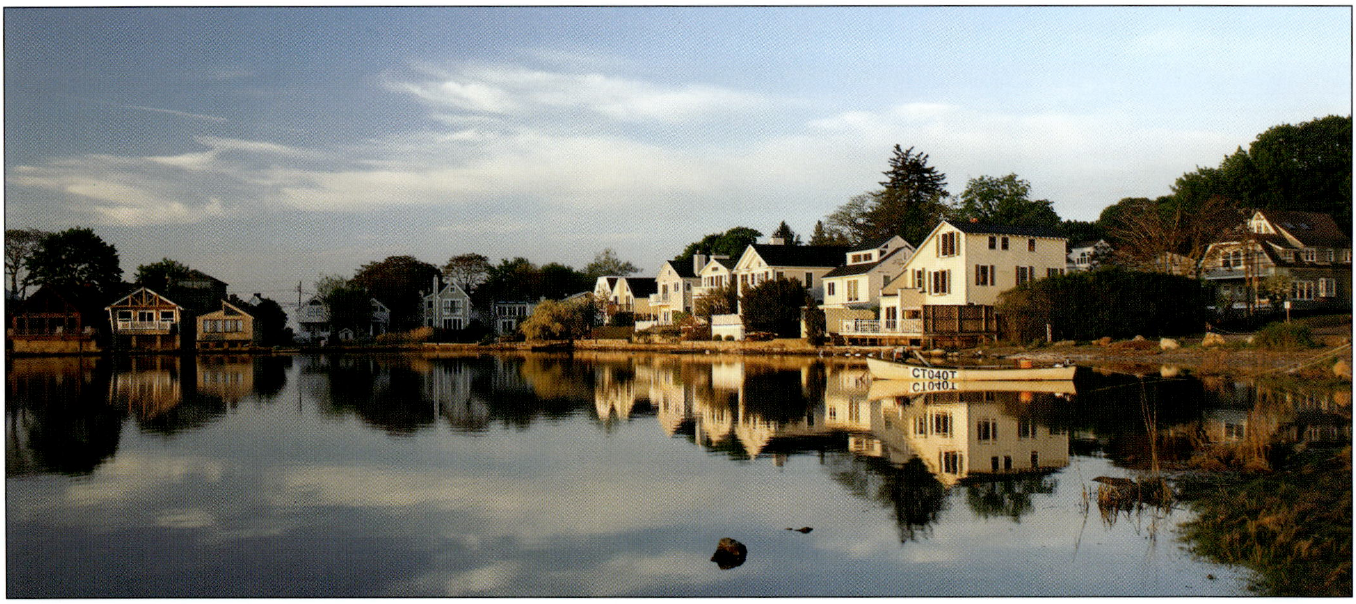

Figure 1—Sunrise, Connecticut coast.

Foreword

Color has changed a lot since I got into the business in 1992. Back then, photographers still took rolls of film to color labs, for instance. Without a doubt, the last ten years has seen its share of paradigm shifts in a field famous for its technological advances. That digital camera thing is right up there with the Daguerrotype. Color-management technology is back stage—it's more akin to the inventions of Kodachrome and Agfacolor, which introduced easy-to-use, stable processes for the making and fixing of color photographic images.

Anyway, the history makes for interesting college fare, but when I saw color management at work for the first time, I knew the world was about to change. I watched as a really high-end Barco was profiled and then watched it measure the same L*a*b values from within Photoshop—version 2.5.1. Crazy!

Today's color technology is a lot better and a lot easier to use. To get good color on a display you don't have to shell out seven grand for a Really Expensive Monitor. The rise of color management has perfectly coincided with the availability of digital cameras and printers. They go together like peas and carrots.

Understanding how to leverage color management will make your work easier, faster, and cheaper. This textbook on color will do just that. Phil manages something extraordinary in this book: he advances the knowledge of color management in photography without the condescension and obfuscation often found in other works on the subject. It's simple, neat, easy to read, and accessible. I admire that, and I'm sure you will too.

Will Holland
X-Rite Color Services
Akron, OH

Introduction

Back in the early 1980s you had to be in the design or publishing business to recognize terms like "font" or "kern." Today, the ubiquity of personal computers and word-processing applications has made these terms commonplace. As individuals tackled the arduous task of learning how to work with a personal computer, they also learned much of the terminology of publishing and typesetting, perhaps without even knowing it. Today, names like Helvetica are known to just about everyone who has spent any time with a PC, and terms like typeface, typestyle, and line spacing are as common as fleas on a dog. It will be interesting to see if the astounding popularity of digital photography will have the same impact on color management.

The Challenges of Digital Photography

Over the past five years, as digital photography has rolled over film photography like a tsunami, it has placed much of the image-processing responsibility back in the hands of the photographer. Handing film off to the lab for processing and printing has been replaced by uploading, ingesting, tagging, converting, color balancing, processing, scaling, and printing—not to mention image archiving. As photographers have made the transition from film to digital, it has become quite apparent that many of the benefits of digital photography are overshadowed by a demanding digital "workflow," the term used to describe the system of digital image management from capture, to output, to archiving, as well as the subsystems that make up the entire process. Without a well-defined and functioning process, moving tens, hundreds, and even thousands of digital images from camera, to computer, to print can be a very time-consuming undertaking.

Many of the benefits of digital photography are overshadowed by a demanding digital "workflow."

Digital photographers who have taken it upon themselves to master this process have had to tackle everything from how to assign a copyright to understanding the proper method for converting a RAW image. There are image ingestion workflows that involve renaming and applying metadata to files. There are RAW conversion workflows for turning camera RAW photographs into standard imaging files. There are image processing workflows, image sharpening workflows, printing workflows, archiving workflows. And, of course, there is the color-management workflow.

Building a Digital Photography Workflow

Just fifteen years ago, building a color-managed workflow was a costly and difficult process. It took a lot of time, effort, and smarts to learn and to im-

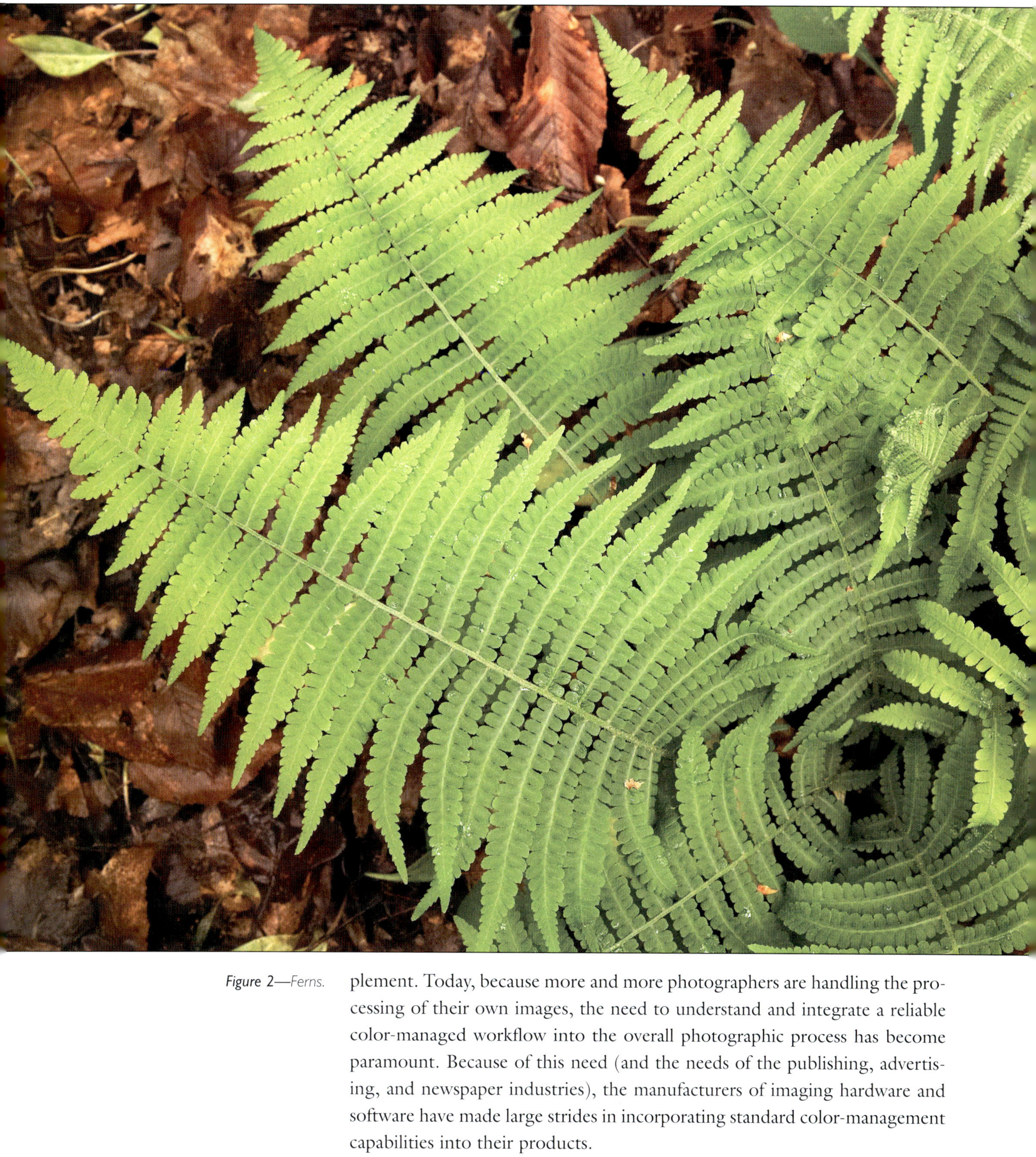

Figure 2—Ferns.

plement. Today, because more and more photographers are handling the processing of their own images, the need to understand and integrate a reliable color-managed workflow into the overall photographic process has become paramount. Because of this need (and the needs of the publishing, advertising, and newspaper industries), the manufacturers of imaging hardware and software have made large strides in incorporating standard color-management capabilities into their products.

In 1993, the International Color Consortium (ICC) was established by eight founding members. Today there are in excess of 65 member companies, and the ICC methodologies are the established industry standard for managing color in publishing, graphic arts, and photography. More and more, the installation and use of ICC color profiles is becoming commonplace. The accessibility of solutions for building a color-managed workflow, including creating custom profiles, is far greater today than it was ten years ago. Still, with all of this progress, color management is complicated. Understanding how to set up the workflow, which buttons to push and which buttons not to push, can be a mystery.

Understanding how to set up the workflow, which buttons to push and which buttons not to push, can be a mystery.

The more the need for accurate color spreads from the pro shooter to everyone clicking the shutter of their digital point-and-shoot cameras, the more the imaging manufacturers will seek to further integrate and simplify the color-management process, trying to make the complexity transparent to the masses. Just as typography has become a common aspect of personal computing, powerful digital imaging is now available to all. Because of this, we may see terms like "ICC profile" become as commonly recognized as the word "font." But, that time is not yet here.

Training, seminars, and books like this are still necessary to help dissolve the cloud of mystery that makes color management difficult to understand. This book intends point out those aspects of color management that are necessary in order to move a photograph all the way through the "workflow" with color intact. It is intended to answer common questions without sliding too far into the technical abyss, which is not always possible. And, it intends to help photographers incorporate color management as a standard, common, and almost invisible part of their everyday workflow and to help make terms like "out of gamut" as universally understood as "Zapf Dingbats."

1. Why Color Management?

Since the first affordable color printers, printing color images has been possible without having to consider "color management" at all. Often individuals were finding that their prints looked pretty good. So why bother? Is the hassle worth it? The emphatic answer is yes, and here are some things to consider that will help you understand why.

The Color Problem

All cameras, scanners, computer displays, software applications, and printing devices perceive, display, and render the same colors differently. If only one

Figure 3—Magnolia blossom.

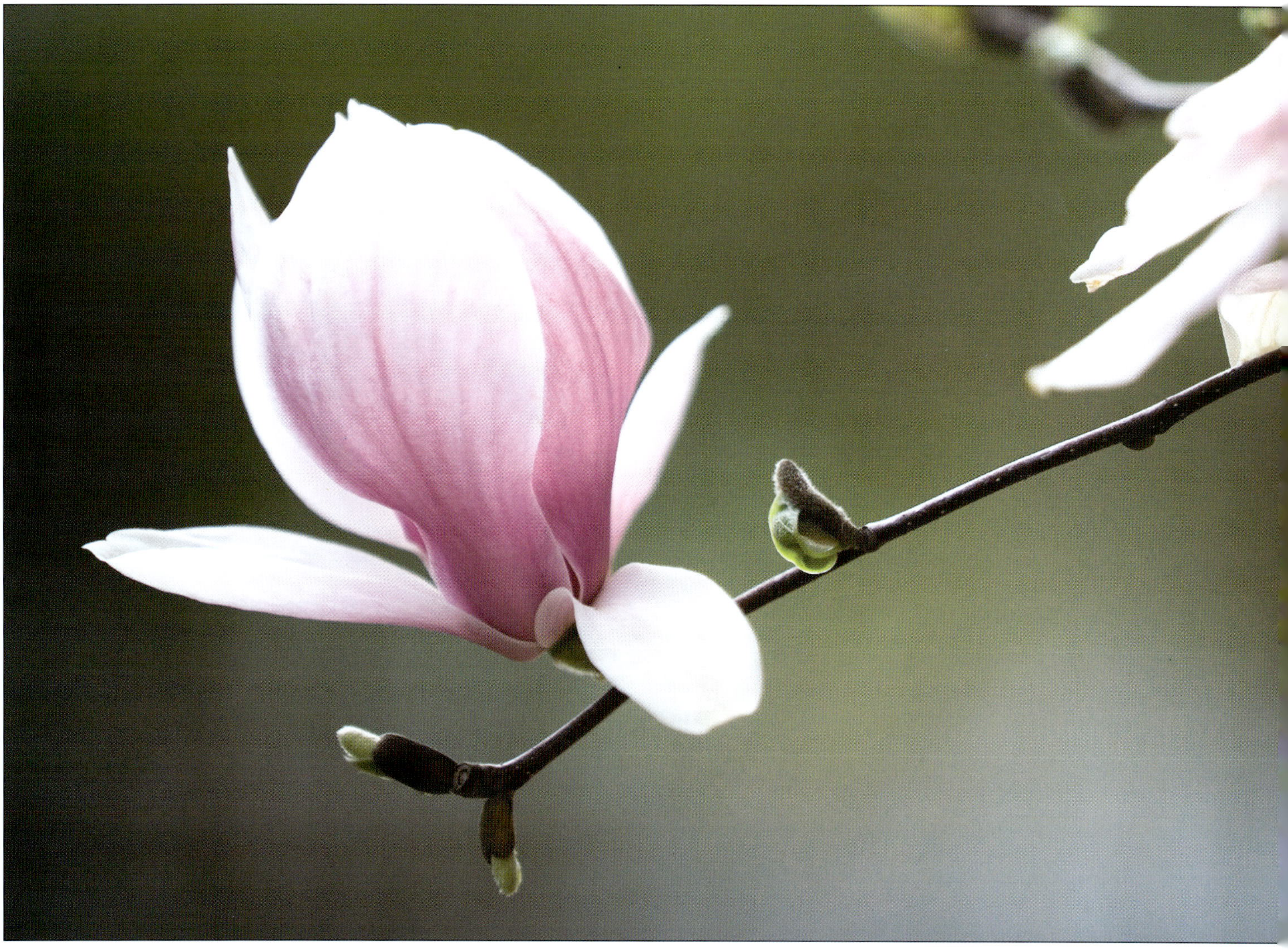

device existed in the photographic workflow, this would not be so much of a problem, but that is not the case. Images are typically moved from camera to editing application. They are viewed on a computer monitor and then sent to a printing device.

Since each of these devices can perceive, display, or render the same color differently, it is necessary to accurately translate the color as it moves from device to device. Without a defined method for color translation, controlling color from device to device and application to application can be very difficult and will produce unexpected and inconsistent results. The image on the computer display could look great with vivid, well-balanced colors, but when printed could look very different.

It is not uncommon for photographers to fall into the trap of altering what already looks great on screen in order to produce a good print. This can lead to numerous iterations of printing, image editing, printing again, editing again, etc.—until the print looks right. This is a huge waste of time, not to mention a waste of ink and paper. Rarely, if ever, does it produce a match between the computer screen and the printout; once the print looks correct, the image on the display usually does not.

Color-management processes are utilized to eliminate these kinds of problems and to provide consistent, predictable results as a photograph moves through the workflow, meeting the expectations of the photographer and everyone else involved in the process.

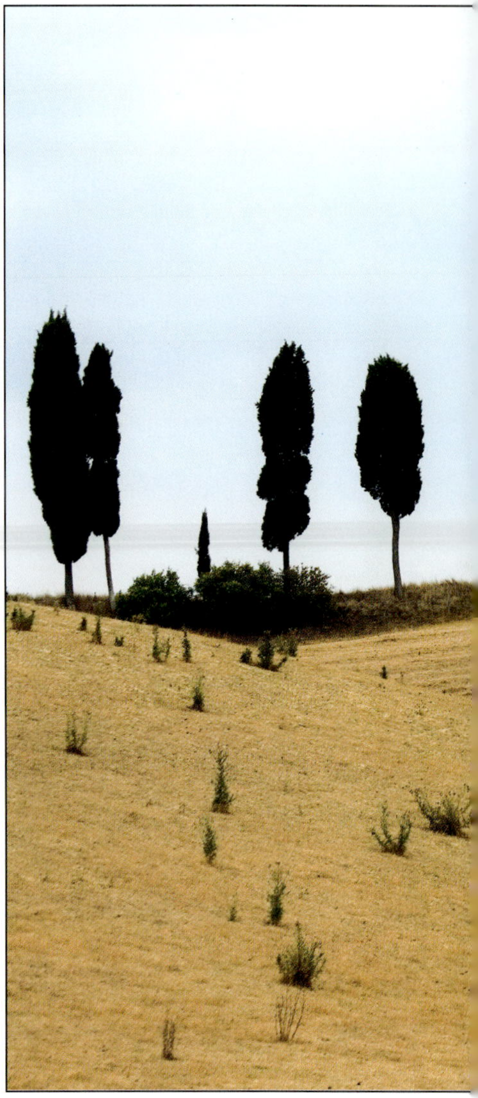

The Extended Photography Workflow: Working with Clients and Service Providers

Even if, without color-management practices, you are seeing a close match between display and printout in your immediate work environment, what happens when you hand your file to your client for display on their computer? Or to a service provider that might be making prints for you? What is the guarantee that what your client sees will be what you see on your computer screen? How are you going to ensure that your print service is going to be able to deliver prints that will match your colors?

Relying on Service Providers. Unless you have the good fortune of completely controlling all aspects of the photographic process, from taking the picture to creating the final print (often referred to as working in a "closed loop" environment), you will have to rely on other participants in the extended workflow to handle your images. Photo labs, photo retouchers, magazine layout departments, ad agencies, prepress, and printing services may all touch your image at one point or another.

It is not uncommon for photographers to fall into the trap of altering what already looks great on screen in order to produce a good print.

All of these services have the capacity to alter the color in your image. This means you may also have to relinquish control over the color in your images. Knowing that the service provider is practicing the same color-management methods as you, however, will give you some confidence that they will be able to handle the color in your images in a predictable manner.

Working with Clients Who Don't Understand Color Management. Clients, like service providers, are active participants of the extended work-

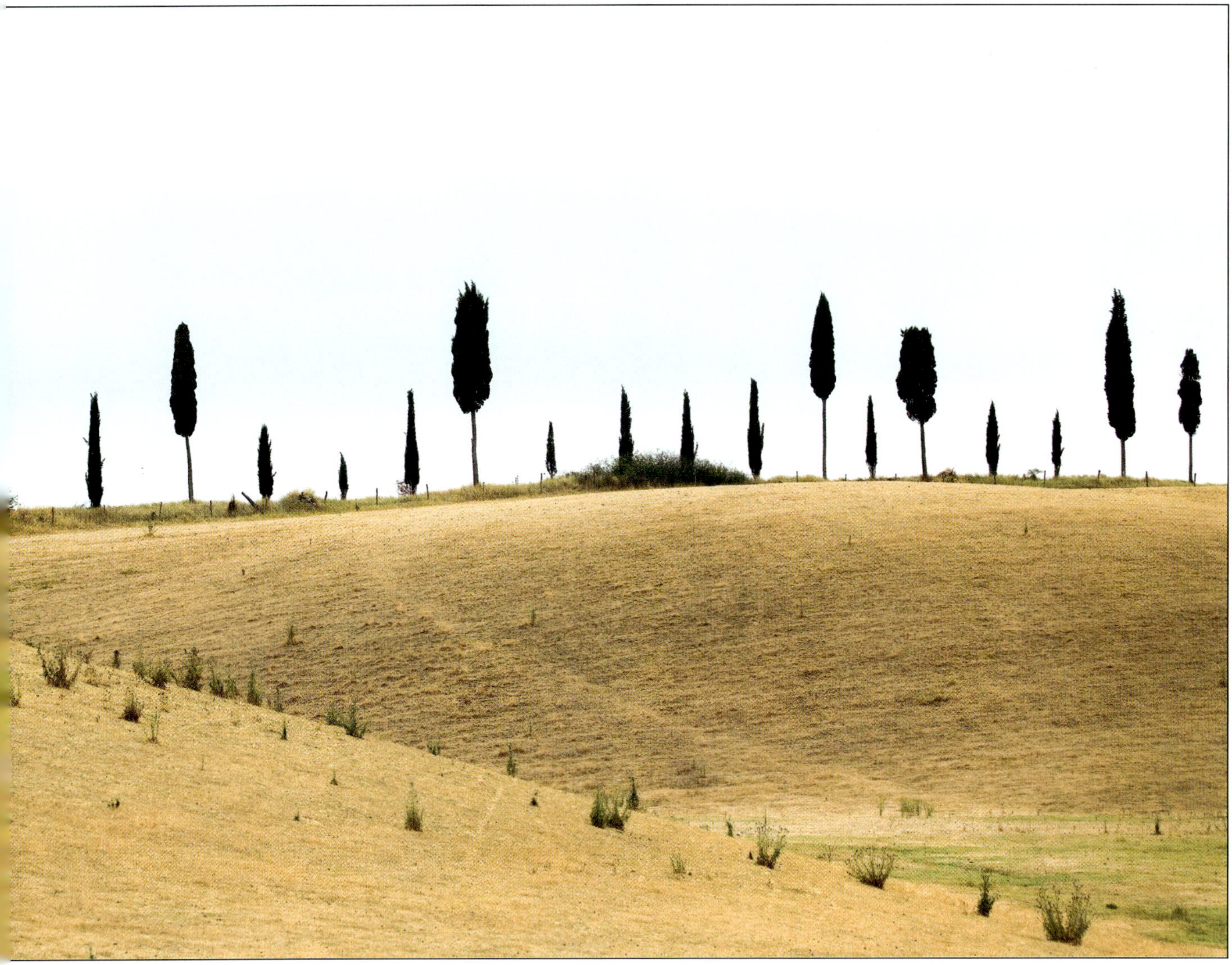

Figure 4—Cypress Trees, Tuscany.

flow, and their decisions are critical to the overall process. Just as service providers have the capacity to alter color in an image, clients make decisions based on how they perceive the image. A client looking at an image on a computer display that has not been properly color calibrated and profiled may be seeing something quite different from what the photographer provided. As a result, they could make some bad decisions based on inaccurate information.

Like service providers, clients also need to practice methods of color management consistent to the photographers. For color management to be effective, it is necessary that all aspects of the extended workflow are practicing the same methods of color management. Chapter 13 describes steps that a photographer can take to ensure that all members of the extended workflow are working in unison to meet the photographer's and the client's expectations.

The Benefits of Color Management

Predictable Color. One of the greatest benefits of color management is the ability to produce predictable color throughout the image processing workflow. As will be discussed shortly, you may not always be able to *match*

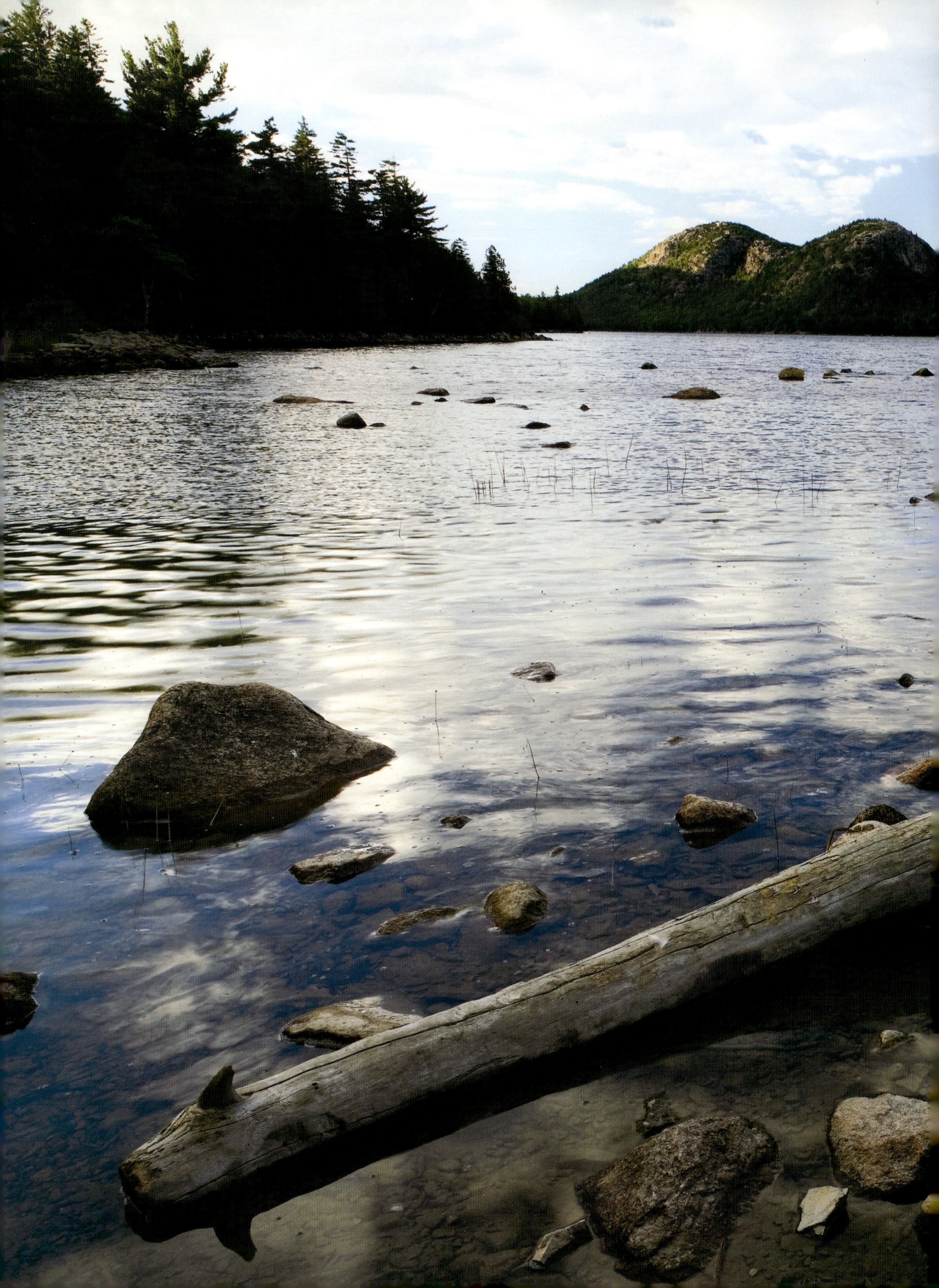

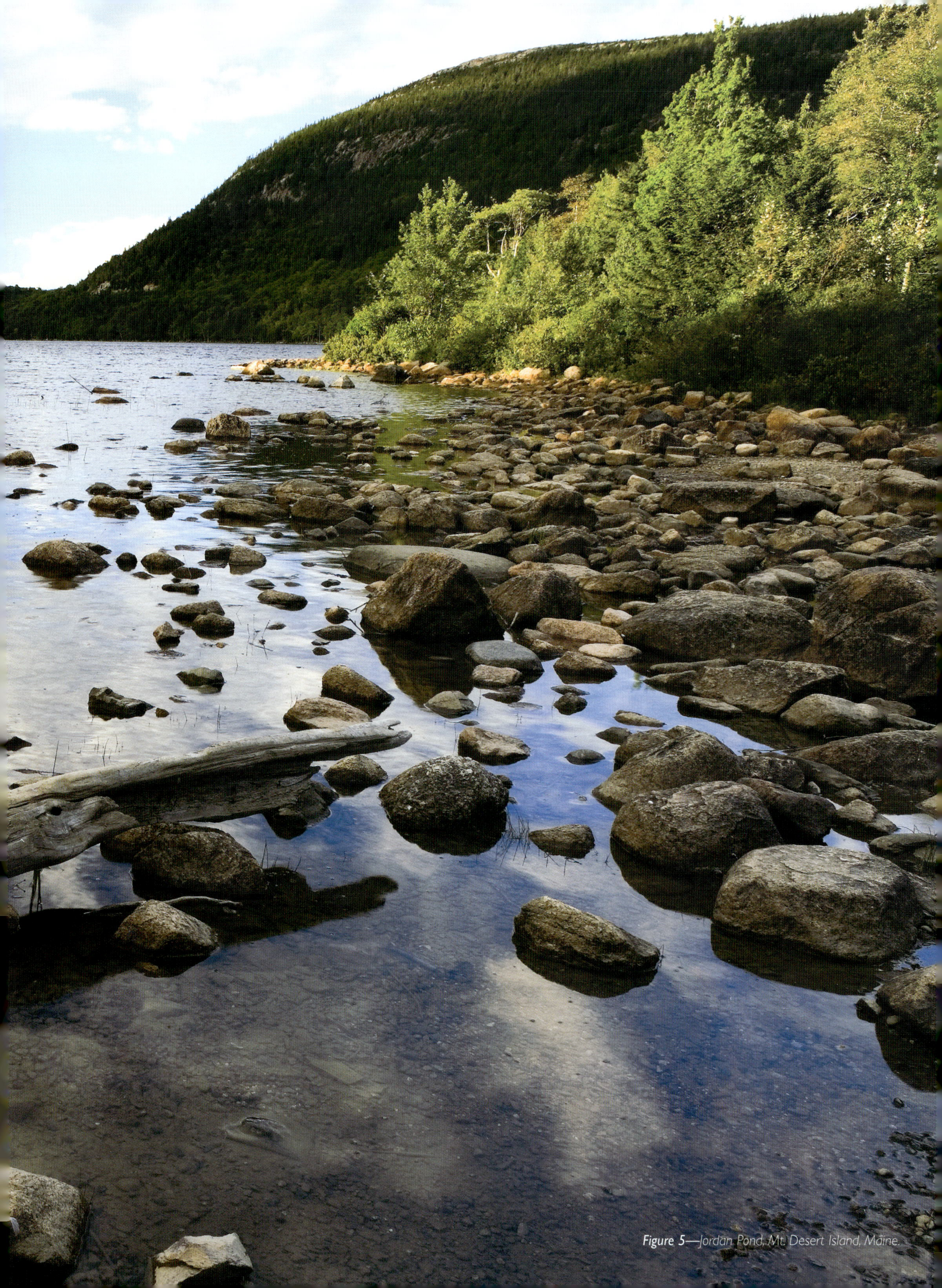

Figure 5—*Jordan Pond, Mt. Desert Island, Maine.*

colors, but if you understand the color capabilities of the devices that you are working with, you will be able to confidently *predict* what will happen to the color in an image as you move it from device to device and application to application. Understanding how a device handles color will, in turn, give you greater control over your image output.

Reduced Waste of Media and Time. Without good color-management practices in place, there is a high level of likelihood that image color will not match as the image is moved through the workflow. Time spent trying to correct the color of a scanned image that does not match the original is time wasted. The trial and error method of printing and editing to try to make a print match the screen is another huge waste of time and materials. Sending inaccurate color proofs to a client can be a huge time waster that could potentially put a job at risk. Good color management can help to minimize these kinds of issues.

Improved Communication with Members of the Extended Workflow. This book is based on the industry standard profile and color conversion methods that were established and are maintained by the International Color Consortium (ICC). Utilizing the methodologies of the ICC also fosters the use of a common color-management language, one that can be used to communicate to members of the extended workflow. Having a common language is useful in effectively communicating with service providers, as well as setting the correct expectations with clients. The color communication language, all the technical terminology that goes along with color management, can seem like a lot of "geek speak," but having an understanding of the fundamentals of the ICC process can go a long way in ensuring you are able to achieve predictable results from your service providers and set correct expectations with your clients.

Real World Expectations: The Colors Will Not Always Match!

Certain Devices Cannot Perceive, Display, or Render All the Colors in Your Image. Let's face it. There are going to be times when the colors are simply not going to match. Not all devices can read, display, or render the colors that human beings can perceive. Output processes like offset printing simply will not be able to reproduce the highly saturated orange that is in your image. As much as you might like to, you can't force the pig to fly. Understanding this will help a great deal in setting the right expectations up front, for both yourself and your client.

Not all devices can read, display, or render the colors that human beings can perceive.

Aspects of the Workspace Can Negatively Impact Color Perception. So much of the color-management process involves managing color conversion as images are moved from one device or computer application to another. Of equal importance is the management of the environment in which we work. Outside elements, like incandescent light from a lamp or bright sunlight streaming through a window onto the computer display, can have a negative impact on how one perceives colors and make it difficult to perceive colors in a consistent way. What seemed blue this morning might seem green this afternoon as the sunlight moves across the room.

Minimizing these "negatives" can greatly improve one's ability to perceive color in a consistent way. Unfortunately, it is not always possible to make the necessary changes in order to minimize the negative aspects of a workspace. The landlord might not allow you to remove the fluorescent lights in your studio. You may work in an environment that is very humid, which impacts how your inkjet printer performs.

Chapter 8 describes some of the things that can be done to improve the photo-editing environment and includes some resources for additional help.

Outside Services Cannot Always "Get It Right." As discussed earlier, it's not unusual for a photographer to have to rely on other members of the production workflow to handle the conversion of colors in his/her images. This conversion may be completely out of the photographer's control, like the final conversion of color for printing a magazine on a web offset press. When relinquishing control, there are steps that a photographer can take before handing over his images. These actions can help mitigate color issues that could occur downstream in the production process. The hard fact is that the outside service can still get it wrong. It is important that photographers do their part to make the conversion process as easy as possible for anyone handling their images. These steps will be discussed in detail in chapter 9.

These actions can help mitigate color issues that could occur downstream in the production process.

The Objective of This Book

Since color inconsistencies naturally arise as an image is moved from one device to another or from one application to another, it should stand to reason that the focus of this book will be directed at the process of translating color to keep it consistent and predictable as it is moved through the workflow, from camera to computer to printer.

Understanding color-management practices does not require a deep knowledge of color theory, but rather, how to address the fact that devices cannot handle color consistently. With the different color-management tools that are available and with an understanding of how color management is implemented in your different photographic tools, you will be able to tackle the beast and take control of your color. This book will focus on implementing a color-managed workflow, creating ICC color profiles for the different devices that you use, and then applying those profiles effectively so that the proper color translations are taking place at the right times in the workflow.

All that being said, it is still a good idea to understand some of the fundamental concepts. If you understand the process, you will know what to look for on your computer to make it happen. This book is intended to get you started.

2. Preview: A Color-Managed Workflow

The day-to-day process of color managing your images will become second nature to you. It's the setup that is a little more difficult. Fortunately, once your color-managed workflow is set up and working well, it doesn't have to be attended to very often.

Think of it this way: Color management is like flying a kite. When you buy a kite, more than likely you have to put it together. This may entail attaching some crossbars, securing a tail, and attaching the kite string. When you fly your kite for the first time, you learn how to judge the wind, the best way to launch your kite, and how to manipulate the kite string so your kite stays aloft. Once mastered, whenever you want to fly your kite, you don't have to go through the setup process again.

Once your color-managed workflow is set up and working well, it doesn't have to be attended to very often.

Color management is fundamentally the same. Once you have it set up and you have worked through the process of successfully moving an image from capture to edit to print, it becomes second nature. Like putting the kite together, setting up color management is done once. It may require some fine-tuning from time to time, but usually you will not have to fuss with the mechanics of it. You will simply use it, like flying your kite.

The following sections outline two photographic workflows. The first is not color managed and points out some of the typical pitfalls that one can encounter. The second illustrates a color-managed workflow and points out some of the steps that are integral to the process. These are typical procedures that a photographer might take when working on a photograph after color management has been set up and is working properly. If some of the terminology is unknown to you, don't worry. All of it will be explained in detail throughout the subsequent chapters.

A Typical Workflow: No Color Management

A photographer completes a studio shoot and loads a series of JPEG images from his digital camera into his computer for sorting, editing, and printing. He opens one of his photographs in Adobe Photoshop for tonal and color correction and general image enhancement.

The color in the image has a slight blue cast that the photographer corrects using the appropriate tools in Photoshop.

When he is finished making his corrections, he is ready to print the image. Choosing File > Print (figure 6), the photographer makes a sample print to see what the printed image will look like and to make sure that the color is accurate.

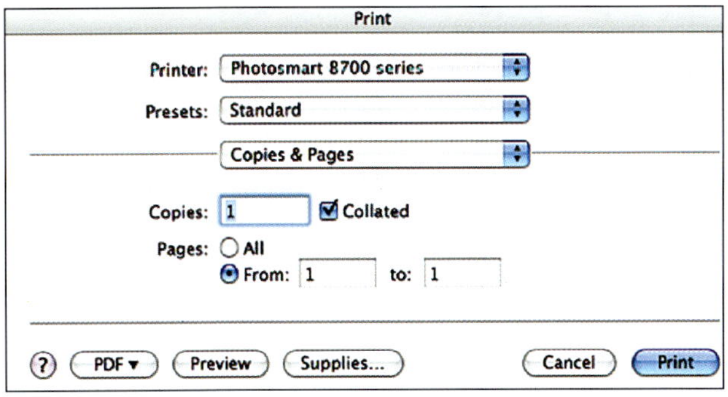

Figure 6—The standard Mac OS X print dialog box. When choosing File > Print in Photoshop, the print job is handed immediately to the print driver. File > Print with Preview must be selected in order to set up color management for output. Once the settings are made in Print with Preview, Photoshop then hands off the image to the print driver.

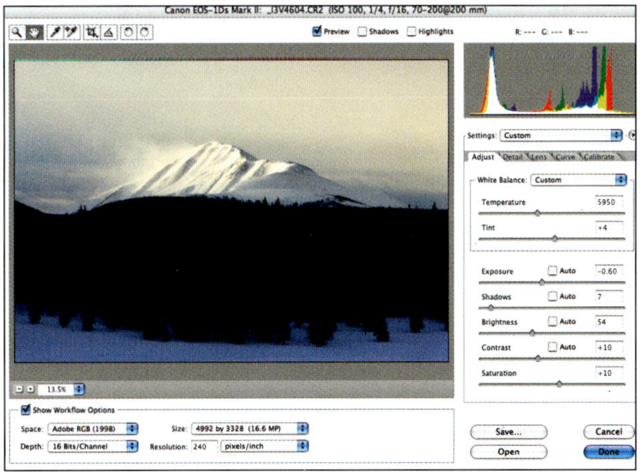

Figure 7—RAW image conversion using Adobe Camera Raw.

The resulting print, when compared to its counterpart on the computer screen, looks dark and does not have the saturated color that the photographer found so pleasing with the image on screen.

To resolve this and attempt to make a more accurate print, the photographer brightens the image in Photoshop and bumps up the image's saturation. The photographer makes another print and compares the results to the image on screen. While the print appears brighter and more saturated, it still does not reflect the appearance of the originally edited image. Since the photographer has had to alter the image in Photoshop for printing, he has to remember what the original looked like. The second print still does not reflect the quality that he desires.

Determined to make a successful print, the photographer makes another attempt to alter the image in Photoshop, adding additional brightness and saturation. A third print is made. Now the printed image is beginning to look more pleasing, similar to how he remembers the image looked after his initial edit. Unfortunately, the screen view of the image is now far too bright and over-saturated, and there is no way that the photographer can make a screen-to-print comparison.

Having successfully made a quality print, the photographer realizes that he now needs to make similar adjustments to all the images in his shoot in order for them to print with the quality he is expecting. Unfortunately, he realizes that he cannot trust the image on his computer display to match what comes out of his printer, and he realizes that he will have to burn through a lot of ink and paper to come up with a set of prints.

A Typical Color-Managed Workflow

After a shoot, a photographer loads the RAW images from his CompactFlash card into his computer.

He loads one of his images into the RAW conversion software that he likes to use and makes adjustments to optimize the color in the image (figure 7). This includes adjusting white balance, exposure, brightness, contrast, and saturation. Adjustments are also made to reduce noise and sharpen the image. The photographer chooses the standard color working space that he likes to work in, Adobe RGB (1998), and leaves the image in 16 bits per channel for maximum editing capabilities in Photoshop.

The image opens in Photoshop where the photographer plans to do some fine-tuning to the image before printing. The image opens in the Adobe RGB working space, because this is what the photographer assigned in the RAW converter.

Because the photographer has also calibrated and created an ICC color profile for his computer display, the color of the image displayed on screen accurately represents what was processed in the RAW converter.

Now in Photoshop, the photographer can make any additional edits that he thinks necessary, removing spots, fine-tuning the color, sharpening, etc.

Once the final edits are made the photographer prepares the image for printing to his local inkjet printer. He scales the image to final output size and then sharpens for output. He then performs a soft-proof of the image so that he can see on screen what the image will look like when printed (figure 8). Before wasting any paper or ink, the photographer can make last minute targeted edits to refine the image and ensure that he gets the most satisfying color in his print.

When outputting to his inkjet printer, the photographer uses File > Print with Preview in Photoshop CS2 (figure 9). He sets the page setup so that the image fits properly on the paper he is printing to. He also chooses the output profile of the printer and paper he is printing to and selects the appropriate rendering intent. Photoshop is now set to convert the color in his image from his standard working space, Adobe RGB, to the color space of the printer and paper he is outputting to. He then presses the Print button.

In the next dialog box that appears (figure 10), the photographer selects the paper type and quality settings for his print. He also turns off the color-management settings. Since Photoshop has already been set up to perform the color conversion, it is not necessary to have the printer perform the conversion again.

After printing, the photographer holds his print under balanced D50 lighting (see page 55) and compares the printed image to the image on his computer display. The two match very closely.

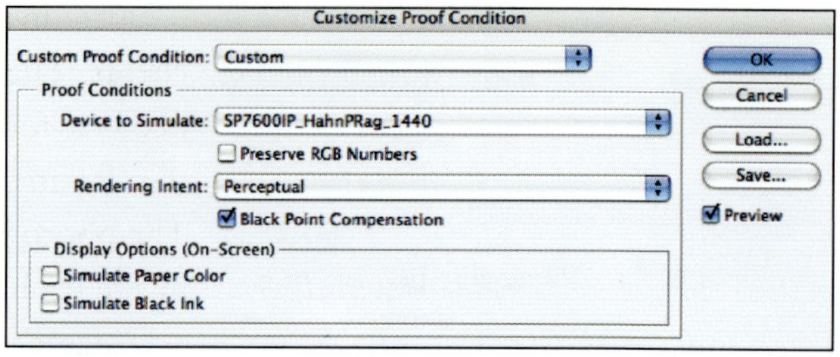

Figure 8—The Customize Proof Condition dialog box (View > Proof Setup > Custom) from Photoshop CS2 provides a means for simulating on screen what an image will look like when printed. The Device to Simulate pop-up menu gives access to the printing profiles installed on the computer. In this example the simulation is set up using the SP7600IP_HahnPRag_1440 output profile, which alters the on-screen image to look like a print from an Epson 7600 inkjet printer using Hahnemühle Photo Rag paper.

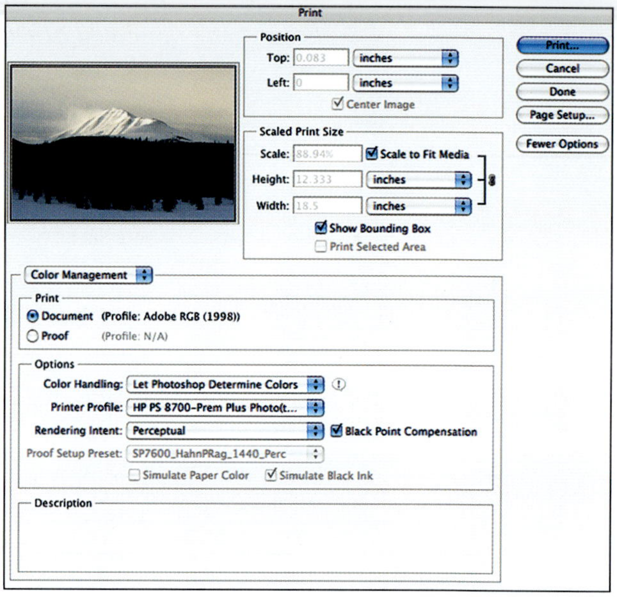

Figure 9—The dialog box opened by going to File > Print with Preview provides access to Photoshop's color-management features for printing an image.

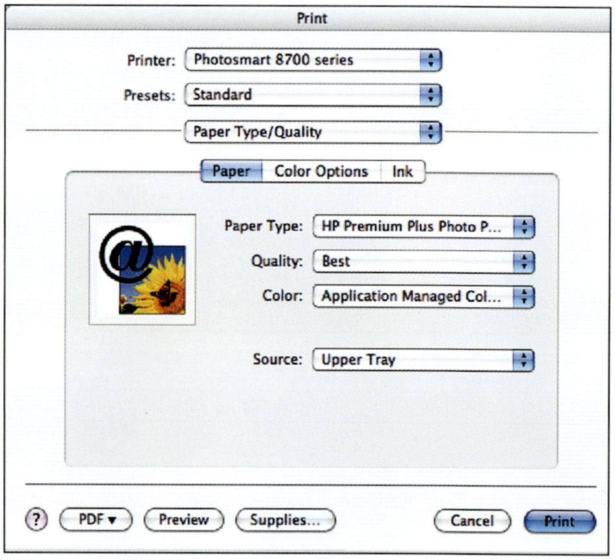

Figure 10—The Mac OS X standard printing dialog box with the features for the HP Photosmart 8750 printer showing. Since Photoshop is handling the color conversion from Adobe RGB to the printer's color space, it is important to turn off all color-management features in the print driver. Converting the image color again in the print driver will create problems. The pop-up Color menu shows that the driver is relinquishing the responsibility of color conversion to the application that is printing—in this case, Photoshop.

After inspecting his print, the photographer receives a call from one of his clients. The client asks if he can send her the same image he just printed. She [illegible] ould he provide her the file in CMYK so [illegible] dy for offset printing? [illegible] d that he will place the

[illegible], the photographer simply [illegible] hoto is in his standard work- [illegible] eet his client's request he will [illegible] d (SWOP), a very common color [illegible]. To make the conversion, the pho- [illegible] ile. Here, he chooses the destination [illegible] enu. He confirms the other settings in [illegible] utton. Photoshop converts the image to [illegible] or space, and he uploads the file to his FTP [illegible].

[illegible] ow to make the proper color conversions will [illegible] book, but before launching into how to set up [illegible] low—and without getting into a lot of color [illegible] help if you first have a basic understanding of some of the concepts and terminology. The next chapter will lay the groundwork for the color-management techniques that follow.

3. Color-Management Concepts

If you have wrestled with controlling color in your images and have attempted to try to color manage your photographic workflow, you will probably agree that color management is pretty complicated. What goes on behind the scenes can seem overwhelming. While it is possible to color manage your images without understanding color theory and all the technical aspects of color conversions, it can be very helpful if you know some of the fundamental concepts, especially when it comes to setting up a color-managed workflow, troubleshooting problems, or trying to understand how a new application handles color. This chapter is intended to introduce you to some of the basics.

RGB and CMYK Color Models

A color model defines color values numerically, most often by grouping three or four primary components. HSL, HSV, LCH, CMY, and RGB are all color

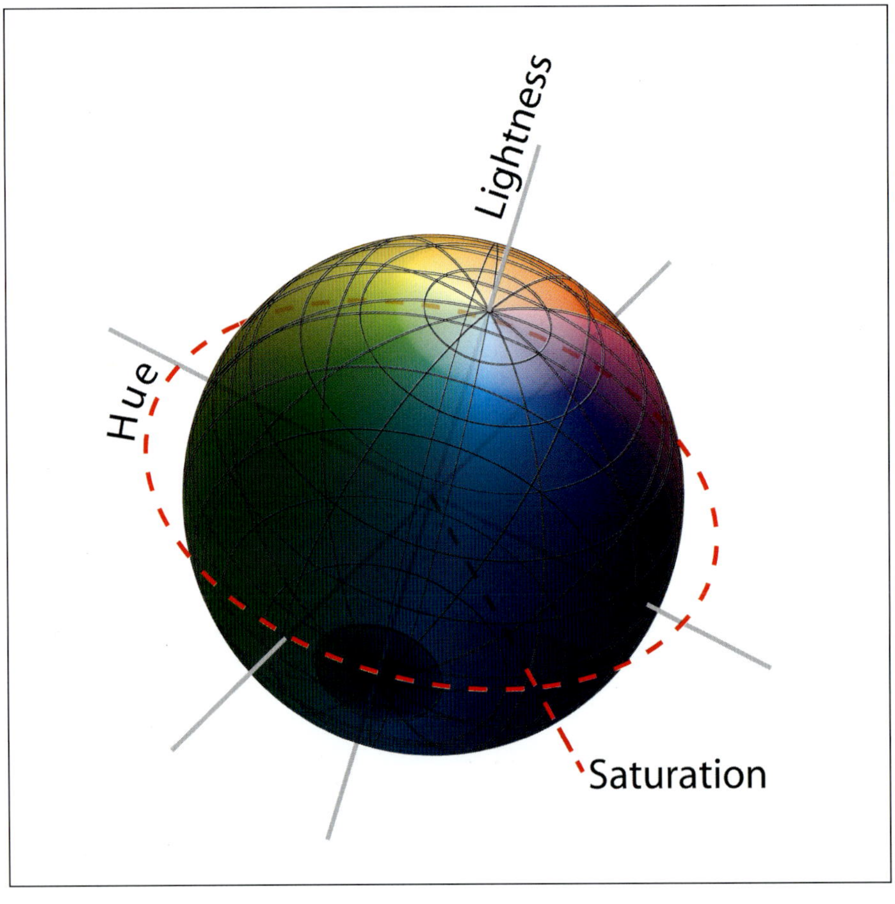

Figure 11—An arbitrary synthetic color space using the HSL Color Model. The color space is plotted in three dimensions where Hue rotates around the vertical access, Saturation increases from the center core outward, and Lightness values increase and decrease up and down the vertical axis. With values assigned for H, S, and L, a point can be plotted within the sphere that defines a color. This three-component model is typical of the different color models that are used to describe color space.

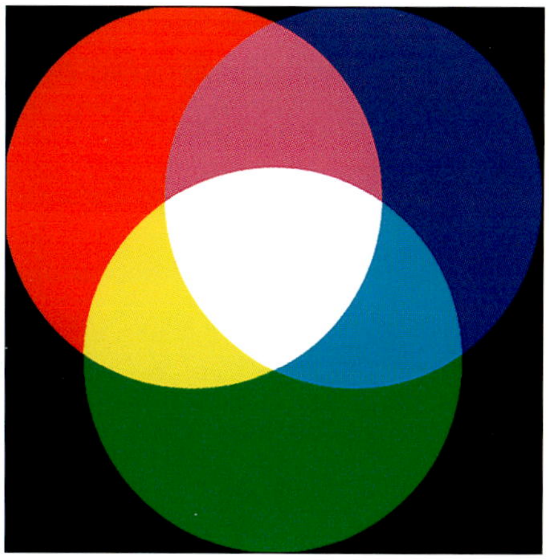

Figure 12—RGB is an additive color model. When all three color channels are assigned maximum values, the result is white.

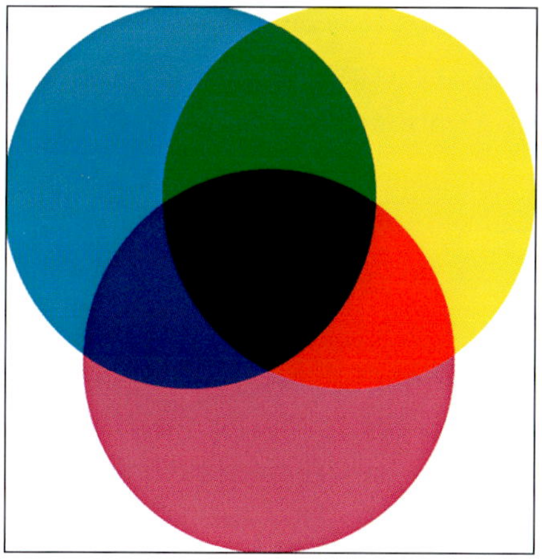

Figure 13—CMYK is a subtractive color model. When all three color channels are assigned maximum values, the result is black.

models that, when associated with instructions for how the three components should be interpreted, will create a color space (figure 11).

RGB. RGB is a basic color model associated with numerous devices that either emit or capture light, like scanners, digital cameras, and computer displays. RGB is referred to as an additive model since the more light that is emitted or captured, the higher the RGB values, and the closer the color is to white. On a computer, in a photo editing application like Adobe Photoshop, we can define colors by assigning individual values of R (red), G (green), and B (blue), typically on a scale from 0 to 255. When assigned in Photoshop's Color Picker, the maximum values (R 255, G 255, and B 255) will produce white (figure 12). The minimum values (R 0, G 0, B 0) represent no light at all—or black.

CMYK. The CMYK color model, typically used by printing devices, is a subtractive process and involves applying ink to a medium. As the individual channels of C (cyan), M (magenta), and Y (yellow) inks are combined on paper, different color values can be achieved depending on how the inks are mixed. This is done using a scale from 0% (or no ink) to 100% (or total ink) for each channel. The less ink that is printed, the closer the resulting color will resemble the color of the medium, which is usually interpreted as white. When combining maximum amounts of ink on paper for each CMY channel, the less light can be reflected off the medium, and the closer the printed color will resemble black (figure 13). (However, applying maximum values of CMY does not achieve a dense black; it produces a muddy brown. This is one of the reasons printers added the additional K [black] ink channel.)

Because of the nature of the offset-printing process, your images will have to be converted to CMYK.

Applications like Photoshop allow you to choose from a number of different color models. Because digital photographic images are in RGB mode at inception, you may spend most of your image-editing and optimization time in RGB. Because of the nature of the offset-printing process, at some point in the workflow, your images will have to be converted to CMYK. This may be a color conversion that you will have to manage yourself—and one that can be problematic if not handled properly. Understanding when and how to make this conversion is a critical factor in the photographic process and can lead to successfully and consistently reproducing images that meet your color expectations.

Color Space and Color Gamut

The term "color gamut" defines the limits of a color space. The sphere in figure 11 (page 18) is an *arbitrary* color space that is illustrated in three dimensions. Other color spaces describe the abilities of a *specific device*—a digital camera, computer display, printer, etc.—to perceive, display, or print colors (for more on this, see the following section on device-dependent color).

If a color falls outside the color space of the device, it is called "out of gamut." In simpler terms, the device is not capable of perceiving, displaying, or printing the color. Many laser printers, for example, have a relatively small color gamut, especially when compared to the larger color gamuts of many inkjet printers on the market today. There are certain colors that the inkjet printer can print that the laser printer cannot. By knowing the color gamut of a device, it is possible to understand its color capabilities or color limitations.

Figure 15 illustrates two device profiles in comparison with one another. The larger red shape represents the color space of a Microtek ScanMaker 1000XL flatbed scanner. The smaller orange area is the color space of an Epson Stylus Pro 7600 inkjet printer when printing on Epson Premium Luster Photo Paper. Both profiles are mapped on a three-dimensional grid based on the LAB color model. It is apparent from this illustration that the scanner has a larger color space than the printer. This means that the scanner can capture far more color than the printer can print. If we scanned an image that contained color outside the color space of the printer, a color conversion conducted when outputting the scanned file would map out-of-gamut colors to the closest "in gamut" color of the printer, rendering the most accurate representation of the color that the printer can print.

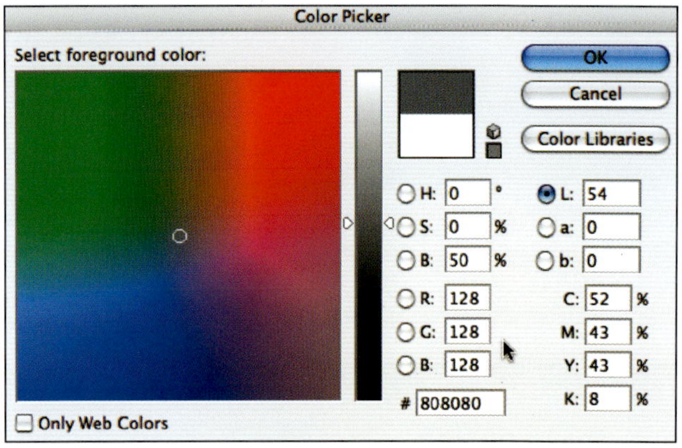

Figure 14—Adobe Photoshop's Color Picker provides a means to assign RGB and CMYK values to define a color. Notice that equal values of RGB will create a neutral gray while the CMYK values for the same gray tone are not equal.

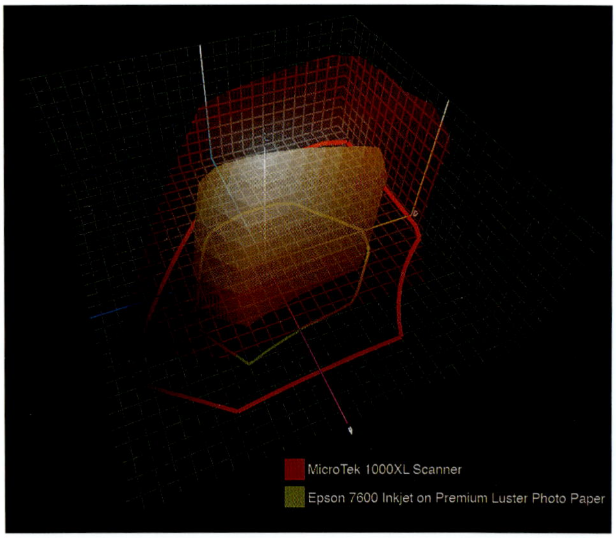

Figure 15—Two device-dependent color spaces illustrate the capabilities and limitations of different devices.

Device-Dependent Color Space

Color spaces that describe the capabilities of a particular device are commonly called "device dependent." They describe the device's color limits in terms of a color gamut. As illustrated in figure 15, every device has unique characteristics.

Different Devices Define the Same Color Differently. Because different devices have their own color spaces, they define the same color differently. In figure 15, the values for a particular blue color (R 42, G 82, B 171) are defined by the scanner's unique color space. Because a computer display's color space is different from the scanner's, however, it interprets this same blue color with RGB values of R 65, G 117,

Figure 16—Each device in the workflow interprets the same blue color with a different set of RGB or CMYK values.

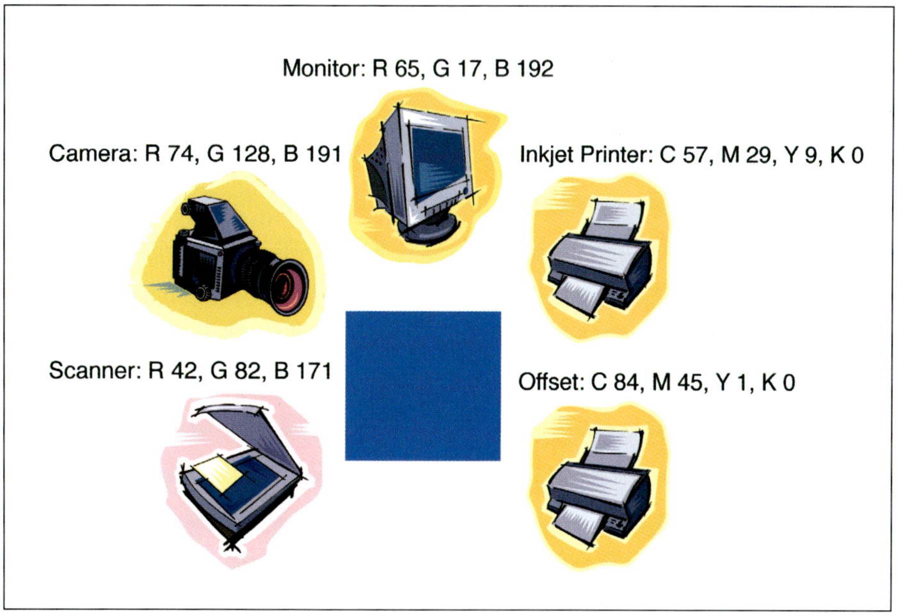

Figure 17—Conversely, they would all interpret the same RGB or CMYK values as a different color.

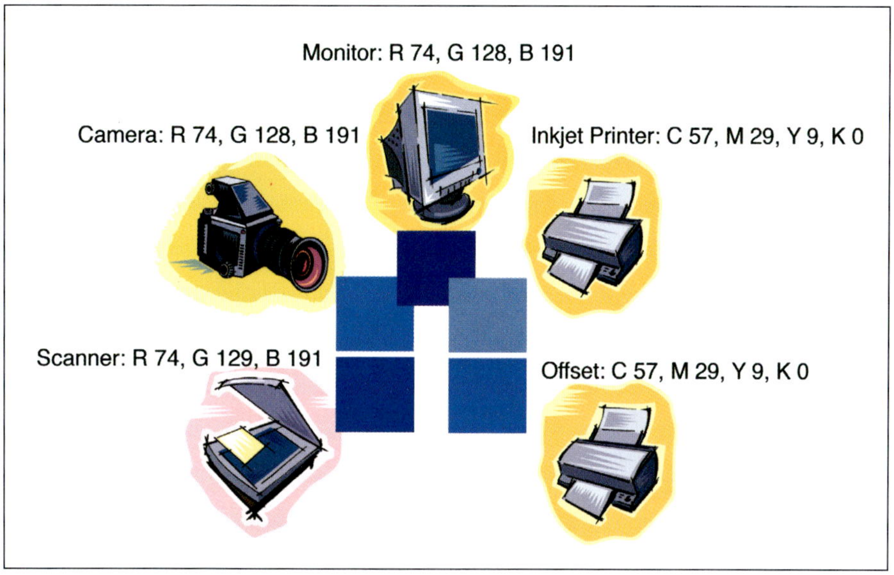

B 192. To reproduce this same color on an offset press would mean converting the RGB values to C 84, M 45, Y 1, K 0—which, again, is defined by the color space of the press.

Since every device interprets the same color in its own relative fashion, the values R 42, G 82, B 171 in the scanner's color space would look different than R 42, G 82, B 171 in the display's color space. Even though the two devices are in the same color mode, RGB, the way their RGB values are interpreted is relative to the device their color model represents. It's as though the two devices are speaking different languages. They are both saying the same thing, but the words they are using are relative to the language they are speaking and are different from one another.

Device-Independent Color Space

Wouldn't it be great if all the devices that we work with spoke the same color language? Unfortunately, that is not the case. Because the photographic workflow requires that we move images between numerous devices and applications, we need a way to translate the image's color from one device's color space to the next. In order to make the translation, there needs to be an absolute reference that can be used to do the translating. Such a reference exists in the form of a device-independent color space

The Importance of Device-Independent Color. In the early 1920s, the International Commission on Illumination (Commission Internationale d'Eclairage, or CIE), conducted a study on the perception of color and developed the color model CIEXYZ. Referred to as XYZ, this is a three-dimensional model that includes all the colors that human beings are able to perceive. Because it does not describe the color space of a specific device, it is device independent.

Absolute color models make it possible to translate color from one device-dependent color space to another.

Additionally, because this color model is so large, all the color spaces of the devices that photographers are working with will fit *inside* XYZ. (Unless you are working with infrared or some color outside of human perception—but it stands to reason that the only color that you are interested in is the color you can see.) Imagine mapping all the colors that you can see into three dimensions using X, Y, and Z axes, and that anywhere in this three-dimensional space, you can plot a point with three specific XYZ coordinates. That point would be the absolute location of a unique color in the XYZ color space. There is no other way to describe this color. XYZ defines all of its colors with unique X, Y, and Z values.

Having an absolute color model makes it possible to translate color from one device-dependent color space to another. This is done by creating an ICC profile for each device to be used in the workflow. These color profiles (described in chapter 5) provide a point of comparison between a color from an absolute, device-independent color space and the color that the device interprets it to be. If there is a difference—and usually there is—it is recorded in the color profile. The profile, then, is a record of how the device handles absolute color values from a device-independent color space and is used in the color-management process as a dictionary of sorts to translate colors between different device color spaces. The profile is a color characterization of the device that maps the device's color space and defines the device's color capabilities.

Imagine the process this way. When making a profile for a scanner, you make a scan of a lot of colors that have absolute XYZ values. Your profile-building software knows what these values are. When the scan is complete, you notice that the scanner's interpretation of a red color is orange. This difference is recorded by the profiling software into the profile. Later, you scan an image of some strawberries. The scanner, as you discovered earlier, makes all the red in the scanned image orange. After scanning you assign the profile you made. The profile knows that all the orange values in the scan are really supposed to be red, and tells the color-management system to make the necessary changes and adjust the colors accordingly.

LAB Color. In the early 1970s, the CIE introduced the color model L*a*b* (or LAB), which is based directly on XYZ and more accurately

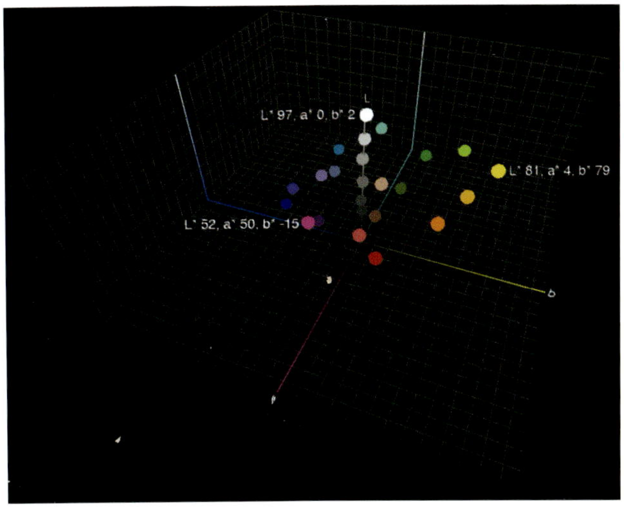

Figure 18—The 24 color Macbeth ColorChecker mapped in LAB. The colored circles plotted in this three-dimensional diagram illustrate how color is mapped in the LAB color model. The L channel is represented by the vertical axis. The a* channel runs from front to back, and the b* channel extends from left to right. The higher a color circle is positioned on the diagram, the lighter its color. Circles positioned to the left are more blue, and to the right they are more yellow. Colors that are positioned to the front are more magenta. Colors toward the back are more green. Each of the circles has a unique LAB coordinate as do all colors in the LAB color model. Several of them are called out in the diagram. On the L* axis a value of 0 equals black and a value of 100 equals white. Any value in between is a value of gray. Negative values on the a* and b* axes move the color toward green and blue respectively, while positive values move the color toward magenta and yellow. The colored circle at the top of the L* axis has a value of L* 97, b* 0, b* 2. Because the a* and b* values are so close to 0, the color represented by these LAB coordinates is very neutral. The yellow sphere to the right with LAB values L* 81, a* 4, b* 79 sits high on the L* axis and close to the a* axis, but far to the positive side of the b* axis, making it a bright and saturated yellow.*

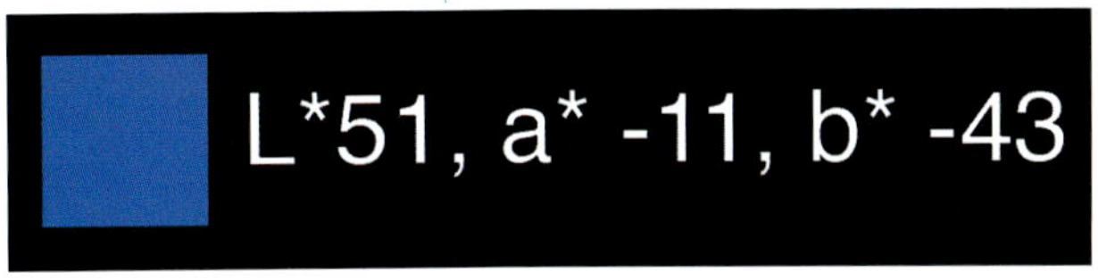

Figure 19—Purplish blue defined in LAB values. This is an absolute definition of this unique color.

defines human perceptible color. Like XYZ, LAB is used as the reference model for many profile-making software applications. Unlike XYZ, LAB maps its color using coordinates for luminance (L*) and two color parameters, blue to yellow (a*) and green to magenta (b*).

Figure 18 illustrates the colors from the Macbeth ColorChecker mapped in a LAB color model in three dimensions. The L* parameter, mapped as the vertical axis, describes the luminance of color—its relative brightness. The a* and b* parameters, mapped horizontally (front to back and left to right) describe color. L* 0 defines black; L* 100 defines white. Negative a* values yield green; positive ones yield magenta. Negative b* values yield blue; positive ones yield yellow. Using this coordinate system, it is possible to plot any color that the human eye can perceive as absolute LAB values.

Profile Connection Spaces. Figure 20 illustrates a common color transformation from one color space to another. In this example, a scanner scans an image in RGB. The color-management system uses the scanner's ICC profile to map scanner RGB values to LAB. These LAB values from the scanner's source profile are then passed to the inkjet printer's destination profile where they are mapped to the printer's CMYK values. This point of interaction between the scanner source profile and the printer destination profile is called the profile connection space (PCS). XYZ and LAB are commonly used as profile connection spaces. In order for an accurate conversion to take place there must always be a source profile and a destination profile. The result of this conversion should be a print that accurately represents the colors that were originally scanned.

ICC Color Profiles

For a well-managed color workflow to work properly, it is necessary to have a profile for every device in the workflow. To understand why, let's return to our analogy, looking at an

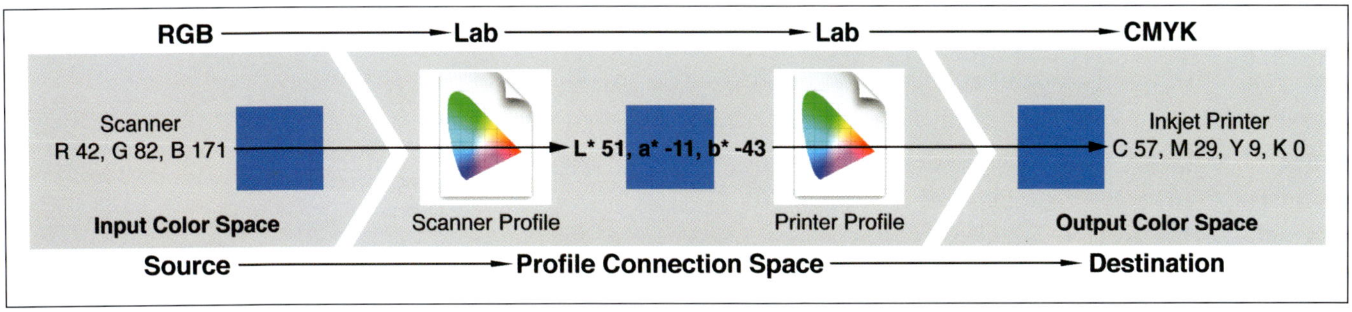

Figure 20—Converting scanner color to inkjet color. When the conversion takes place, the scanner's source profile maps its relative RGB values to absolute LAB values. The LAB values are passed to the printer's destination profile where they are mapped to relative CMYK values for output.

ICC profile as a translation dictionary. Imagine you are trying to speak to a person from Kenya. You speak Russian and the Kenyan speaks Swahili. You have a Russian-to-German dictionary and the Kenyan has a German-to-Swahili dictionary. With these two dictionaries it would be possible to communicate—you could translate the Russian into German and the German into Swahili.

In this example, the dictionaries are profiles, and German is the profile connection space. Now, imagine that a third person enters your conversation—but this person speaks French. In order to communicate with this person, he just needs to have a French-to-German dictionary. In fact, you could continue to have a conversation with anyone who enters the group as long as the person has a dictionary that uses the profile connection space.

The most accurate profiles are the ones that are custom made for individual devices. It is possible to acquire profiles from the manufacturers of input, display, and output devices. Many manufacturers will install ICC color profiles onto your computer when you install their device drivers or applications. While these profiles can be very good, they are built for an entire product line, like all HP Designjet 130s, as opposed to the individual Designjet 130 that you might own. In chapter 5, you will learn how to create custom ICC profiles for all the devices in your workflow.

The International Color Consortium

The ICC has been mentioned a lot so far. What is this? The International Color Consortium, or ICC, is made up of a group of like-minded companies that came together to create a standard way of solving "the color problem" when sharing images and files between different hardware devices and computer applications. Founded in 1993 by eight technology companies, the ICC now has an impressive member list that includes all the usual suspects—Apple, Adobe, Sun, Kodak, Agfa, Canon, Quark, GretagMacbeth and X-Rite, R.R. Donnelly, Pantone, Nikon, Nokia, and about sixty more. The ICC developed the methodologies most widely used for color management and promotes their adoption as an open, cross-platform, and vendor-neutral standard. If you look at the device drivers and applications that you are using for photography, you may find that many of them subscribe to the industry standards of the ICC. Unfortunately, each color-management implementation is not always exactly the same when you compare one manufacturer's device driver or application to another. This has created some confusion with end users. However, understanding the ICC's color-conversion methods and the process of color management can go a long way in helping you figure out what a vendor is attempting, if it is not initially clear.

Working Spaces

In addition to device profiles, photographers should be familiar with the concept of a working space. Introduced by Adobe Systems, working spaces—like Adobe RGB (1998), ProPhoto RGB, or ColorMatch RGB—are ICC color profiles that do not represent the color capabilities of any given device. These profiles provide a uniform, neutral environment that is well suited for image editing. Usually they have a color gamut that is large enough to give the photographer ample headroom for manipulating color and the flexibility to convert, on output, to numerous different output destinations—like inkjet prints, CMYK color spaces for press output, and the Internet. Working spaces are a great place to hold your color until you are ready to output, at which time you convert to the output color space of the device you are printing to. If you archive your edited images in a standard working space, then you will increase the chances of being able to successfully output to all different types of devices, even those that might not exist today.

The most accurate profiles are the ones that are custom made for individual devices.

Each working space profile has its own unique color gamut. ProPhoto-RGB has an extremely large color space, while sRGB is relatively small. Typically what they have in common is "neutrality," meaning that they translate equal amounts of RGB as a gray value. This is often also referred to as being "well behaved." Assigning equal amounts of RGB may not result in a neutral value if you are editing in a device's color space. Device color spaces are not usually well behaved.

For ideal results, a working space should meet the needs of the photographer's workflow. Because not all workflows are equal, there are many working spaces available. Some, like Adobe RGB, are widely used. Others can be more obscure—like Don Hutchison's Don RGB. When choosing a working space for your images, you will want to consider the following:

1. What is the color space of the output device that you will be sending your image to?
2. Are you outputting to multiple output devices and mediums, like inkjet, offset, a sign printer, the web?
3. Are you archiving your images with the expectation that you might be outputting to some unknown device in the distant future?

RGB working spaces have a relatively large color gamut when compared to the color gamut of many printing devices. For example, Adobe RGB completely encompasses the CMYK color space based on the SWOP specification for offset printing. Ideally, a working space should contain all the color from the input device and encompass the color space of all the output destinations you may be sending your image to. This is a pretty tall order considering that many input devices today can capture a very large amount of color data, and the numerous output devices that you might send your image to could vary dramatically.

So why not just use the largest working space available, like ProPhoto-RGB? Simply put, in a color space as large as ProPhoto RGB or Wide Gamut RGB, you may be able to assign highly saturated color that current printing technology could never reproduce. When converting for output, the color-management system will do its best to map the saturated ProPhoto RGB color to the closest in-gamut color that the printer can reproduce. These colors could be very far apart, and the end result could be a very drastic shift in color that is far from meeting your expectations.

Figure 21 (next page) shows an an extreme example, comparing ProPhoto RGB to the CMYK color space U.S. Sheetfed Coated. As you can see, a color assigned at the periphery of ProPhoto RGB would have to undergo a significant transformation to be output in this CMYK color space. The transformed color would be quite different from the original. Additionally, editing an 8-bit per pixel image with only 256 tonal levels in a large working space like ProPhoto RGB, where the colors are spread out over a wide space, can easily introduce posterization into an image. This creates visible bands,

The SWOP Specification and Color Management

In the mission statement on www.swop.org, SWOP (Specifications Web Offset Publications) is defined as "the specifications for everyone involved in the graphic arts workflow, which includes all forms of magazine advertising and editorial input, whether analog or digital. Adherence to these specifications ensures that all input received by the printer can be reproduced as intended and desired by the advertiser/publisher with minimal difficulty." The ICC profile called U.S. Web Coated (SWOP) v2 was developed to adhere to the SWOP specification. By converting color into this CMYK color space, the user ensures that the color in his graphic material will be printable by any printer that adheres to the SWOP specification.

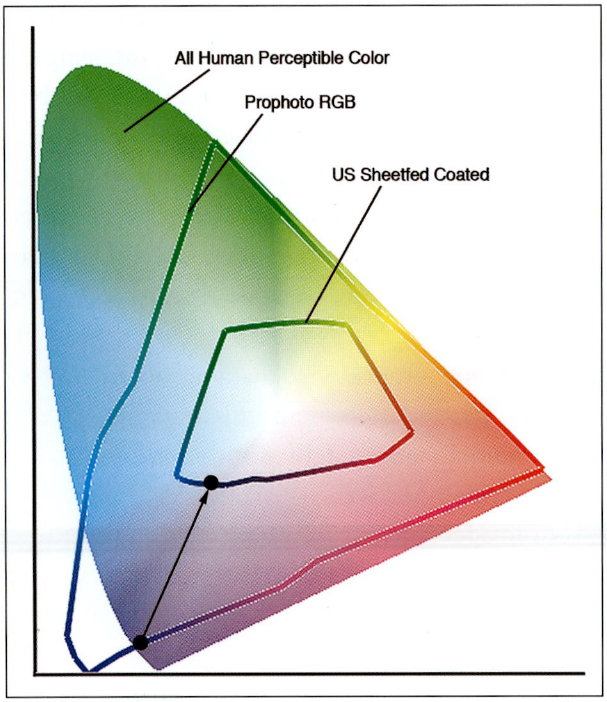

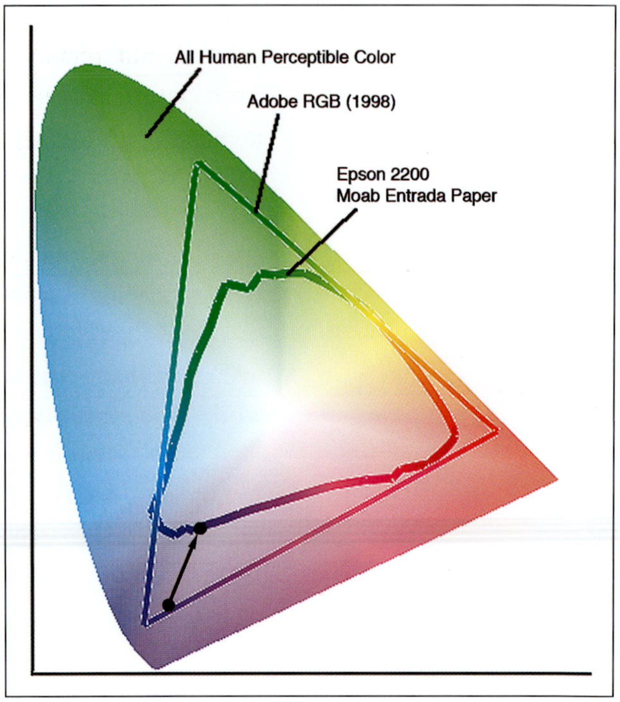

Figure 21 (left)—This chromaticity diagram illustrates the extreme difference between two color gamuts. The larger, ProPhoto RGB, is so large that it extends outside of what the human eye can perceive. Converting from this large space to a much smaller one, like U.S. Sheetfed Coated, could drastically alter the highly saturated colors that reside at the periphery of ProPhoto RGB as they are transformed to the closest match inside the printer's color space. Simply put, there are a lot of colors in ProPhoto RGB that the printer simply cannot print. ***Figure 22 (right)—*** *Putting image color in a working space of a more moderate size, like Adobe RGB (1998), will provide ample editing headroom and will help minimize color transformation on output.*

especially in areas of subtle gradation. It is better to edit 8-bit images in smaller working spaces where the color is closer together and where the potential of introducing banding will be less of an issue.

For these reasons, it is a good idea to try to convert the large amount of color that you might capture with your digital camera or scanner into a working space that will not drastically alter your color and will give you enough headroom to make color adjustments without pushing your color out of gamut. Additionally, you will want to be able to convert your color, upon output, to devices that have the majority of their color space contained within your working space. Ideally, you would want to have all of the printer's color contained within your working space, but that is not always possible—especially when you plan to output to numerous output devices or mediums.

Working spaces are good places to "hold" color if you are not sure what your output device will be.

Figure 22 shows the output color space for an Epson 2200 inkjet printer when printing on Moab Entrada paper. The printer's color space is fully contained within Adobe RGB. It is large enough that any colors assigned within Adobe RGB that are outside the 2200's color gamut will not have to go through a drastic transformation when converted for printing.

Working spaces are good places to "hold" color if you are not sure what your output device will be—especially if you are archiving your images for future use. Because most high-end digital cameras provide RAW capture into 16-bit files, many photographers are putting their images into large color spaces like ProPhoto RGB. Not only does a 16-bit file, with a potential of 65,536 tonal levels, give the photographer enough image data to edit his images without the risk of introducing banding, but archiving into a large color gamut retains a maximum amount of color data for future output. Anticipating that future printers will have much greater color output capabilities with a much larger color gamut, it makes good sense to retain as much color data as possible.

In this example, putting image color in a large working space ensures that the photographer will be able to take full advantage of future printing technology. Even if the photographer needs to provide his image today to a client or outside service provider, spinning off an interim conversion to a smaller working space like Adobe RGB while maintaining the original in a larger working space is a viable solution. Figure 23 illustrates this workflow.

Figure 23—Converting a RAW image into a color space like ProPhoto RGB preserves most of the color data because ProPhoto is a relatively large color space. When preparing a file for a client, it would be wise to first run an additional conversion to a smaller RGB color space.

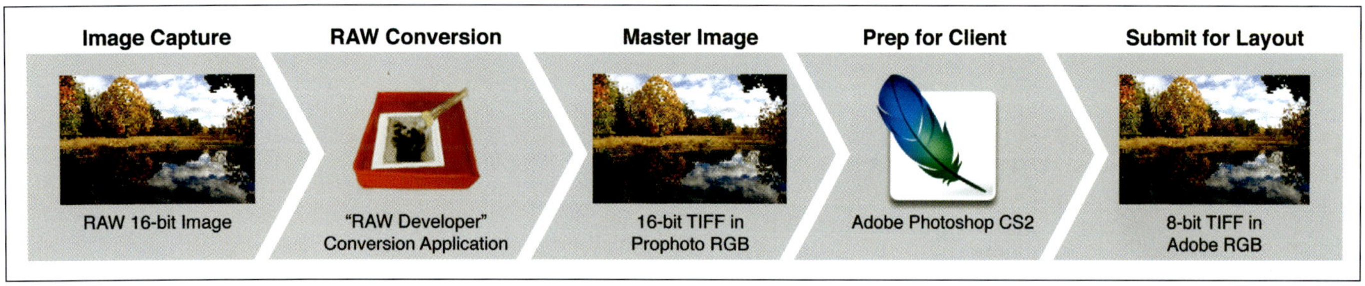

Color-Management Methods

So far there has been a lot of discussion about device-dependent color spaces, ICC color profiles, device-independent color, and the importance of the profile connection space in the color-conversion process.

Since the color within an image file is defined by a long series of numbers, color conversion from one color space to another is a process of mapping source color space numbers to destination color space numbers. The conversion process is the function of the color-management method (CMM). (*Note:* This is sometimes called a color-management module or a color engine.) The CMM does all the "heavy lifting" in the color conversion. Utilizing ICC profiles that define the source and destination color spaces, it conducts the translation between the two. There are numerous CMMs in use today. The computer platform and applications you are using will determine which color engine(s) will be available to you. In some cases, applications will give you several choices. The best strategy is to pick one and try to stick to it if you can.

Application-Level Color Management. Consider that each color engine performs its own mathematical operations. Yet, even though all should follow the ICC specifications, they don't necessarily perform the same math. As a result, not all conversions are equal. For this reason, Adobe created its own CMM for its Creative Suite of applications. The Adobe Color Engine (ACE) performs all of the color conversion functions for Photoshop, Illustrator, Acrobat, InDesign, and GoLive and is the same on both Mac and Windows platforms. If you happen to share your images across platforms, the Adobe (ACE) color engine is a good choice.

System-Level Color Management. Both Apple and Microsoft provide a Color Management System (CMS) that is installed with Mac OS X and

Windows XP. Apple's ColorSync and Microsoft's Image Color Management (ICM) both incorporate color management methods (CMMs) for converting color. ColorSync uses the Apple CMM, and ICM uses the LinoColor CMM as its default conversion engine.

With ColorSync and ICM, both Apple and Microsoft have made considerable effort to provide technology that will solve the device color mismatch problem at the operating system level in a way that is very transparent to the end user. Both systems rely on all the components of the ICC's methodologies for color conversion and provide control that end users can employ to pair ICC color profiles with scanners, cameras, displays, and printers. Once set, applications that support the CMS will transparently apply color conversions so that colors remain consistent as they are off-loaded from a camera, edited, and printed. Both systems also provide an application programming interface so that developers who choose to do so can incorporate the system-level resources for color conversion into their device drivers and applications.

Most high-end applications for image editing and optimization have incorporated their own ICC color support.

For anyone using a consumer-grade camera, Image Capture, and iPhoto on the Mac, ColorSync can be a powerful and very straightforward solution. As you will see, when the setup for ICM and ColorSync are described in the next chapter, this is not a complete solution for photographers at a professional level. To provide a higher level of functionality and customization, most high-end applications for image editing and optimization have incorporated their own ICC color support in addition to utilizing ColorSync and ICM, or they bypass ColorSync and ICM altogether.

Assigning Color Meaning vs. *Converting Color Data*

Some applications and device drivers give you the opportunity to assign a color profile as opposed to converting from one color space to another. This has often been a point of confusion. As you would expect there are reasons for choosing one or the other.

Assigning a Profile. Assigning a profile utilizes the profile to alter image color on screen without actually changing the data in the file. Remember, color information in image files is defined by a lot of numbers. Assigning a profile does not *change* these numbers. It will, however, change how the numbers are *interpreted* as defined by the profile that is assigned.

The reason for assigning a profile is to give meaning to the color data in the file in accordance to the color characteristics of the device that captured it. Consider a digital camera that inherently captures color with a slightly red color cast. An ICC profile is created for the camera that records the camera's color characteristics—it knows about the red problem. Then, imagine photographing a gray card; the captured image will look slightly pink. When *assigning* the profile to the image, it will translate what the camera really meant when capturing the image without altering the underlying image data. The appearance of the image on screen will be changed to accurately represent the gray value of the card that was photographed.

This profile assignment is giving meaning to the color data in the image file. It is saying that the color was captured by a particular camera that happens to have a red color problem. Once the assignment is made and the color appearance is corrected, the image can be accurately converted to other color spaces as it is moved through the photo workflow.

Converting to a Color Space. Converting from one color space to another *will* change the data in the image file. Using the previous example, once the camera's profile is assigned and the image has color meaning, it can be accurately converted to another color space, like a working space. When this happens, the RGB color values in the image will shift and will be mapped to the working space's color values. If the captured image had color that was outside the color gamut of the destination working space, those colors will be translated to the closest in-gamut colors. The out-of-gamut colors will be eliminated from the file. For this reason, it is important that you are careful when converting from one space to another. Colors that are converted out of a file *cannot be restored.*

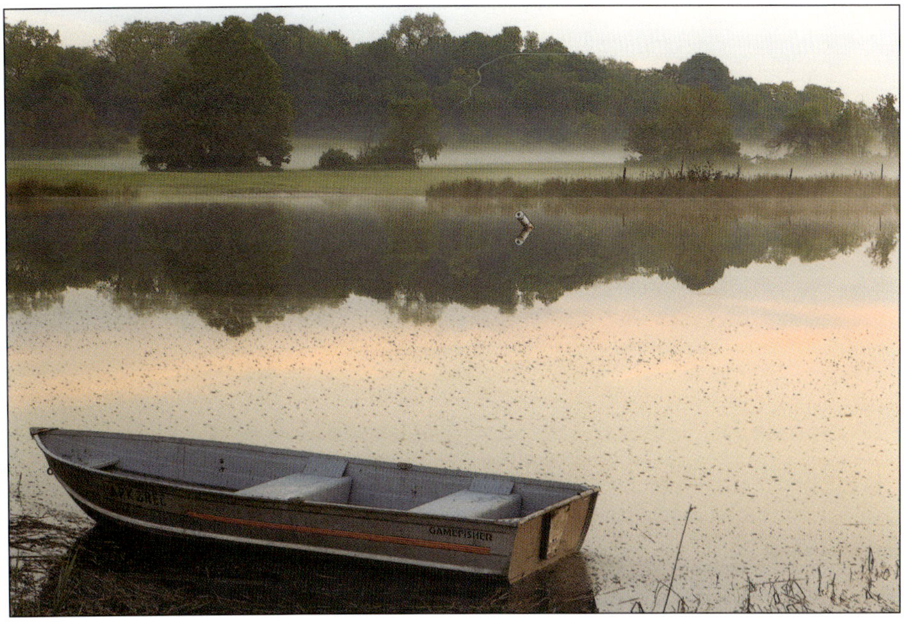

Figure 24—*A scanned image that does not have a source profile assigned.*

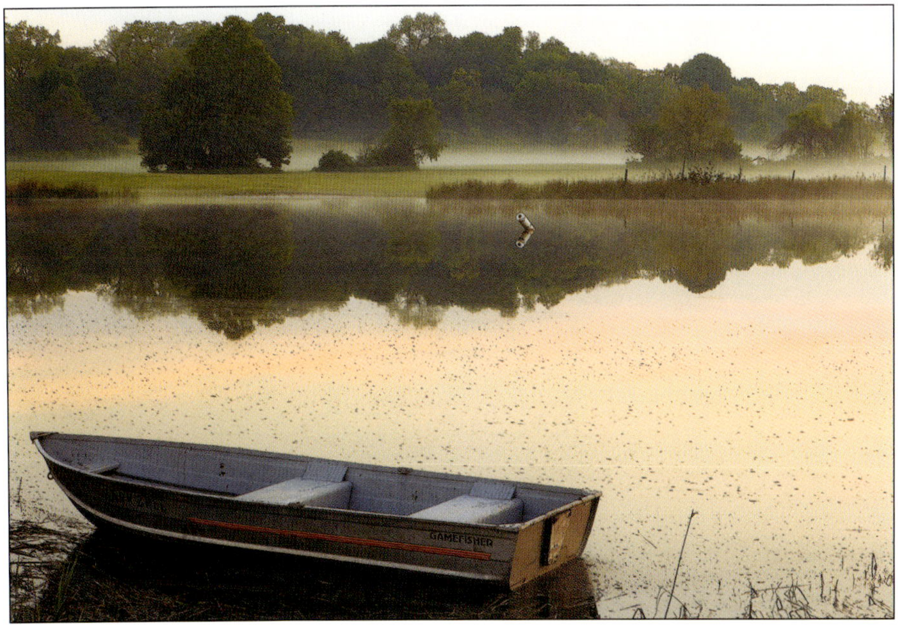

Figure 25—*The same image after assigning the scanner's source input profile and converting to Adobe RGB (1998).*

The image of the metal boat in figure 24 is an example of what happens when a device-dependent input profile, in this case a scanner profile, is *not* assigned. It shows how the scanner interpreted the color in the image—dark and muddy. The profile that was created for this scanner records these characteristics and can be used to convert the color accurately. Without first assigning the scanner profile and giving the image color meaning, it is not possible to match the color of the image that was scanned.

Figure 25 shows the same image after the scanner profile has been assigned. The color in this image accurately describes the color of the image that was scanned. When entering images into a color-managed workflow, it is always important to make sure that the image has color meaning. Color meaning is given to an image by assigning a profile for the device that captured the image. Once the profile is assigned, the color can be accurately converted to other color spaces.

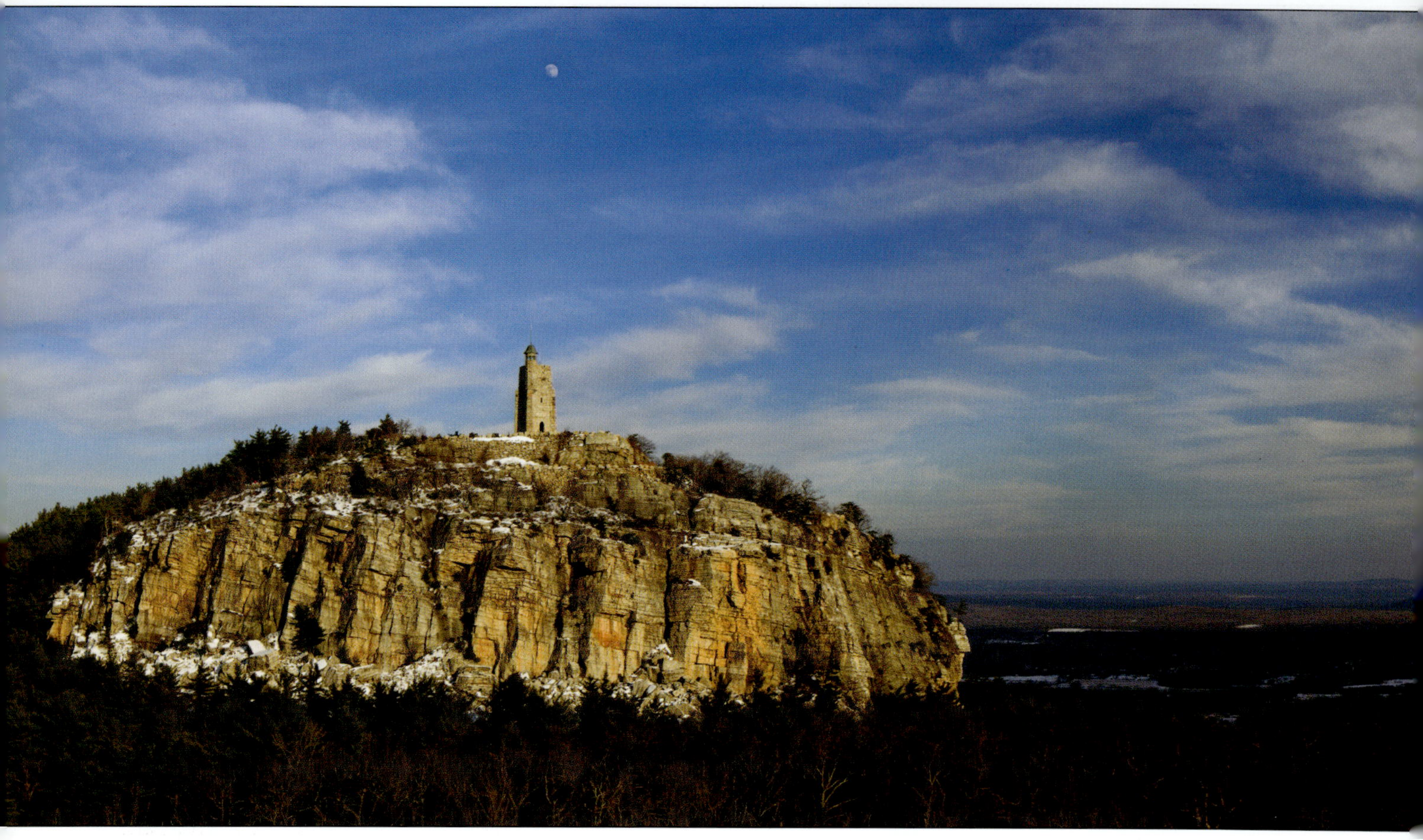

Figure 26—Skytop, Mohonk Mountain House.

Think of it this way. You call your travel agent and tell him that you want to fly to Denver. The travel agent asks you where you are flying from. You say you do not know. The travel agent says that he cannot book you a flight to Denver if you do not know where you are. You tell him that you are going to find out and will call him back. If you do not know where you are, you cannot get to where you want to go. In terms of color management, if you do not have an input profile assigned, the likelihood of your scanned image looking like the original is very slim.

You decide that the only way to find out where you are is to go outside and walk around and see if any of the characteristics of your current location can help the travel agent figure out where you are. As you are walking around, you take a lot of notes. You then call your travel agent and tell him that you are on an island with miles and miles of huge skyscrapers. The travel agent said he knows where you are. The characteristics of the place you describe could only describe one place: New York. Now you know your source location, and the travel agent can book your flight to Denver.

You take a cab to the airport, and the nice agent at the ticket counter issues you a boarding pass and a ticket. On the boarding pass it says that you are in New York. This is like assigning a profile. You know where you are, but you haven't gone anywhere yet. Because you are still in New York, you could go back to the ticket counter and trade in your Denver ticket for a new ticket to Barcelona. This would be the same as assigning a different profile to your image. Since you know where you are, you can go just about anywhere. You

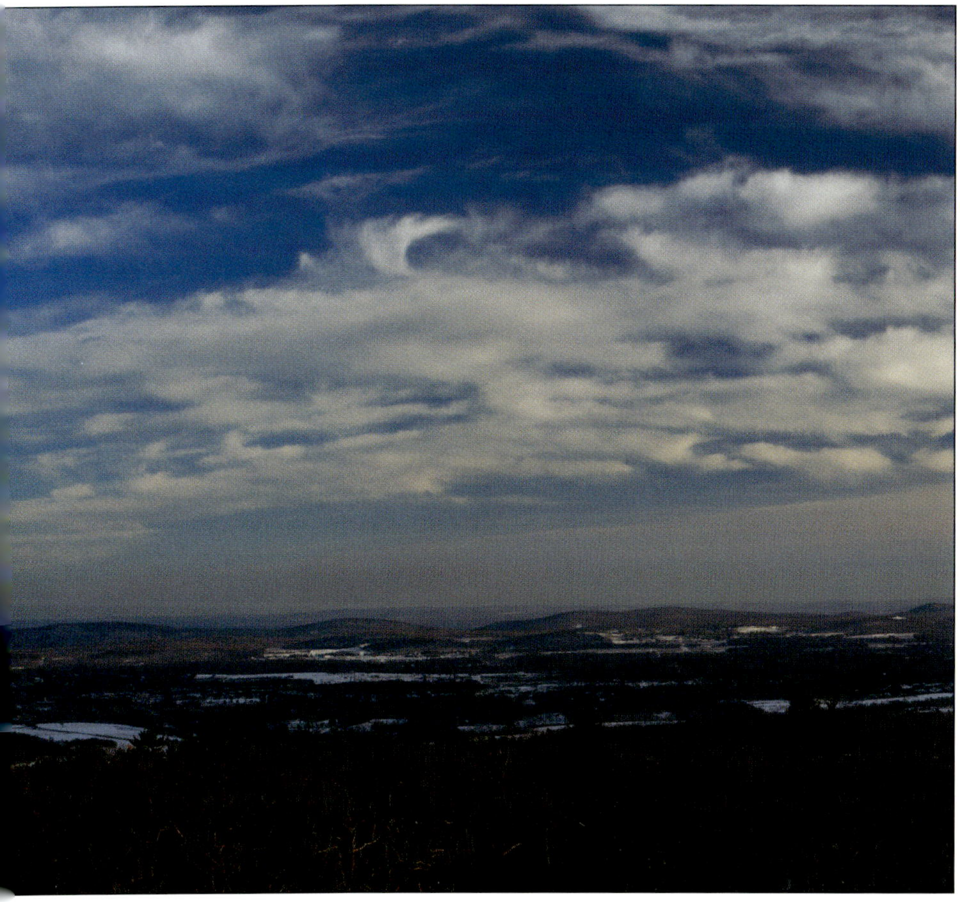

decide to keep your ticket to Denver. You board the plane and several hours later you are at Denver International Airport. This would be similar to converting your color. Think of converting as "taking the color trip." When you arrive in Denver, you are no longer in New York. You have converted to your destination color space.

Taking this analogy one step further, suppose that when you were flying from New York to Denver, you had to stop at the airline's hub in Chicago. Think of the hub as a working space. Airlines place hubs in strategic locations so that they do not have to make direct flights from every city to every other city. They know that they can accommodate far more destinations simply by moving their passengers through several centralized locations. Imagine an airline scheduling flights from Los Angeles to Newburgh, NY. Newburgh has a small airport just off the Hudson River called Stewart International Airport. The airline would never be able to fill a flight. This would be a losing proposition. So instead of scheduling flights directly to Newburgh, the airline could fly people from LA and many other cities to Chicago, and then fly everyone from Chicago to Newburgh. People flying from Newburgh could fly to the airline's hub and from there fly just about anywhere.

Similarly, when you put your color in a working space, you open up the options for outputting to numerous destinations. You have taken your color from, perhaps, an obscure source location like your scanner's color space to a much more common interim destination—a working space. From the working space, the likelihood of successfully traveling to many different output destinations is very high.

When you put your color in a working space, you open up the options for outputting to numerous destinations.

Assigning color profiles is like being handed a boarding pass. You know where you are. You know where you are going, and you know what the destination looks like. But you haven't gone anywhere.

Converting color is like boarding a plane and making the trip, moving your color data from its source color space to its destination color space. When you arrive, you have made the conversion.

Rendering Intents. When converting to a color space, in addition to choosing what color space you would like to convert to, you will have the option to choose a rendering intent. This will determine how the conversion is performed and how colors that are outside the destination color space are handled. There are four rendering intents that define how a color conversion is performed.

Relative Colorimetric. Relative colorimetric will convert all out-of-gamut source color to the closest in-gamut color of the destination color space. Essentially, the out-of-gamut color is "clipped" off. Relative colorimetric will also map the white value in the source color space to the white value in the destination color space. When printing, white is typically defined by the color of the paper—even though the paper might have a distinct color, like newsprint gray. When using relative colorimetric to print to newsprint, the white in the image is mapped to the gray value in the newsprint's profile. Because this gray value represents white in the image, the printer is instructed not to print any ink. Essentially, anything that is white in the source image will be translated to the white of the destination color space.

Absolute Colorimetric. Like relative colorimetric, absolute colorimetric will clip out-of-gamut colors, shifting them to the closest in-gamut color. Unlike relative colorimetric, absolute colorimetric will not map source white to destination white; it will change the destination white to the color of the source

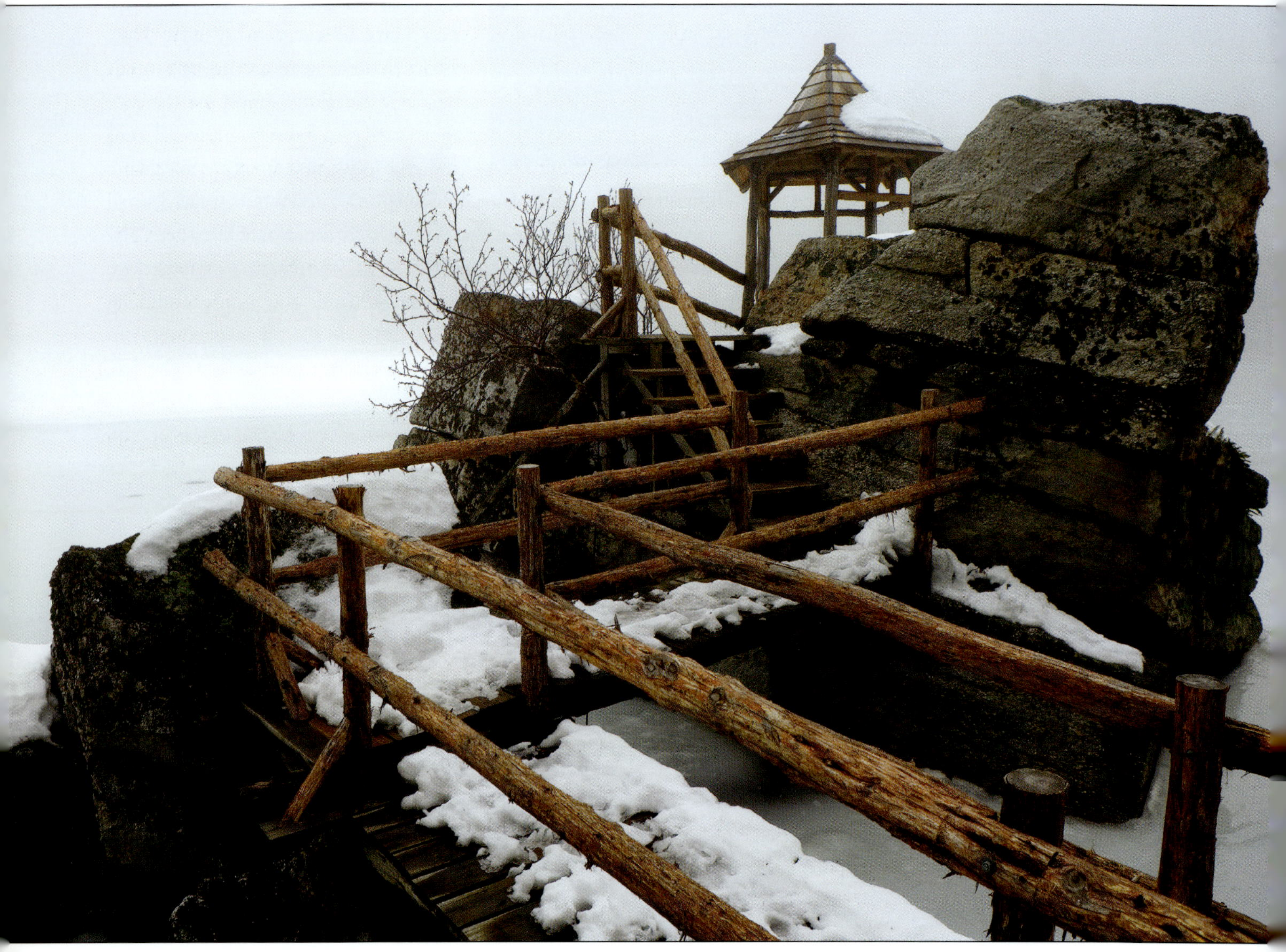

Figure 27—*Gazebo on Lake Mohonk, Mohonk Mountain House.*

white. Suppose the white in the source color space is not pure white but slightly gray. The destination white point will be changed to this slight gray value.

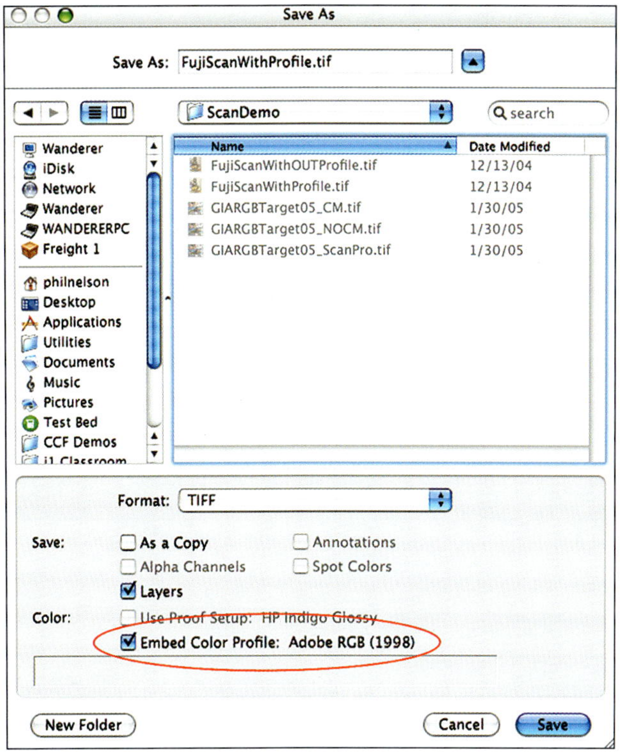

Figure 28—The Photoshop Save As dialog box has an option for embedding ICC color profiles within certain document types. It is always a good practice to embed the appropriate profile into an image file. This is especially true if you are providing your image to someone outside of your work environment, like a client, graphic designer, prepress shop, or printer.

Perceptual. Perceptual will try to maintain color and tonal relationships. So instead of clipping out-of-gamut colors, it compresses all colors inward to try to maintain color relationships. This can be important if your image has a lot of subtle detail and a lot of out-of-gamut colors. By compressing the colors inward, even the in-gamut colors are shifted. Perceptual is often referred to as the "photographic" rendering intent. While it is a good choice for converting photographic images, it is best used when you are converting a lot of out-of-gamut color. If the source color in your image is inside the gamut of your destination color space, relative colorimetric rendering is a better choice, since it will not shift the in-gamut colors as much as perceptual rendering will.

Saturation. Saturation is not as concerned with color accuracy as the other rendering intents. Its purpose is to provide a result with saturated color, even if it means shifting hue. Saturation is the best choice when reproducing saturated, "punchy" color is important and matching color is a secondary concern. The saturation rendering intent is also a good method for converting color from a smaller color space to a larger one.

So how do you determine which one of these to use when you are ready to print your photograph? When you soft-proof your image on screen (see chapter 7), you will have the opportunity to select the different rendering intents and to see how each can affect your print.

Embedding Profiles

When introducing a photograph into a digital imaging workflow, it is always a good practice to ensure that the image has color meaning by embedding the color profile in the image file. An embedded profile will help ensure that as the image moves through the workflow, the different applications and users handling it have a potential to know the color meaning of the file and to make accurate conversions further downstream in the imaging workflow. Profile embedding is often handled behind the scenes by applications and device drivers with color-management capabilities. The Adobe CS2 applications provide this option in the Save As dialog box (figure 28).

Images without an assigned or embedded profile are commonly referred to as "untagged." It is best *never* to leave an image untagged.

4. Software Setup

Setting up your photo-editing applications so that they handle your color in a predictable fashion is an important part of the color-management process. Along with display calibration and profiling, it is one of the first things that you will want to do when initially setting up color management or when opening a photo editing program for the first time. Additionally, if you are relying on ColorSync or ICM, the Mac and Windows Color Management Systems, to perform color handling for you, you will want to make sure that you set the preferences for these as well.

Define a Standard Working Space and Source-to-Destination Conversions

There are numerous applications available for photo editing—too many to mention in this book—and not all of them handle color management in the

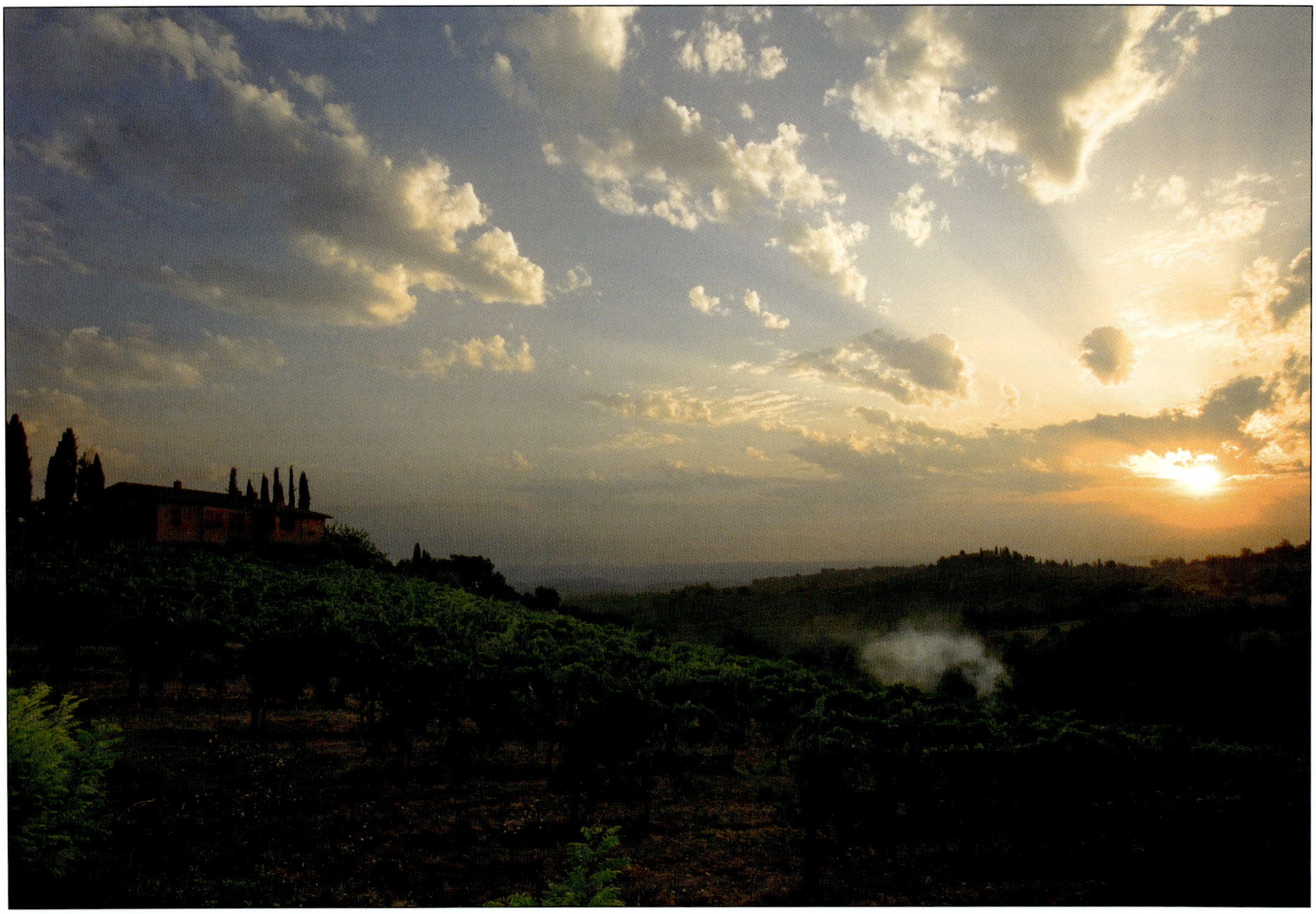

Figure 29—*Sunrise, Tuscany.*

same way. However, if you have an understanding of the color-management process, you will know what to look for in your applications.

With an understanding of the color-management process, you will know what to look for in your applications.

Essentially, you will want to define a standard working space. This will be the common color space into which you will put your image so that you can work on it, like Adobe RGB, ProPhoto RGB, or one of the many other working spaces. Since your image will be coming from a camera or scanner, it will be necessary to convert the image's color from the device's source color space to the destination working space. When printing, a second conversion will need to take place from the working space, now the source color space, to the destination color space of your output device.

Using the preference settings of many applications, you will be able to predefine these settings. This will help you ensure that the color conversions that take place are consistent. Setting up standard source-to-destination conversions for input and output is what you will want to look for in your imaging applications when you are setting them up.

Where Do ICC Profiles Come From?

Since setting up for color management involves assigning ICC color profiles for the different devices and applications you work with, it makes sense to first explore where profiles come from, as well as how and where they are installed on your computer.

Device Manufacturers, Application Developers, Paper Manufacturers. Almost all device manufacturers supporting professional photography will incorporate some form of color management in their device driver or application. When installing this software on your computer, a generic ICC color profile is installed on your system. These profiles are built by the manufacturer to support every model of the particular device that they build. For example, Microtek provides an ICC profile for their ScanMaker 1000XL flatbed scanner. This same profile accompanies every ScanMaker 1000XL that Microtek ships. While every ScanMaker 1000XL is very similar in functionality, not all devices are the same when it comes to color—even when they are the same device from a single manufacturer. Microtek understands this and also ships an application and color target with the ScanMaker 1000XL so that a custom profile can be created for every individual scanner.

Printer manufacturers will also install color profiles that support both their printer and the different papers that the printer supports. Again, these profiles are generic and are built for every printer model that is manufactured. Also, not all papers are alike, and in order for color to translate properly when printing, different profiles are needed for different papers. Most printer manufacturers will install several ICC profiles for the variety of papers that they support. Just keep in mind that a printer profile needs to support both the printer *and* the paper. For this reason, printer profiles are named to describe the printer and paper that they support.

Some application developers that provide photo-editing tools will also install ICC color profiles on your computer. For example, Adobe installs a long list of working-space profiles, like Adobe RGB, sRGB, U.S. Web Coated

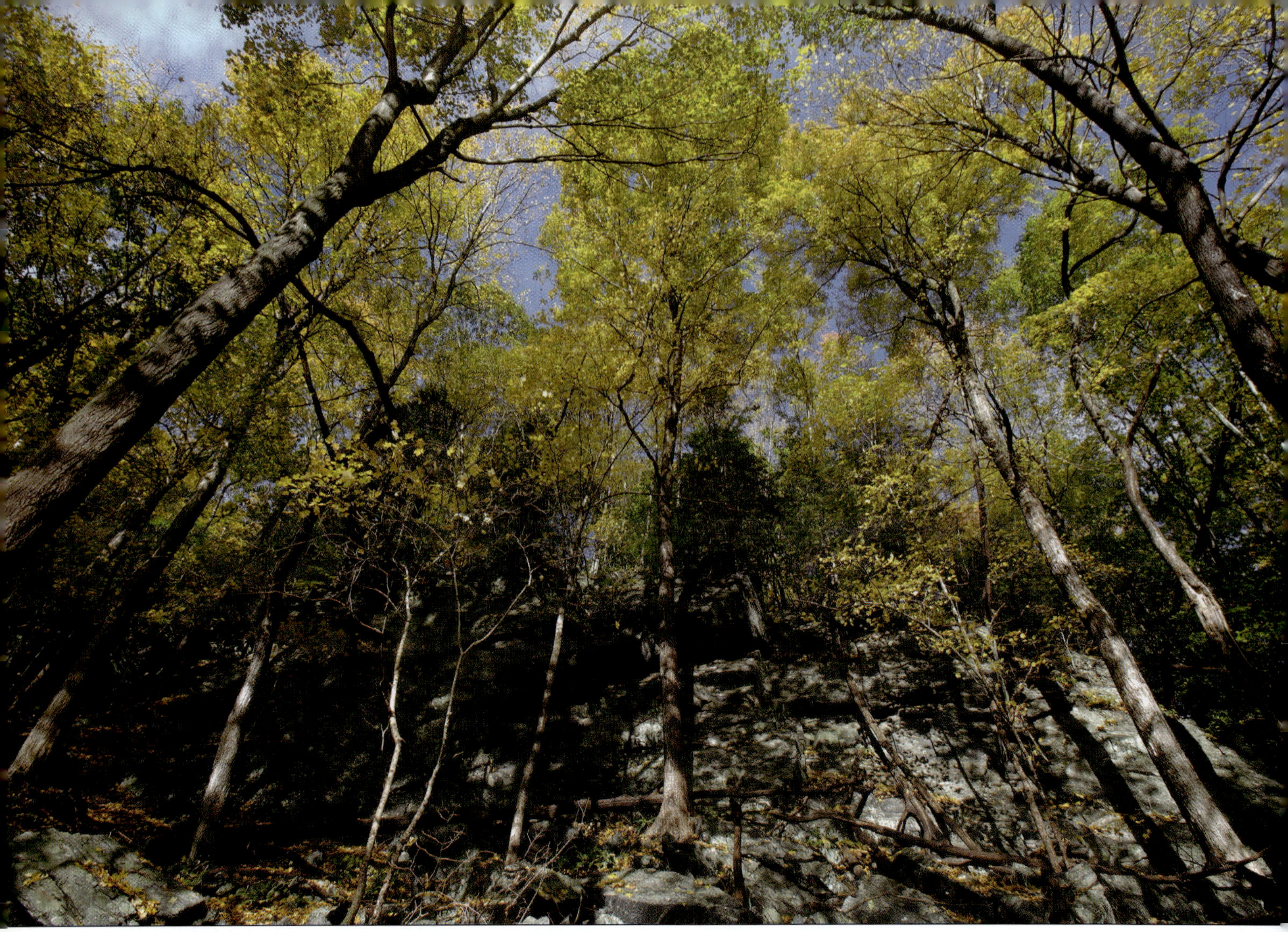

Figure 30—Spring Woods, Bedford, NY.

(SWOP), etc. Phase One installs a very long list of camera profiles that it uses in its Capture One software. Software RIPs developers like ColorByte, which makes the very popular RGB RIP ImagePrint, has a very long list of output profiles that it provides from its FTP site for many of the different papers that are available for the printers that ImagePrint supports.

You may decide that you want to experiment with a new paper that is not supported by your printer, like printing Hahnemühle Photo Rag on a Canon ipf5000. Some paper manufacturers, like Hahnemühle, will provide profiles for their papers and the most popular inkjet printers. If you do not have the tools to build your own custom printer profile, it is always a good idea to check the manufacturer's web site to see if a generic profile is available.

Profile Services. A profile service can build a custom profile for your device if you do not want to invest in the equipment to do it yourself. Having a service build a profile for your printer, for example, would require that you print a color target on your printer and provide the print-out to the profiling service. The service would scan the color target using their color-management equipment and send you the profile. This kind of service can be found by doing a search on the Internet.

Build Your Own. The process of building your own profile is described in the next chapter. Being able to build your own custom profile will give you the greatest flexibility and the maximum control over the individual devices that you work with.

Where Do ICC Profiles Live?

When profiles are installed on your system there are a number of different directories where they can reside. The following paths describe where you can find ICC color profiles on your computer:

Macintosh

Hard Drive > Library > ColorSync > Profiles
Username > Library > ColorSync > Profiles

- Many of the applications that you might work with to edit images will look in the system-level ColorSync > Profiles folder when launching.
- Adobe installs their profiles in Hard Drive > Library > Application Support > Adobe > Color > Profiles. In this folder there is an additional directory named Recommended. This folder contains all of Adobe's working space profiles.
- Some applications, like the ImagePrint RIP, prefer to store their profiles inside their individual application folder.

Windows

Local Drive > Windows > system32 > spool > drivers > color

- Adobe installs their profiles in C: > Program Files > Common Files > Adobe > Color > Profiles. In this directory there is an additional folder named Recommended. This folder contains all of Adobe's working space profiles.
- If you have difficulty locating a profile, try conducting a search for ".icc" or ".icm" files.

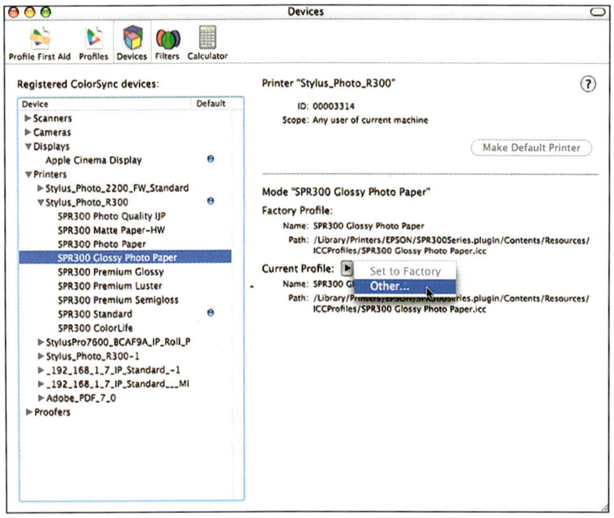

Figure 31—The Devices section of ColorSync Utilities allows custom ICC profiles to be assigned for different devices attached to the computer. For printers, the ColorSync Utility will allow you to assign individual profiles for each default paper type for the printer you select. In this example, when selecting Glossy Photo Paper for the Epson R300, information about the profile assigned to this paper is displayed on the right. Using the pop-up menu next to Current Profile, a custom profile can be assigned to Glossy Photo Paper on the R300. Anytime Glossy Photo Paper is chosen in the R300's print dialog box when printing, ColorSync will automatically assign the custom profile you assigned.

System-Level Color Management: Setting Up

Macintosh. ColorSync can provide color transformations on images coming into your computer from your camera or scanner, for your display, and for your output devices. Apple programs like iPhoto, Preview, and Image Capture will utilize the settings made in the ColorSync Utility application that is installed with OS X. Once ColorSync is set up, color conversions will take place behind the scenes.

Open the ColorSync Utility (Applications > Utilities > ColorSync Utility). There are a number of icons in the toolbar at the top of the ColorSync Utility window (see figure 31).

To set up ColorSync, select the Devices icon. In the list on the left, the ColorSync Utility will display all the imaging devices that are attached to your computer. These are organized in classes, like scanner, camera, display, printer, etc. By clicking the triangle next to the device class name, you can reveal the names of the actual devices that are attached to your computer. (The blue dot to the right of the device name indicates that it is the default.)

Clicking on the device name will reveal information about the device to the right. Here, it is possible to see which profiles are being utilized by ColorSync for any of the devices you are working with. There is a Factory Profile that ColorSync automatically assigns, and a Current Profile, which is the profile that you can assign. If you want to use a profile other than the factory default, simply click on the arrow to the right of Current Profile and select Other from the pop-up menu. Navigate to the profiles folder and select the color profile that you want to use with the device.

If you are setting up your digital camera, for instance, the camera profile you select is what will be used by ColorSync as the input profile for images that you import from your camera. As long as the application you are working with supports ColorSync, like iPhoto, then the proper color profile assignment will take place.

When assigning the Current Profile for a printer, the ColorSync Utility will list the standard default paper types for your printer. When the printer is connected to your Mac, ColorSync assigns these profiles to each of the printer's papers. If a profile does not exist for the printer and paper, a generic profile is assigned. Like the camera profile, a custom profile can be assigned as the Current Profile. When printing, ColorSync will utilize the assigned output profile as the destination color space and make the necessary color conversion. When printing, many printer drivers provide an option to select ColorSync as a method for color conversion. Figure 32 shows this option in the Epson R300 print dialog box. When you select a paper type when printing, ColorSync automatically uses the ICC profile you assigned in the ColorSync Utility for that paper.

The display profile, like the other device profiles, can also be assigned in the ColorSync Utility. In addition, the System Preferences in Mac OS X also provide a function for assigning a display profile. Open System Preferences (under the Apple menu) and click the Displays icon. Then, click the Color tab. The box to the left lists all the display profiles on your system. Selecting a profile here will also assign it as the Current Profile in the ColorSync Utility.

Windows. Microsoft Windows XP has similar functionality to ColorSync. However, the Color Settings control panel that is needed to assign ICC profiles is not part of the standard Windows XP installation (figure 33). A trip to Microsoft's web site is

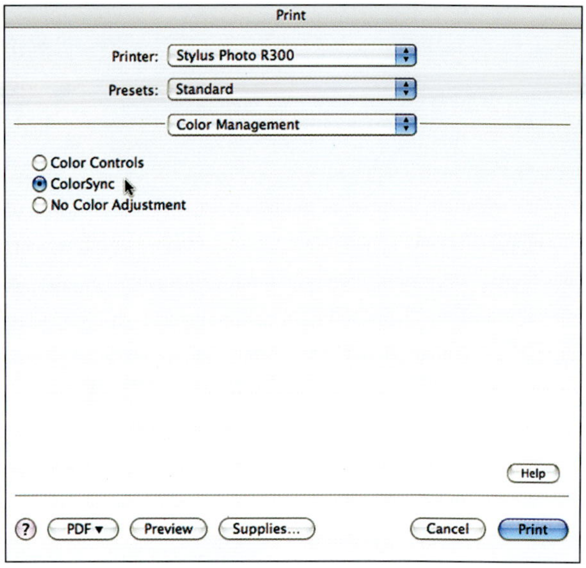

Figure 32—The Color Management panel of the print driver for the Epson R300 printer has an option for selecting ColorSync as the color-conversion process. This will utilize the settings in the ColorSync Utilities for color managing output to the R300 using the Current Profile that is set for whatever default papers are available for the printer. Simply selecting the paper you are printing on will assign the proper ICC profile.

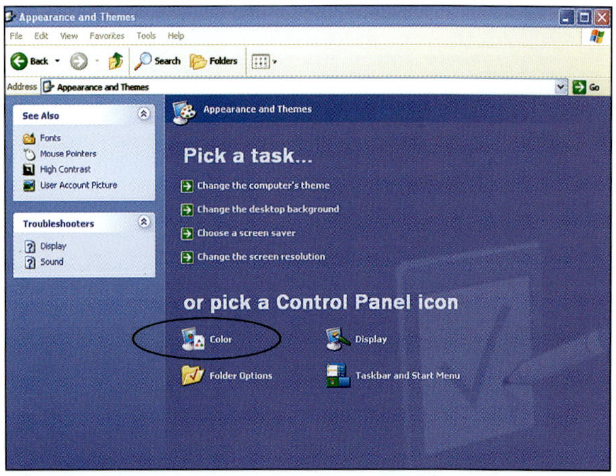

Figure 33—The Color Settings Control Panel is not installed with Windows XP and requires an additional installation. The Color Settings control panel can be downloaded from Microsoft's web site.

It is possible to select different profiles for the different video cards installed on your computer.

necessary in order to acquire, download, and install the Control Panel (search the Microsoft site for "Control Panel"). Once installed, Color Settings will appear in the control panel under Appearance and Themes.

Selecting the Devices tab will provide a means for associating ICC color profiles with the different devices that you use (figures 34 and 35). The pop-up menu at the top of the dialog box presents a selection of device classes like display, printer, etc. When a device class is selected, all devices of this class are listed in the box below the menu. Selecting the device will reveal the profile currently associated with the device. To change the device/profile association, click the Add button and select the ICC profile that you want to add. Selecting the profile and setting it as the default will bind the two to one another. When assigning a display profile, it is possible to select different profiles for the different video cards installed on your computer.

Shortcomings of System-Level Color Management. Fundamentally, ICM and ColorSync provide a valuable service for anyone using a consumer-level digital camera, an application like iPhoto, and an inkjet printer.

ICM and ColorSync are not as valuable to anyone using high-end professional tools like Photoshop, simply because many professional tools provide their own, more sophisticated color-management systems and will bypass ColorSync or ICM. Also, many manufacturers of professional scanners and digital cameras will provide software that has its own methods for handling color. Even though ColorSync or ICM can assign a profile for the device, there is a chance that the device's software will not use it. The Microtek example in the previous section is a good example of this.

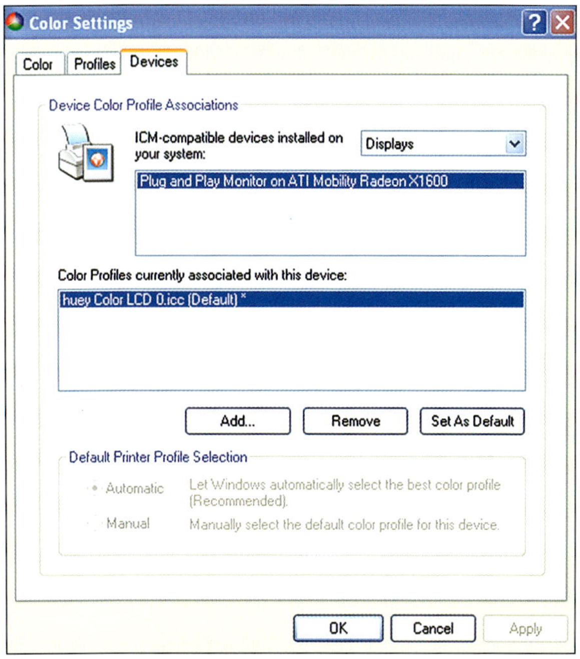

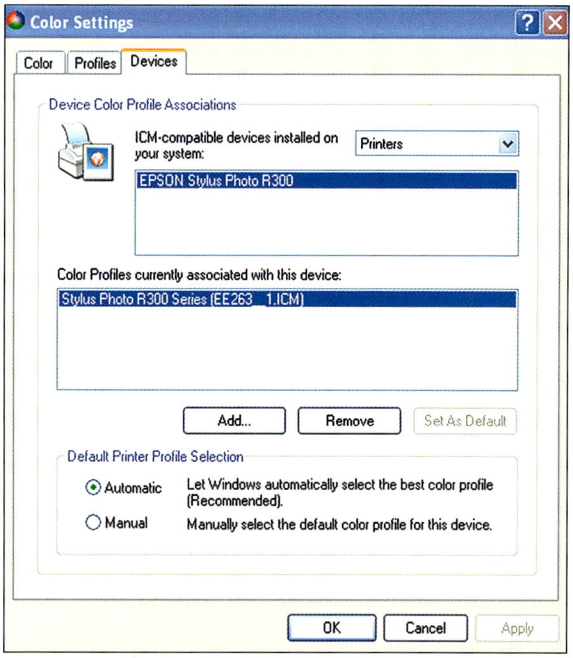

Figure 34 (left)—The Devices tab in Window's Color Settings control panel. In this example, it is possible to change the display profile by adding the new profile to the Color Profiles list and selecting it. ***Figure 35 (right)****—Selecting the class of device in the pop-up menu at the top of the dialog box will reveal a list of the different devices available and the profiles associated with them. In this example, the file "Stylus Photo R300 Series (EE263_1.ICM)" is a package of ICC color profiles that was installed with the print driver. The package contains output profiles for the standard default paper supported by the Epson R300 printer, like Epson Enhanced Matte, Epson Premium Glossy Photo, Epson Premium Luster Photo, etc.*

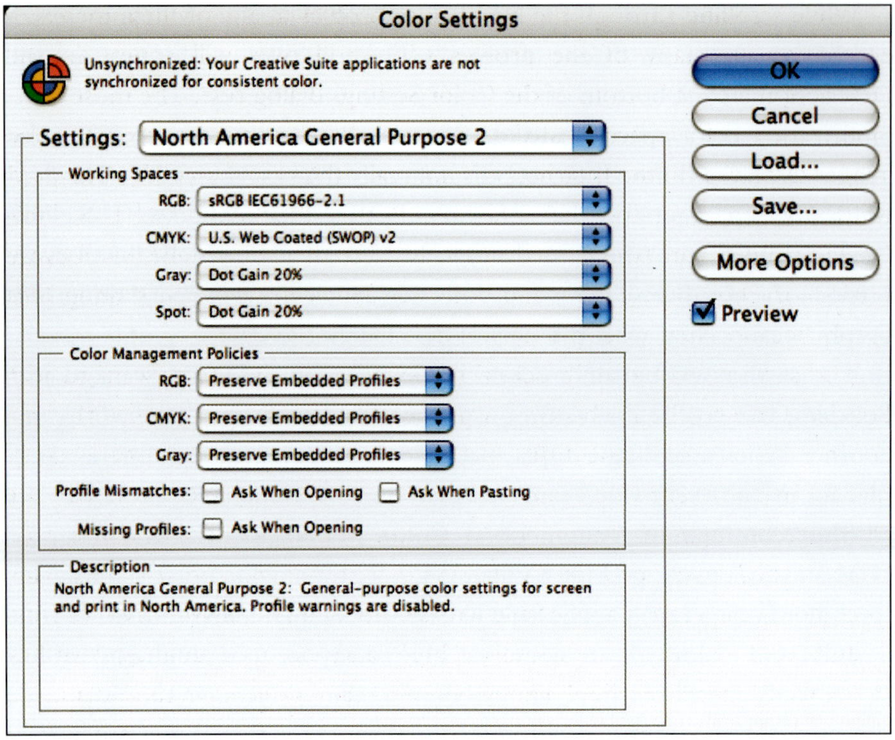

Figure 36—Adobe Photoshop's Color Settings dialog box (Mac OS X).

If you are using professional-level equipment and software, you will want to pay close attention to how these devices and programs handle color management.

Application-Level Color Management: Setting Up

Color Settings in Photoshop CS2. Of all applications used by professional photographers, Adobe Photoshop is the most common. Photoshop incorporates sophisticated color handling so that you can be confident that the color in your image is being handled properly when you open it, work on it, proof it on screen, and output it. Photoshop's color-handling preferences are accessible from the Color Settings dialog box (Edit > Color Settings). It is here that you will define your standard working spaces and some important color handling policies. These settings help minimize guesswork, a lot of wasted time and effort, and the potential for making a mess out of your photograph.

When opened for the first time, Photoshop CS2 will ask you if you want to define your color settings.

When opened for the first time, Photoshop CS2 (and several of the previous versions) will ask you if you want to define your color settings. Essentially, Adobe is recommending that you do this. The default color settings are set to North America General Purpose 2 (see figure 36). You can change these to meet your specific needs.

In the area designated for working spaces, you can choose your default working spaces from the pop-up menus. You establish this default setting for RGB, CMYK, Gray, and Spot settings. If you determine that Adobe RGB (1998) is your preferred working space, then set this in the RGB pop-up menu. If you will be providing CMYK versions of your files to designers and ad agencies for page layout, you may decide to define a standard CMYK color space like U.S. Web Coated (SWOP) v2.

While scrolling through the list of color profiles in any of these menus, a description of many of the profiles you scroll over will appear in the Description area at bottom of the Color Settings dialog box. The most commonly used color space is sRGB. Because sRGB is most appropriate for images displayed on the Internet, it is not really the best choice for a standard RGB working space for photographers. Both Adobe RGB and U.S. Web Coated (SWOP) are widely used simply because they are installed with every version of Photoshop. These are both excellent choices when sharing files simply because they are so widely used.

The section immediately below Working Spaces is Color Management Policies. Here you define how you would like to have images handled that are not in the same color spaces that you have defined as your standard working spaces. In the three pop-up menus for RGB, CMYK, and Gray, you set whether you want to have Photoshop Convert to the Working Space or Preserve the Embedded Profile of the document when you open it, if its color space does not match your default setting. For example, if you have set your default RGB working space to Adobe RGB, and you open an image that has the embedded profile, ProPhoto RGB, you can either have the document automatically converted to Adobe RGB, or you can have Photoshop open the image in its original color space, ProPhoto RGB.

It is highly recommended that you check each of the three check boxes below the pop-up menus. If the check boxes for profile mismatches and missing profiles are checked, any time that you open an image or paste content from an image that is in a color space that does not match your standard working space settings or does not have an embedded profile, Photoshop will present you with a warning (see figure 37). Before actually opening the file, Photoshop will ask how you would like to proceed, whether you would like to open the file in its original color space or convert to your standard color space, or, perhaps, you would like to discard the color profile altogether and not color manage the document. If the file being opened does not have an embedded profile, Photoshop will ask whether you would like to assign a profile and then, perhaps, convert the color to your working space (see figure 38). This option will be discussed further in the next chapter. As long as these three boxes are checked, you will always be forewarned if there is a color mismatch and given the opportunity to make adjustments that suit your current work objectives.

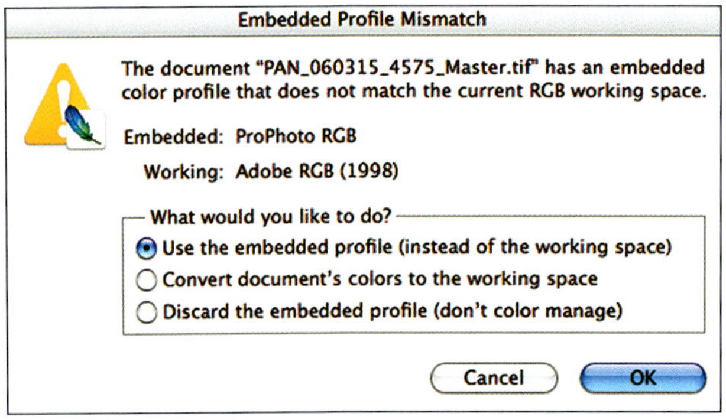

Figure 37—Photoshop's Embedded Profile Mismatch dialog box. Photoshop will present this dialog box if the image that is being opened has an embedded profile that does not match the user's standard working space as defined under Color Settings.

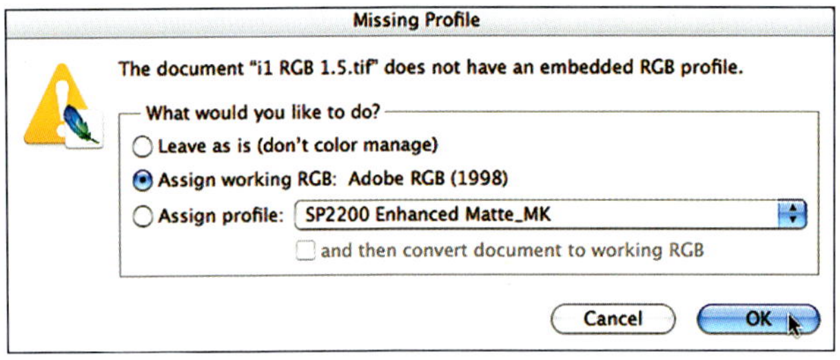

Figure 38—Photoshop's Missing Profile dialog box. When a file is being opened and does not have an embedded profile, Photoshop presents the user with these options. This dialog only appears if the Missing Profile: Ask When Opening box is checked in Photoshop's Color Settings.

Just above the Preview check box in the Color Settings dialog box there is a More Options button (figure 39; next page) that will open two additional sections: Conversion Options and Advanced Controls. Conversion Options provides a means for selecting a desired color engine (or CMM; see page 31) and default rendering intent, and whether to use black-point compensation and 8-bit dithering. Advanced Controls provides options for desaturating monitor colors and changing the blending behavior of RGB colors. These settings are covered in detail below.

The default color engine is Adobe's proprietary one. This is listed as Adobe (ACE)—short for Adobe Color Engine. Since Adobe provides Photoshop and the Adobe Creative Suite for both the Macintosh and Windows operating systems, having a common conversion engine across platforms ensures that the color transformations on both platforms will be the same. If you are consistently moving your images from one platform to the other or you do work in other Adobe applications like Illustrator or InDesign, Adobe (ACE) is a good choice.

Choosing ColorSync (for Mac users) or ICM (for Windows users) will tell Photoshop to use the default color engine that is set in either ColorSync or ICM control panels. The Apple CMM is a good choice if you are working with different applications from different developers on your Mac and you want to make sure that they all use the same CMM.

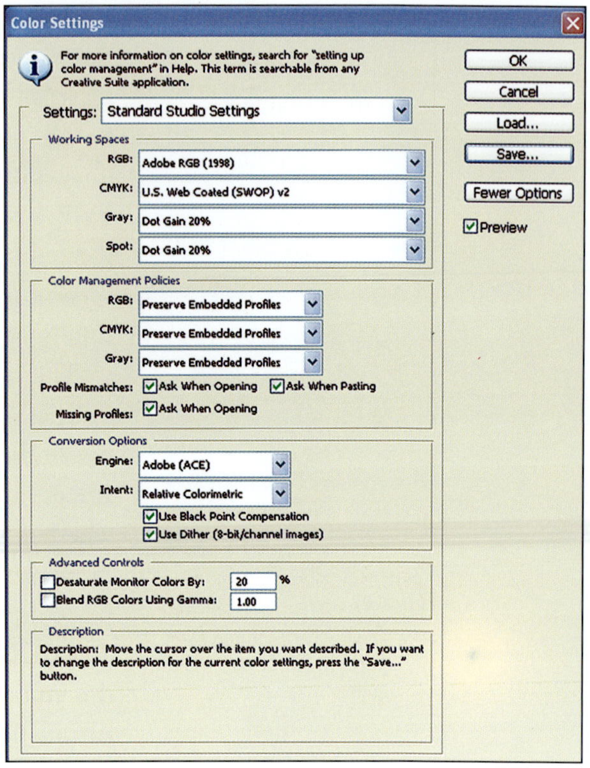

Figure 39—Photoshop's Color Settings dialog box with More Options showing (Windows XP). This reveals access to Conversion Options and Advanced Controls.

In addition to selecting the color engine, you can also set the default rendering intent. When performing a color conversion in Photoshop, there will be occasions when you will be able to choose the rendering intent that you want to use, and there will be occasions when you will not. For example, in figure 37 (previous page), the Embedded Profile Mismatch dialog, there is an option to convert the document's colors to the working space, but there is no choice in this dialog box for a rendering intent. In these situations, when Photoshop does not give you an option, it will use the default rendering intent that you select in Color Settings.

The Use Black Point Compensation setting will map the black point of your source color to the black point of your destination color space. Adobe is trying to ensure that you will achieve the best black response and the maximum dynamic range when you use this feature. In some circumstances, when Use Black Point Compensation is turned off, the black values are clipped when running the conversion and the blackest black in the destination color space ends up being gray or washed out. In other circumstances, blacks can fill in and eliminate detail if this setting is not checked. It is strongly recommended that you keep Black Point Compensation turned on.

The Use Dither (8-bit/channel images) setting is used to minimize potential banding when converting images. It is best left turned on.

In the Advanced Controls panel, Desaturate Monitor Colors and Blend RGB Colors options should be left turned off. Desaturate Monitor Colors is intended for use when the color space of the image being edited is larger than the color space of the display. In this situation, it is not possible to accurately see the colors outside the display's color gamut. By desaturating display colors, it might be possible to see the out-of-gamut colors. Unfortunately, the screen representation of the image will not translate accurately on output.

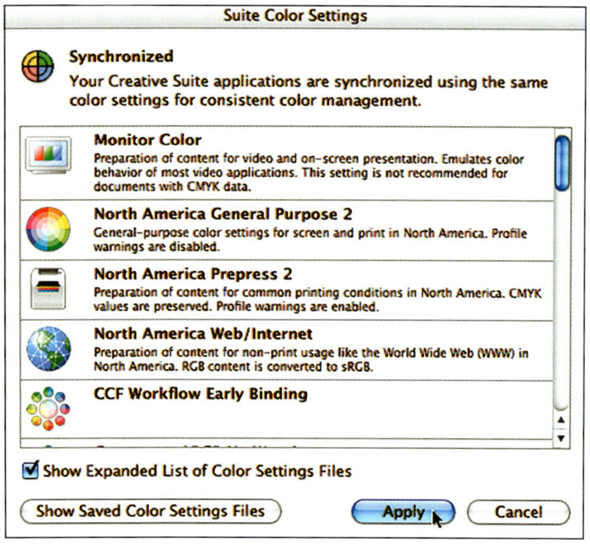

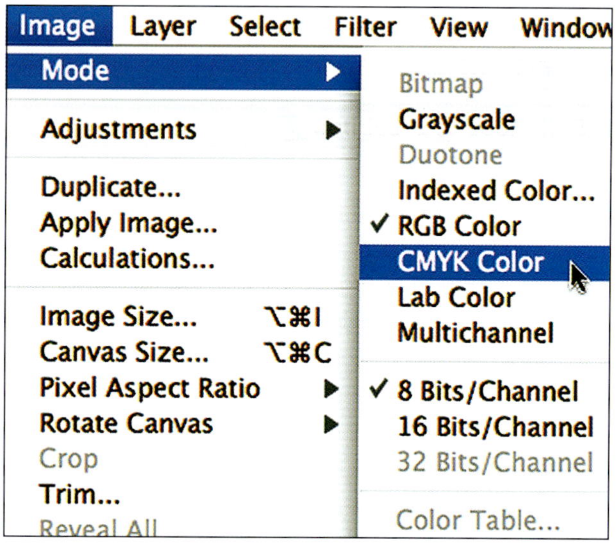

Figure 40 (left)—The Suite Color Settings in Adobe Bridge allow you to synchronize your color settings with all applications in Adobe CS2. *Figure 41 (right)*—Conducting a color mode change from the Image menu will call on the settings that have been established in the Color Settings dialog box. If you have set up your standard CMYK color space to U.S. Web Coated (SWOP) v2 and the standard rendering intent to Perceptual, Photoshop will use these settings when invoking Image > Mode > CMYK Color.

The Blend RGB Colors setting allows the user to alter the way Photoshop blends adjacent colors. Again, these are both best left turned off.

Once you have defined all of the settings in the Color Settings dialog box, it is possible to save them. Pushing the Save button will allow you to give your settings a name and save them to an Adobe Color Settings File (or .csf). These files can be used by other applications in the Adobe Creative Suite. Using the Load button in Adobe Illustrator CS2, for example, you could load the saved .csf file that was created in Photoshop. This is an easy way to match the color settings between applications.

Adobe has taken this a step further in the CS2 suite of applications by allowing you to synchronize your color settings across all applications in the suite. In Adobe Bridge, the CS2 file-browsing application, there is a setting under the Edit menu, called Suite Color Settings (figure 40). Once a .csf file has been created, invoking this feature in Bridge will allow you to select your previously saved settings and push them out to all the Adobe Suite applications in one step.

The settings that are established in the Color Settings dialog box are also used when conducting a standard color mode change from the Image menu (figure 41). If you invoke a mode change from RGB to CMYK by selecting Image > Mode > CMYK Color, for example, Photoshop will use the working space setting for CMYK as the destination color space and the rendering intent that is set under Conversion Options.

Also, any readings in the Info palette (figure 42) for color spaces other than the one the image is in will utilize the settings in the Color Settings dialog box.

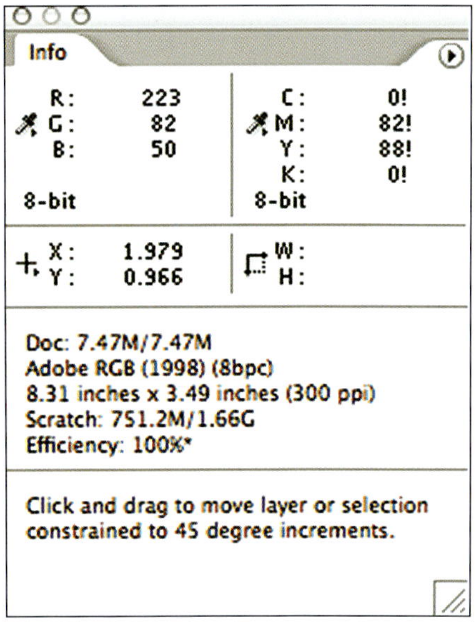

Figure 42—Photoshop's Info palette uses the Color Settings when calculating color values for color modes other than those of the current document. For example, if you have opened an RGB image, the Info palette will use the settings in the Color Settings dialog box to calculate CMYK values.

Setting Up Phase One Capture One Pro. The Capture One Pro RAW conversion software from Phase One is a powerful tool for organizing and processing RAW images. Phase One has built full ICC support into their

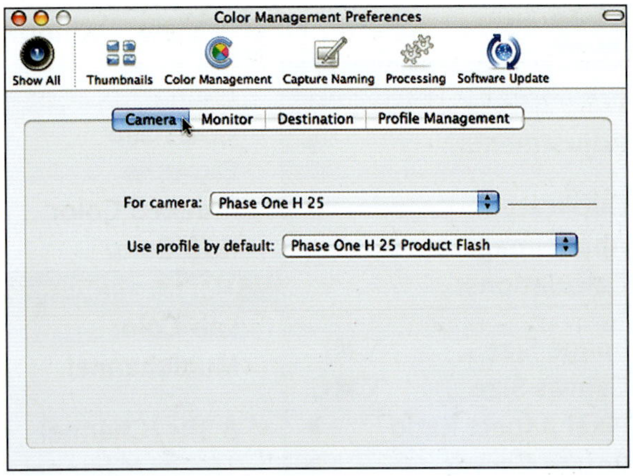

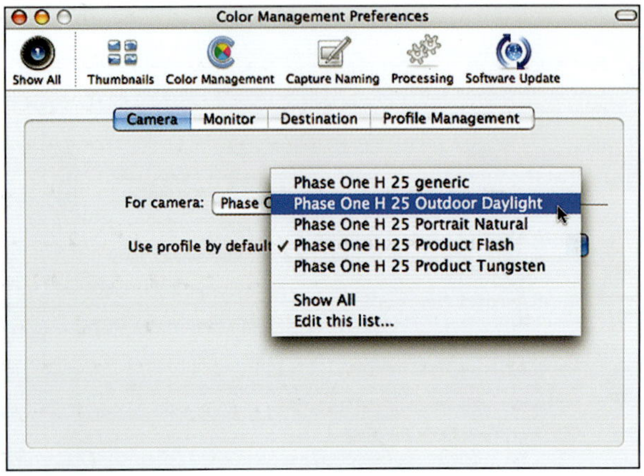

Figure 43 (left)—The Camera tab in Phase One Capture One. Figure 44 (right)—C1's Preference window gives the user the ability to define his default camera profile.

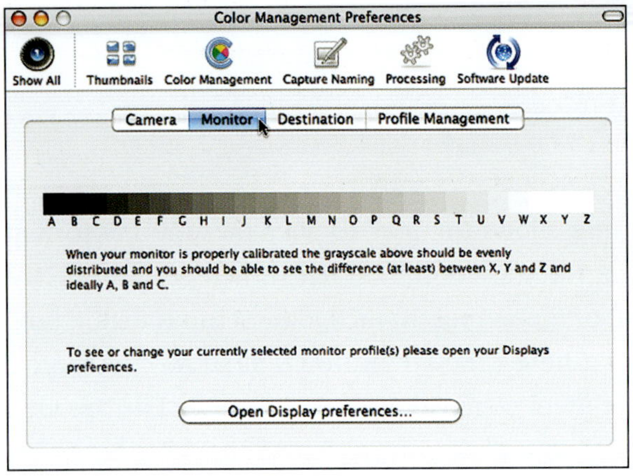

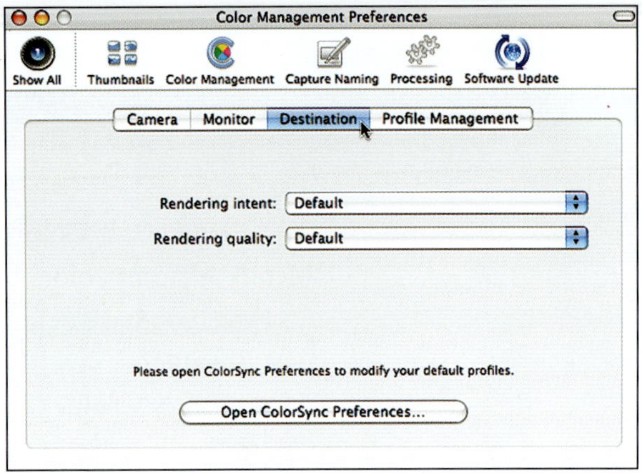

Figure 45 (left)—C1's Monitor tab helps evaluate whether the user's display is calibrated. Figure 46 (right)—C1's Destination tab provides settings for Rendering Intent and Rendering Quality

application. Setting up Capture One (C1) is initiated in the software's preferences.

From within C1's Preferences you can select the Color Management tools. Here, Capture One Pro lets you set color handling for your camera, monitor, and output. It also provides a profile manager so that you can choose which profiles you will work with from within C1. The Camera tab allows you to define an input profile for your camera (figure 43). Phase One provides a very long list of profiles for many of the most popular cameras on the market. These profiles are loaded on your system when you install C1.

The Camera tab allows you to define an input profile for your camera.

In the Camera tab you can select your camera from the For Camera menu. This will shorten the list of profiles in the second menu to include just the profiles for the camera you selected (figure 44).

Under the Monitor tab, C1 presents a gray scale (figure 45). If you cannot see an even distribution from black to white, C1 suggests that you calibrate and profile your display. The button at the bottom provides direct access to the Display System Preferences so that you can change the profile if necessary. Chapter 5 describes how to build an ICC profile for your monitor.

The Destination tab provides a choice of default rendering intents and rendering qualities (figure 46). When C1 converts an image for output, it will use the rendering intent and quality setting that you define here. C1's default settings are a Perceptual rendering intent and Best Quality. The quality settings provide a tradeoff between quality and performance, where the Draft quality is the best performer.

The last tab under Color Management is Profile Management (figure 47). Here, C1 provides a list of all the profiles on your computer (provided they are located in the common directory for profiles). The list is separated into two groups: Camera and Destination/Proof. These can be selected from the menu above the list. The Camera list shows all the input profiles on your system. This will include all the camera profiles that were installed with the C1 software. By selecting the profiles for just the cameras that you work with, you can limit the size of the profile menus in C1 to include just the profiles that you select here, making profile selection a lot easier. The Destination/Proof list shows all the working-space and output profiles on your system. Here again, you can limit the number of profiles in C1's profile menus by selecting only the profiles that you work with.

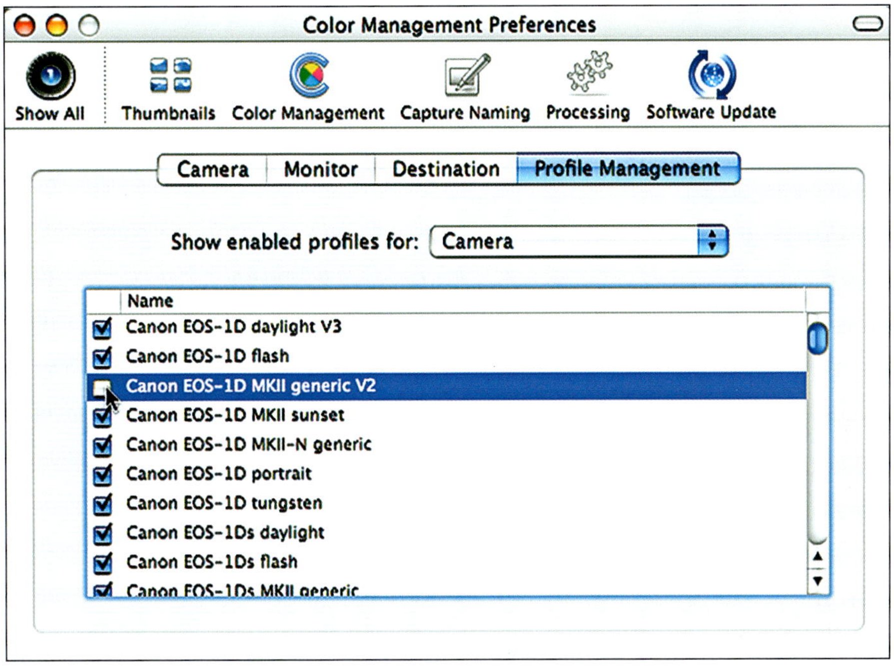

Figure 47—The Profile Management tab in C1 provides the option to turn off profiles that are not used. This shortens the list when selecting a profile from a menu in C1, providing only the profiles that the user needs.

Once the C1 color-management preferences are set, you will have the application ready for image input and output. The process for handling these tasks will follow in the next two chapters.

5. Building a Color-Managed Workflow

Just as you set up your applications for color management, you will also want to make sure that your input and output devices, like your camera, scanner, or printer are set up and working properly as well. Part of the setup process entails working with the hardware to ensure that it is functioning at peak performance and working with the device drivers for your hardware to make sure that it understands your color-management needs. Additionally, you will want an ICC color profile for all of your devices.

This chapter describes how to calibrate your hardware and generate your own custom profiles. If you do not want to invest in the necessary equipment for building profiles, you will find other alternatives for acquiring custom profiles at the end of the chapter.

What Is Needed?

There are numerous solutions available for calibrating and profiling the different equipment that you work with. A quick search for "color-management solutions for photographers" on the web will turn up a long list that varies widely on price and functionality. Setting up a photographic workflow will require both color-management hardware and software. The hardware is packaged with the necessary software to make it run. Also, there are additional software packages from third parties that will work with the most popular color-management hardware.

Hardware for Setting Up Color Management. There are two primary hardware components for calibrating and building ICC color profiles: colorimeters and spectrophotometers. Both can be used to calibrate and create profiles for output devices and displays, but they have distinct differences in the way that they capture color information.

Colorimeters capture light data using colored filters to imitate the way that the human eye sees color.

Colorimeters. Colorimeters capture light data using colored filters to imitate the way that the human eye sees color. Typically these devices read light emitted from another source. Most commercial monitor-calibration devices on the market for photographers are colorimeters and only have the ability to calibrate and build an ICC profile for a computer display. The GretagMacbeth Eye-One Display2, the MonicoOptixxr, and the Pantone Huey are examples of popular solutions for color managing a computer display.

Spectrophotometers. Spectrophotometers, on the other hand, have their own light source and record light wavelengths by bouncing light off of a colored surface and recording the spectral data as it is reflected back to the measurement device. Capturing spectral data provides some unique advantages

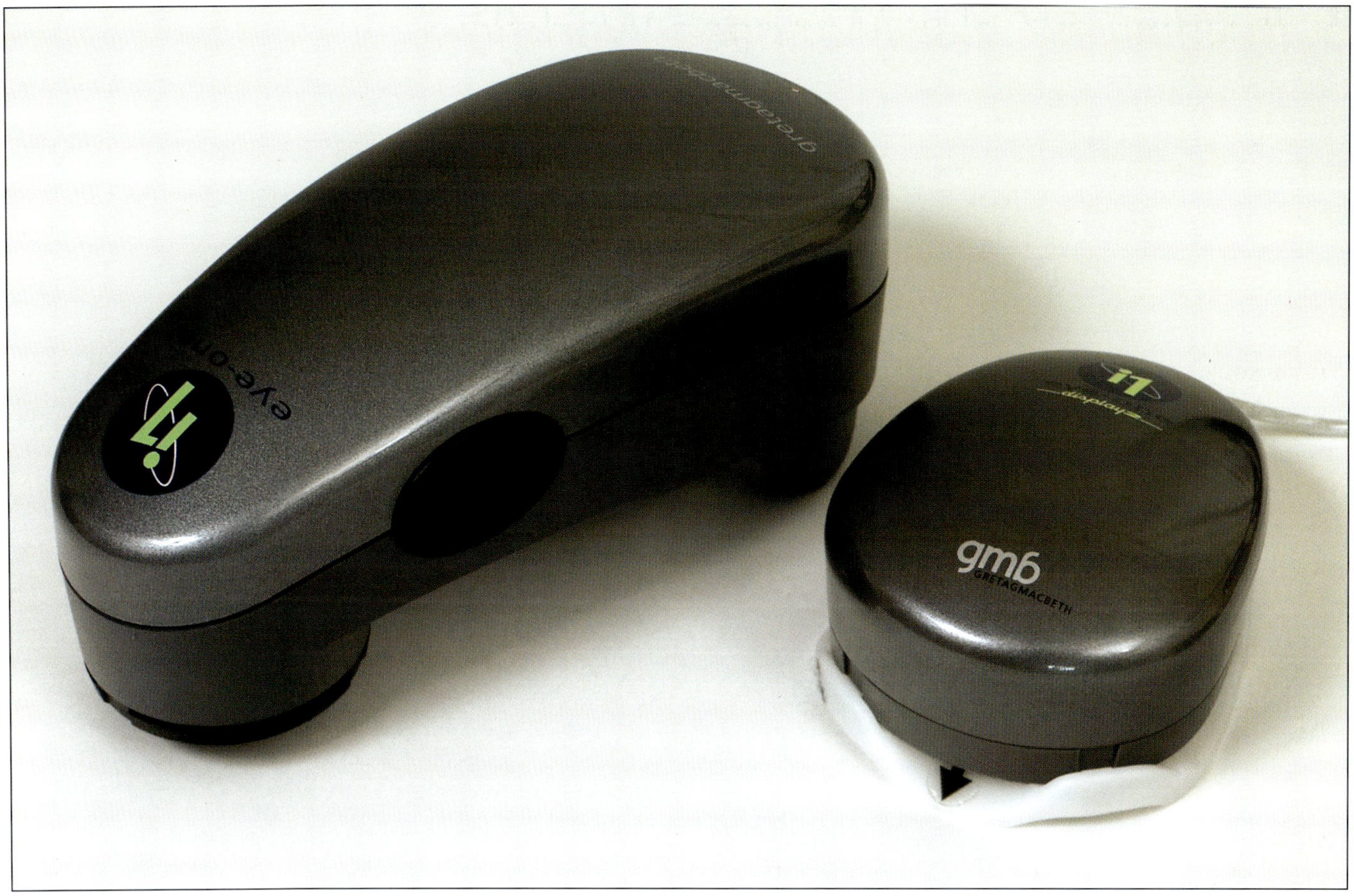

Figure 48—GretagMacbeth's i1 Spectrophotometer (left) and i1 Display 2 Colorimeter (right).

over a colorimeter. For instance, spectrophotometers can create great printer profiles and also double as a colorimeter for display profiling. Spectrophotometers typically cost more than colorimeters, but the flexibility they offer can offset the cost of the device. The X-Rite Pulse ColorElite, GretagMacbeth Eye-One Photo, and ColorVisionPrintFIX Pro Suite are examples of full color-management solutions for photographers.

Software for Setting Up Color Management. In addition to hardware solutions, there are software solutions that work with a variety of the most popular hardware devices. GretagMacbeth's ProfileMaker is a high-end suite of profile-making applications with a package specifically made for photographers: PM5 Photostudio. ProfileMaker works with X-Rite and GretagMacbeth hardware. Another solution, Integrated Color Corp's ColorEyes Display boasts that its monitor profiler works with just about any measurement instrument.

Device Calibration vs. Profiling

It is not uncommon to hear the terms calibration and profiling used to describe the process of building an ICC color profile. In actuality, these are two distinctly different processes.

Calibration. A calibration is performed to fine-tune a device by physically changing its performance so that it closely matches the manufacturer's specifications. Think of taking your car to the dealership for service. When the service department tunes your car, the mechanic is trying to make the car perform as though it was brand new. This makes the car run the best it can. Over time, as you drive it, your car will drift out of tune, and you will take it back to the dealership for another tune up.

When calibrating a device in a digital photographic workflow, like your monitor, the purpose is to manipulate the display into a state of peak performance, a state that can be repeated if the display drifts out of calibration. Once the device is calibrated, it can then be profiled. For the profile to work effectively, the device should always be in its calibrated state.

Profiling. Profiling a device is similar to what the FBI does when they profile a criminal. (Hopefully, you don't think of your photographic equipment as criminals.) Profiling is the process of characterizing the device. When the FBI profiles a criminal they are pursuing, they are trying to gain an understanding of the person's psyche—his personality traits, strengths, weaknesses, etc. This information helps the FBI anticipate what the criminal will do and gives them a better chance of tracking him down.

When profiling a scanner, monitor, or printer, the objective of the profiling process is to gain an understanding of how the device perceives, displays, or outputs color. To make this process work, the profile-building tools will ask the device to record, display, or print color samples. It will then compare how the device handled the color by comparing it to a reference file for the color samples. It will make note of the color differences and build this information into an ICC color profile. This data will also define the color gamut of the device. The profile can then be used to translate color from one color space to another.

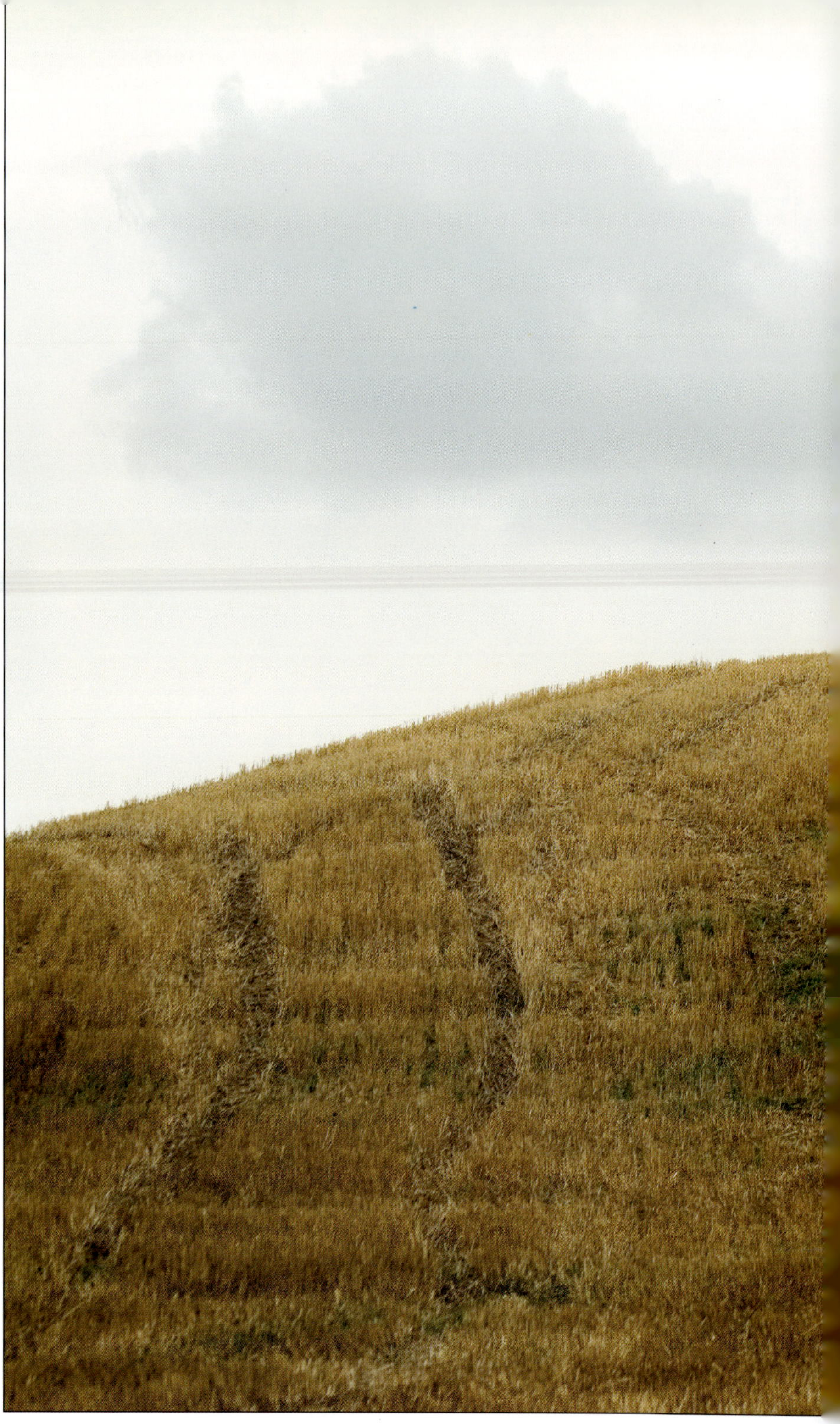

Figure 49—*Lone shed, Tuscany.*

Display Calibration and Profiling

Types of Displays. There are displays available today of all shapes and sizes. For the most part, manufacturers have ceased to build cathode ray tube

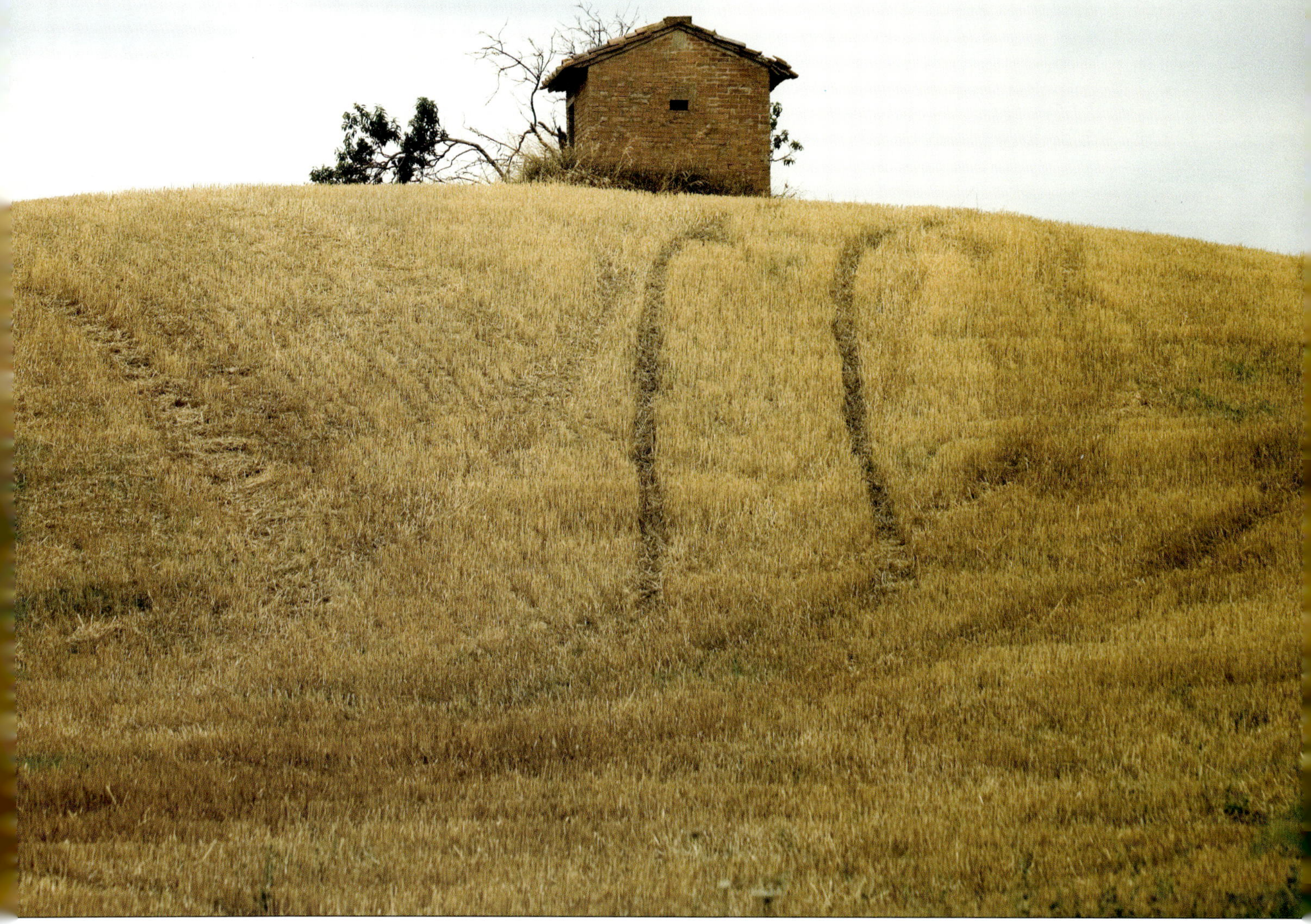

(CRT) monitors in favor of liquid crystal displays (LCD). If anything, the fact that LCDs have allowed individuals to replace bulky CRTs and reclaim desk space has led to their success. Additionally, CRTs have an inherent, barely perceptible flicker that can lead to eye strain when viewed for long periods of time. LCDs don't have this problem and offer greater luminance, a larger color gamut, reduced power consumption, and less magnetic radiation.

Display Calibration. Depending on the make and model, some displays have buttons on the front panel that will allow you to adjust white point, gamma, and luminance (or color temperature, contrast, and brightness).

Some displays, like the Apple Cinema Display, do not provide these features and cannot be calibrated. This does not mean that you cannot build a profile for an Apple display. You simply bypass the manual calibration steps in the color-management software. Most packages for display profiling do this by providing an easy mode and an advanced mode, where advanced gives you full calibration using the controls on the display. Assuming that your display can be calibrated, once this process is finished, the color-management software will make

Display Calibration and Profiling Solutions

GretagMacbeth	X-Rite MonacoEZColor
i1 Photo	Integrated Color Corporation ColorEyes
Eye-One Display2	Pantone Huey
ProfileMaker Pro	

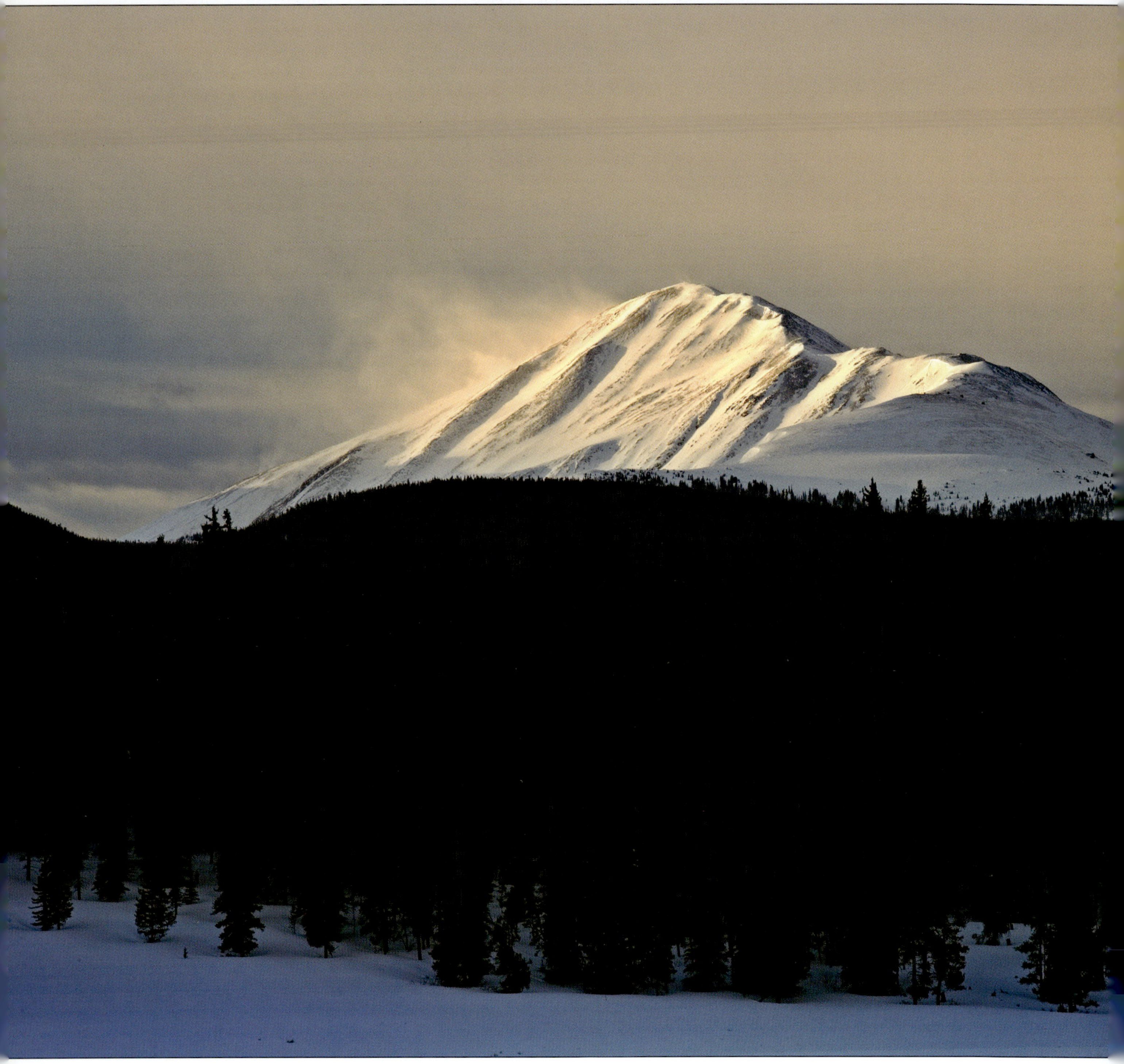

adjustments to the color lookup table (CLUT) in the computer's video card. After this adjustment is made, the software will build an ICC profile and store it in the proper directory on your computer's hard drive.

Using a colorimeter or spectrophotometer to run your calibration, you will launch the software application that came with the device to begin the display calibration process.

The software will ask you some questions about your display (whether it is a CRT or LCD, etc.). It will then ask you to define a target for three standard settings: the display's white point, gamma, and luminance. When defined, these settings establish the target calibration that the color-management software and hardware will try to hit. The settings will not take effect until the calibration process is completed.

White Point. The white point defines the color temperature of the display—whether white on the display looks cool or warm, orange or blue. When adjusting white point, you want to try to approximate the white point of the light under which you are viewing your prints (explained further in chapter 8). This makes a more accurate screen-to-print comparison.

White point is defined in values of D illuminants. Standard settings are D50 and D65 (see figure 51). Although this may seem backward, the higher the number, the cooler the display will appear. In early prepress days, the common standard was established as D50. Setting a display's white point at D50 helped match the screen to the paper white of the stock that was being printed. That standard has expanded over the years to include D65 as more and more inkjet papers with optical brighteners are used for output. These papers are cooler in tone, so trying to make a match may require a cooler (or bluer) white-point setting. If you are using an inkjet printer, try setting your white point to D65. (By the way, if your display or the software you are using describes a white point in Kelvin measurements like 6500K, don't let this confuse you. Many manufacturers will describe D65 as 6500K.)

Another common setting in display-calibration software is Native White Point. If you target a Native White Point, the calibration software will set the white point to the value it measures. This is a good solution if your display does not have calibration capabilities. If you are calibrating several displays and want them to match, it is better to specify a fixed setting like D65.

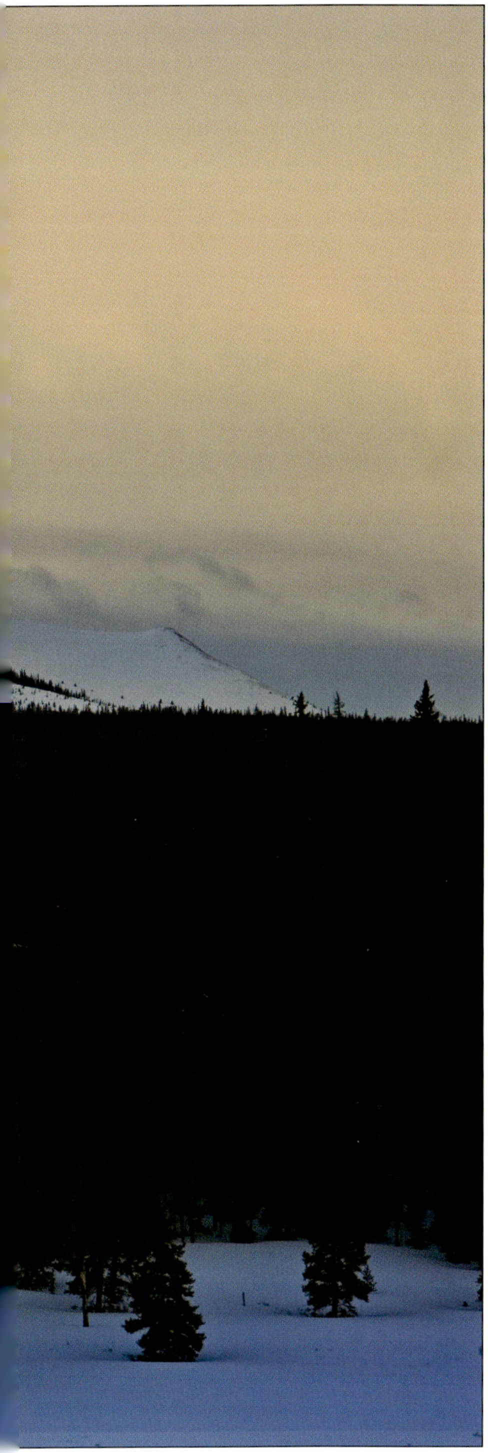

Figure 50—Mount Baldy, Colorado.

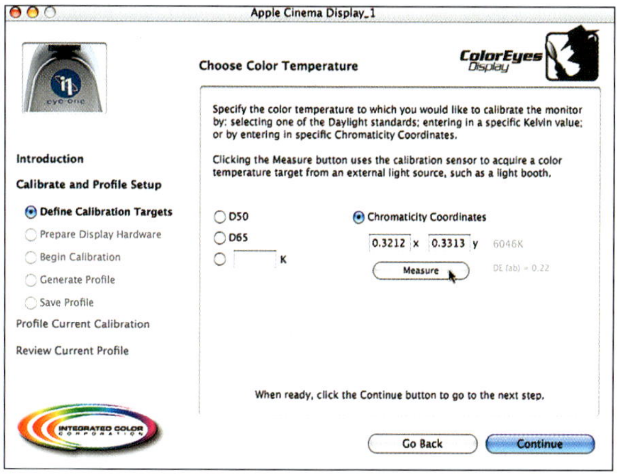

Figure 51—Integrated Color Corp's ColorEyes Display solution works with a variety of spectrophotometers and colorimeters. This dialog box allows the user to define a target white-point setting either by selecting D50 or D65, the standards, or by entering a Kelvin value. Additionally, ColorEyes Display provides a facility for measuring the luminance and color temperature values of a light source. This a great way to match the display's white point to the light under which prints are viewed.

Since the standard lighting for viewing prints is D50 (equivalent to noon daylight), you would think that D50 would be the proper target setting for the white point of your monitor. A display set to D50, however, can tend to look a little orange—especially if you are comparing your screen to inkjet prints, which tend to be more cool. Many photographers set their displays to D65 even when viewing under D50 light. While this may sound rather confusing, the best approach is to start with a setting of D65, make some prints, hold them under a D50-balanced light, and make a comparison. If the screen seems too blue, try building a profile with a warmer white point.

Gamma. Loosely put, gamma refers to the contrast of your display and the distribution of tonal values from black to white. The goal of adjusting gamma settings when calibrating is to distribute the tonal values as evenly as possible so that your display presents your photograph as accurately as it can. Critical areas of an image are in the darkest and lightest tonal regions, where image detail is defined by subtle differences in tone. Displays that "fill in" the darker tones may not be able to represent detail as anything but black. The most common setting for gamma is 2.2. The Windows operating system has been using this gamma setting for years. Apple, back in the days of the original Macs and monochrome displays, set their system to a gamma of 1.8 to provide a better match for laser printers. This has caused a lot of confusion over the years. The best choice you can make, especially if you work with a Mac and you share your images over the web, is to set your display gamma to 2.2. An image edited on a Mac set to gamma 1.8 will look dark on Windows systems.

Luminance. The luminance setting is very important for evaluating color, especially if you are working in an environment with multiple displays. You will want to make sure that the displays are set with the same luminance value. Luminance is measured by candelas per meter squared, or cd/m^2. Most of the current LCD displays are able to achieve a luminance of greater than 400 cd/m^2, which is far too bright for normal viewing. A good target for an LCD is between 90 and 120 cd/m^2. CRTs should be set around 100 cd/m^2.

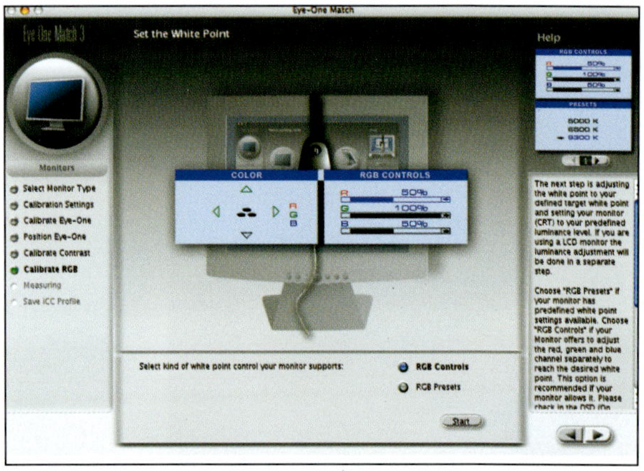

Figure 52—*GretagMacbeth's Eye-One Match instructs the user step by step through the screen calibration and profiling process. Clicking the Start button on this screen will initiate the process of setting the white point of the display.*

Once the targets for white point, gamma, and luminance are entered, the software will guide you through the process of manipulating the controls on your display until you hit your target settings. A spectrophotometer or colorimeter placed on the front of the display keeps track of your progress as you change the display's settings for RGB values, contrast, and brightness. When all three targets are hit, the display is calibrated. Figure 52 shows a sample of the interface from GretagMacbeth's Eye-One Match software.

Display Profiling. After the calibration process is complete, the color-management software will fine-tune the color lookup table on the computer's video card and then start the profiling process. Once the display is in its peak operating condition, it can be profiled. From a reference file of known color values, the software sends a series of color swatches to the screen, and

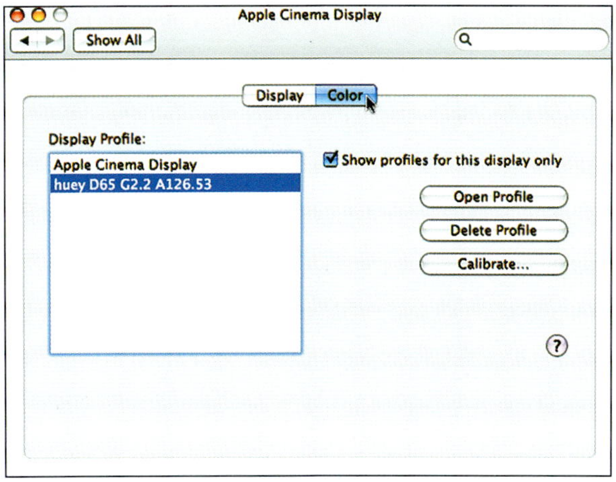

Figure 53—The Mac OS X Displays System Preferences has a tab for Color. Here it is possible to assign the display profile.

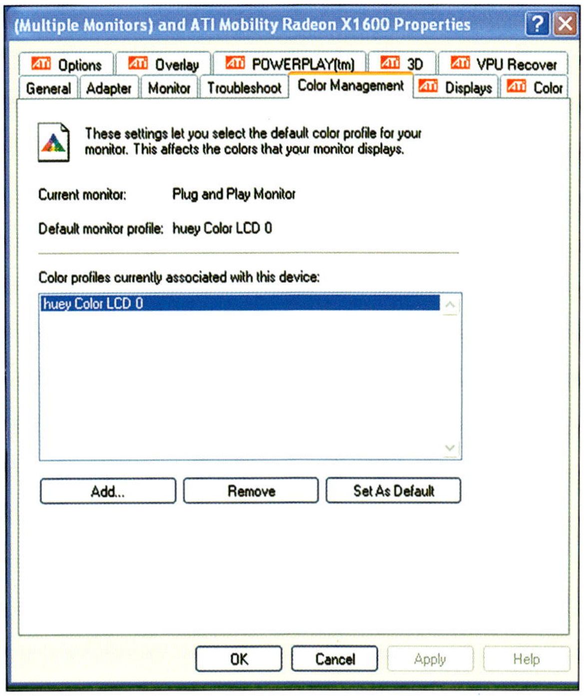

Figure 54—To access the display profiles under Microsoft Windows XP, access Display Preferences, and click on the Advanced button. Under the Color Management tab, you will find the settings for selecting and changing the profile.

the spectrophotometer or colorimeter reads these values as the display renders them. Once the software has completed this step, the values that were read are saved in tables of numbers in an ICC color profile along with the values from the reference file. The values that were read are RGB and the values in the reference file are LAB. Having this data, the profile can be used to transform colors so that they are accurately rendered to screen. Additionally, the data that is collected in the profile will describe the color gamut of the display.

When asked to save the profile, it is a good idea to give it a descriptive name. If you choose, the name can also include the date so that you know when it was made and how long it has been since you last calibrated and profiled your monitor. Some display-profiling software provides an optional function that will remind you on a regular basis, like once a week, that it is time to recalibrate. Once named, the profile is saved in the proper folder on your computer and is assigned to the display. It is always a good idea to double check to make sure that the profile is actually the one that is in use (figures 53 and 54).

Testing Your Calibration and Profile. The last part of the display calibration and profiling process is testing to see how well your display is working. There are two tests that you might consider, one that checks the black threshold and another to evaluate gamma. The following steps describe how to check the black threshold of your monitor.

1. Open Photoshop and create a new RGB document. Assign your working-space profile.
2. File the document with a solid black background of R 0, G 0, B 0.
3. Using the Marquee tool, make a rectangular selection on the left side of the window. Fill the rectangle with the following RGB values: R 8, G 8, B 8.
4. Draw a second rectangle to the right of the first. Fill this with the following RGB values: R 12, G 12, B 12.
5. Select the following from the View menu: View > Proof Setup > Monitor RGB.
6. Put Photoshop in Full Screen Mode by going to View > Screen Mode > Full Screen Mode or typing the letter F twice.
7. Hide all of Photoshop's palettes by hitting the Tab key.
8. The display should appear solid black, and you want to look for the two rectangles that you filled with RGB 8 and RGB 12 (figure 55, next page).
9. If you *cannot* see the RGB 8 rectangle but *can* see the RGB 12 rectangle, then your monitor is not able to display black values less than level 8. In other words, any black tone defined

by RGB 8 or less will appear black on your screen. This is not a big problem.

10. If you cannot see either rectangle, then your monitor is not able to display tones less than level 12. In other words, any tonal value of RGB 12 or less is displayed as black. If you cannot see the RGB 12 rectangle, you really cannot tell the limit of the black threshold. It could be greater than 12. If you have this problem, then it is worth investing the time to run a second display calibration and to make another profile. If after several calibrations your display is still performing the same way, then chances are that you are not going to be able to correct it. If seeing details in the shadow areas of your photographs is important, it might be time to invest in a new display.

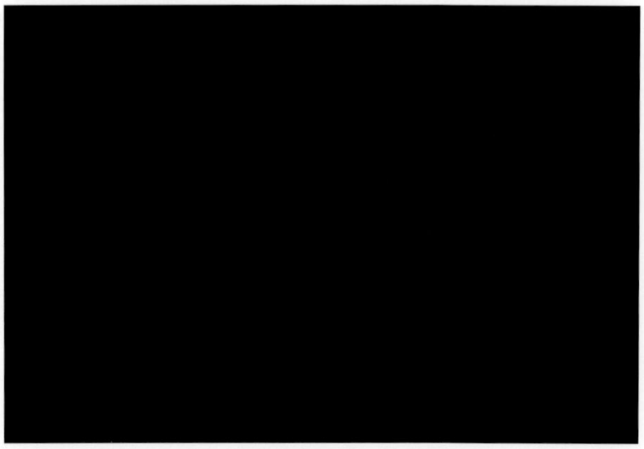

Figure 55—The black threshold test is a good way to find out how well your display can render black values and differentiate values at the lower part of the tonal scale. This image represents what you might see when running this test. The ability of the display to render subtle differences in black tones is critical for displaying shadow detail in photographs.

Another test that you can run to check the performance of your display is a gradient test. Try the following:

1. Create a new RGB document in Photoshop that is 512 pixels wide by 172 pixels high at 72 ppi. Assign your working-space profile.
2. Using the Linear Gradient tool set to build an even ramp from black (R 0, G 0, B 0) to white (R 255, G 255, B 255), draw a gradient horizontally across the document starting on the left border and ending on the right border. Hold the Shift key while drawing to constrain your movement to an exact horizontal. This should create a smooth black-to-white gradient.
3. Select View > Proof Setup > Monitor RGB.
4. Put Photoshop in Full Screen Mode by selecting View > Screen Mode > Full Screen Mode or typing F twice.
5. Hit the Tab key to hide Photoshop's palettes.
6. The gradient ramp should show no banding (see figure 56). Some banding might be slightly perceptible, but if you are seeing strong vertical bars in the ramp, try recalibrating your display. Also, if you are perceiving strong color anywhere in the ramp, try recalibrating.

Figure 56—A gradient test like the one shown here is a great way to evaluate the gamma of your display. An even ramp from black to white is desirable; banding is not.

Creating Input Profiles

When creating a profile for input devices, it is necessary to scan or take a photograph of a color test chart or target with the device that is being profiled (figure 57). The image that is captured of the target is imported into the profiling software. The profiling software compares the color data from the scanned or photographed target with the target's reference, which is included with the profiling software. The reference data describes what the color values of the physical target actually are. If there are differences between the color in the reference file and the way the device perceived the color in the physical target, this is recorded in the profile. This record of how the device perceives the reference colors not only characterizes the device but also is used to accurately translate the device's color to any other color space.

This record is used to accurately translate the device's color to any other color space.

Digital Cameras. The reason for profiling a digital camera (or camera back) is to minimize the work that might be necessary if the camera captures color incorrectly. If, for example, a camera characteristically creates images with a slightly red cast, the photographer will continually have to correct for this in an image-editing program. This can be time consuming. On the other hand, if this characteristic is recorded in an ICC profile, then the color-management system can take care of this problem automatically when the camera's profile is assigned.

RAW Files. An important consideration prior to profiling a camera is whether or not you photograph and process RAW images. Working with RAW files requires adding a conversion application into your photographic workflow. These applications differ in the way that they handle color management and assign ICC profiles.

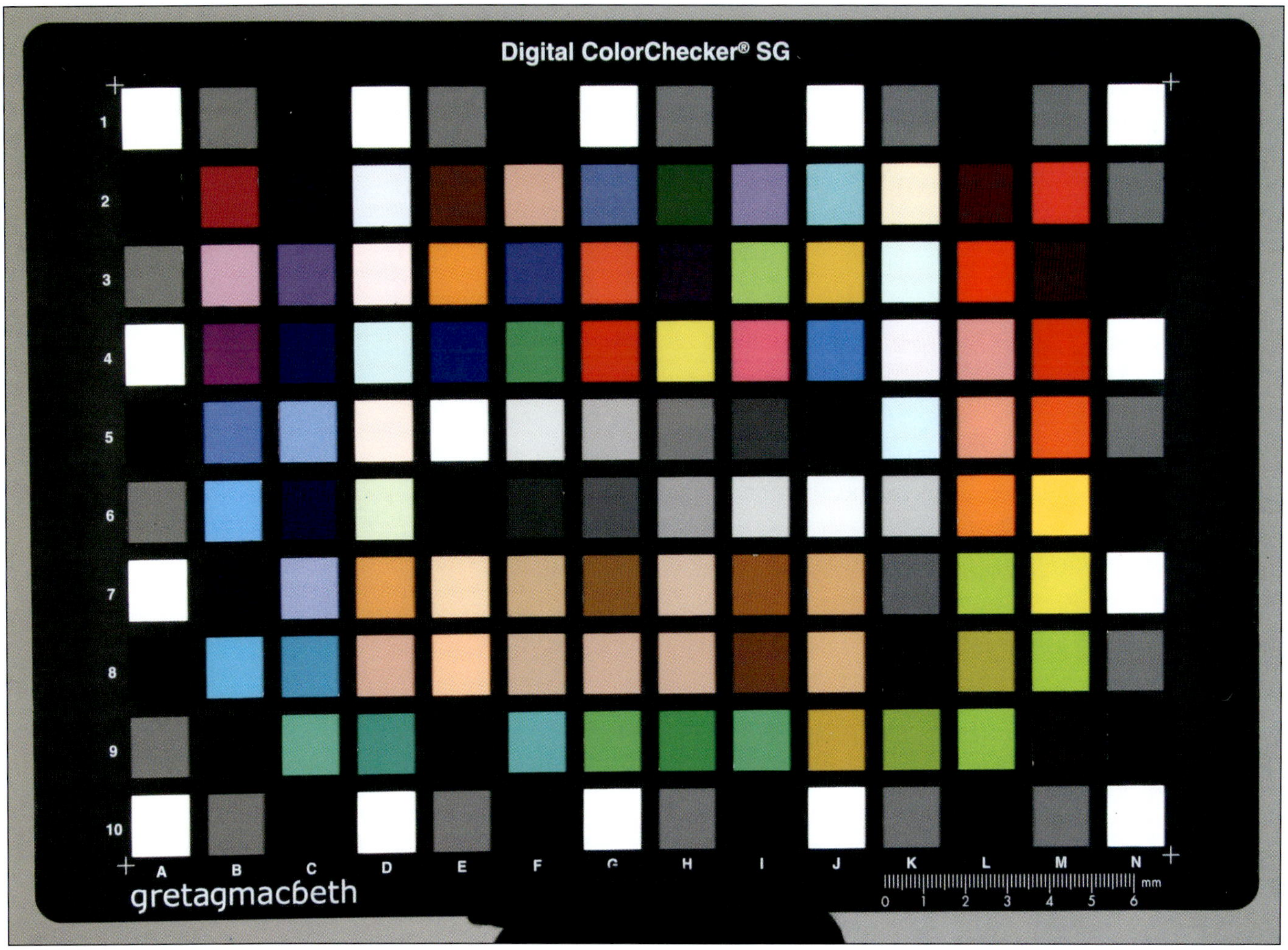

Figure 57—GretagMacbeth's Digital ColorChecker SG. This color target was designed specifically for creating scanner and camera profiles. The gray, black, and white swatches around the perimeter help the software calculate whether the chart has been evenly lit when photographing. Also, GretagMacbeth has included the standard 24-patch ColorChecker within the ColorChecker SG (patches E2 to J5). Photograph by Mark Gundlach, GretagMacbeth Global Services.

As noted in the sidebar (right), when shooting RAW images, the settings that are made to optimize the image are recorded as instructions on how the image should be converted, but nothing is actually being changed in the RAW image file. Therefore, you can think of the RAW file as an unprocessed negative that can be developed over and over again. Each time that you process the film, you can change the chemistry and get a different result. If you do not like the results or think of a new idea for how you would like the film to be developed, you can start all over again. This is what Apple's Aperture software refers to as "versioning"—creating multiple renditions from one RAW file. With many RAW converters, your image will not enter the ICC color-managed workflow until after it has been processed and exported out of the conversion application. Even if your camera tags your RAW images with sRGB or Adobe RGB profiles, these profiles are disregarded by the RAW converter.

In order for anyone to be able to work on a RAW image, the RAW conversion application has to interpret the RAW file and provide an RGB preview on screen. The converters developed by the camera manufacturers, like Canon's DPP or Nikon's Capture Editor, support the conversion of images from their respective cameras. Others, like Adobe Camera Raw, Phase One Capture One (C1 provides support for cameras other than just Phase One's camera backs), DxO, Bibble Pro, BreezeBrowser Pro, RawShooter Premium, and RAW Developer—just to name a few—are built to support numerous camera models. These converters include specific support for each and every camera and/or camera back whose RAW files they convert. Since RAW files are proprietary to the camera manufacturer, every developer of RAW conversion software has to build custom support for the RAW files for each camera, hence the lag time between a new camera's introduction and support for the camera's RAW files in the RAW-conversion applications.

When opening a RAW image, the RAW converter interprets the camera's RAW data and provides an RGB preview of the image on screen so that it can be edited. A RAW image displayed on screen without interpretation would appear as a very dark grayscale. Each RAW conversion application interprets RAW files in its own particular fashion. In order for a color-accurate preview of the image to be displayed, the image's color has to be passed through the display's ICC profile to the screen.

In order to make an accurate conversion to the screen's color space, the RAW converter has to provide RGB source color data to the monitor's dis-

Two Modes of Capture: RAW and Camera Processed

One simple distinction between images captured in a RAW format and those captured in JPEG or TIFF format is where the image data is processed.

When shooting in the JPEG or TIFF mode, image data from the camera's sensor is processed in-camera utilizing the camera manufacturer's conversion algorithms. Settings made on the camera by the photographer for contrast, saturation, white point, and desired color space are taken into account when the process takes place. The resulting image is saved as a JPEG or TIFF file that has been converted to either sRGB or Adobe RGB, depending on whether the camera supports these color spaces, which is the trend with most digital SLRs today.

RAW images, on the other hand, require processing on a computer system with a conversion application. When processing, the settings that are made to optimize the image (contrast, saturation, white point,) are simply recorded as instructions on how the image should be converted; even though you can see the changes that are applied as they happen, nothing is actually being changed in the image file. It is not until the RAW data is exported to a standard computer image file, like JPEG, TIFF or Photoshop's PSD file format, that the color is "fixed." This means that, after the shoot, you can change the settings and come up with different results.

Another distinct advantage of a RAW capture is the higher bit-depth of the image. Digital SLRs typically deliver RAW files with 12-bit per pixel (bpp) image data compared to 8-bit JPEG and TIFF files. (Photoshop treats 12bpp RAW files as 16-bit images.) The tonal range of a 12-bit image is 4,096 tonal levels as opposed to an 8-bit file that has 256 tonal levels. This additional image data while adding to the file size, gives a 12-bit image a great deal more editing flexibility. Pushing an 8-bit file around by making drastic edits can easily introduce posterization or banding into the photograph, while 12bpp images will be able to handle significantly more abuse.

play profile. For this reason, most RAW converters have their own internal RGB color space. Apple, for instance, describes their "preview" color space as Wide Gamut. Whatever it is, the RAW converter has to interpret color from every camera it supports in order to provide an RGB preview. In a way this could be described as an internal camera profile—not an ICC color profile per se, but a characterization of the camera nonetheless.

Apple's Aperture even takes the screen presentation one step further by allowing the user to see the RAW image in the color space of an output device, simulating what the image will look like when printed (see chapter 7 on proofing). This would not be possible if the color in the image did not have a source definition that could effectively be translated to the color space of an output device.

Adobe Camera Raw (ACR) uses built-in camera "profiles" to render and convert RAW color from the different cameras that it supports. Camera Raw also provides tools that allow the user to alter ACR's default interpretation of a RAW image, changing and saving ACR's settings as a new camera default. This can be very useful for fine-tuning or correcting an individual camera's RAW color interpretation and then applying it to every new RAW image coming from the camera.

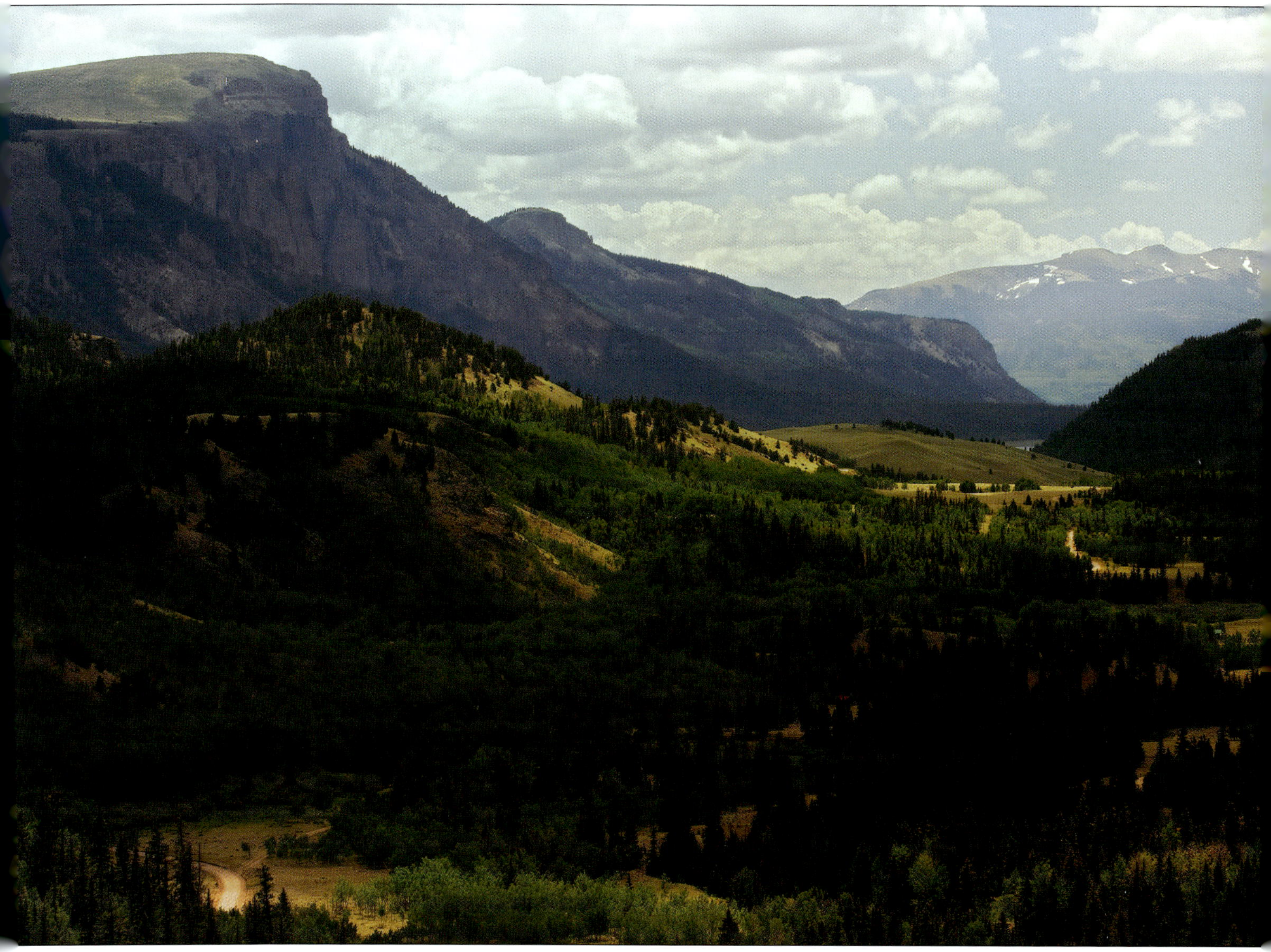

Figure 58—Southwestern Colorado.

Phase One's Capture One Pro is one of a number of RAW conversion packages that include a long list of very good ICC camera profiles that can be selected and assigned to RAW images in the application. C1 also allows users to assign their own custom camera profiles (figure 59). These profiles are used to interpret the camera's RAW color data within the RAW converter so that the image can be accurately displayed on screen and the RAW image can be edited before conversion.

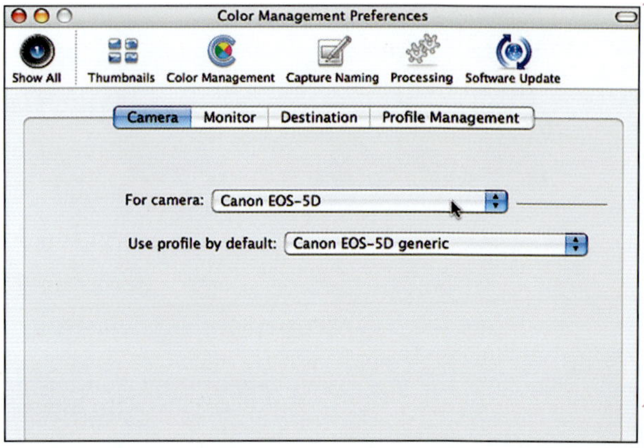

Figure 59—Phase One Capture One's color-management preferences allow an ICC profile to be assigned as a default for each camera used.

Because some RAW conversion applications provide their RAW interpretation "profiles," an ICC color profile for the camera is not necessary. Other applications utilize ICC profiles built purposely for the cameras whose RAW images they support. Some of these allow the user to assign his own custom camera profile. Whichever converter you have decided to work with, you will have significant opportunities to modify the RAW image's color prior to conversion—opportunities that are not available for JPEG or TIFF files that are converted in the camera.

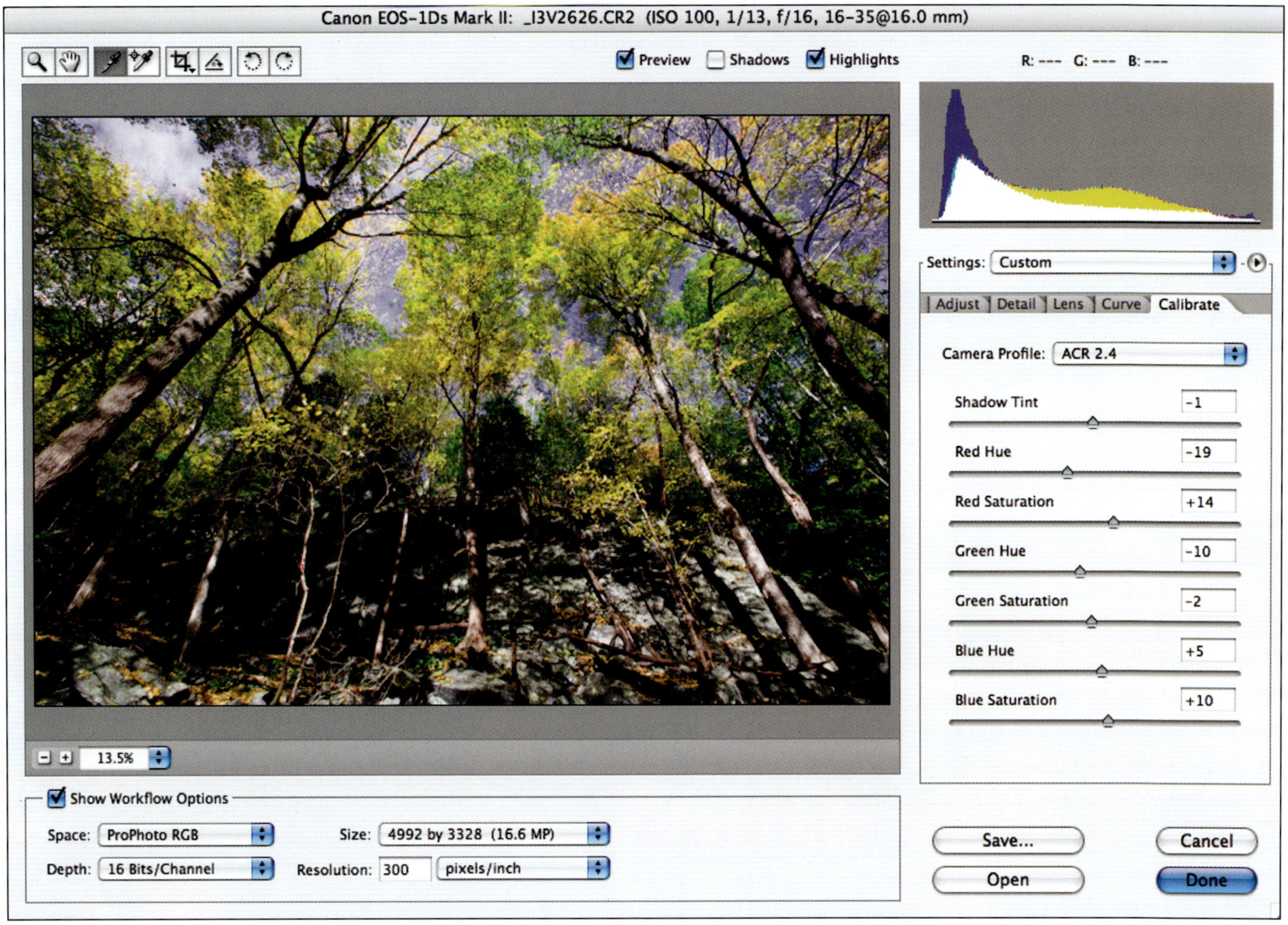

Figure 60—The Calibrate tab in Adobe Camera Raw provides the user the ability to make detailed color adjustments. Adjustments can be made to take into account a camera's color deficiencies. These settings can be saved and set as the default for an individual camera. When new images for the camera are opened in ACR the new default settings are applied. This has great potential for both color correction and an enhanced workflow since images are "color managed" on the fly. Note also the Space menu under Show Workflow Options. This provides the user a choice of four working spaces that the image can be saved to.

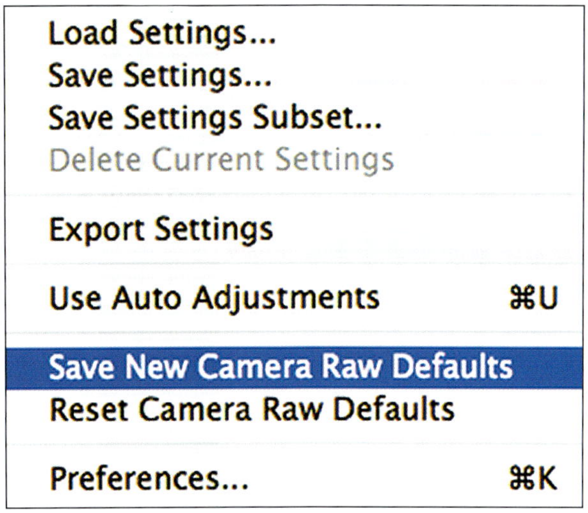

Figure 61—This menu from within Adobe Camera Raw can be used to save custom calibration settings and assign them as the default for a camera. The new default settings are used every time that an image from the camera is opened in Adobe Camera Raw and Adobe Bridge.

All RAW conversion programs also provide a means for saving a converted image into a working space (figure 60). Some provide access to all the working-space profiles that are available on your hard drive while others give you a more targeted choice. ACR, for example, provides four working spaces to output to: sRGB, Adobe RGB, ColorMatch RGB, and ProPhoto RGB. Adobe Lightroom Beta 4 provides three. Canon DPP provides five common working spaces.

JPEG and TIFF Formats. JPEG and TIFF images that are processed in-camera can benefit from an ICC profile. Cameras, like all other devices, will render image color in their own unique way. Unfortunately you cannot climb into your *camera* and control the color conversion of an image the way you can if you are processing the RAW image on your *computer.* For this reason, when shooting in the JPEG and TIFF modes, you are at the mercy of what the camera gives you—even if your camera provides custom settings for color tone, saturation, and contrast.

The following describes the process for creating a camera profile for JPEG and TIFF images using GretagMacbeth's Digital ColorChecker SG target and Eye-One Match software. The process is similar when using other targets and profile-building applications.

Prior to photographing the color checker (or target) that will be used to build the camera profile, it is important that your camera is set up properly. First, all settings that increase, decrease, or alter contrast, sharpness, color tone, or saturation need to be set to their zero or off position. Some cameras provide preset settings like Canon's Picture Styles. If your camera has this type of functionality, make sure that it is either turned off or set to zero.

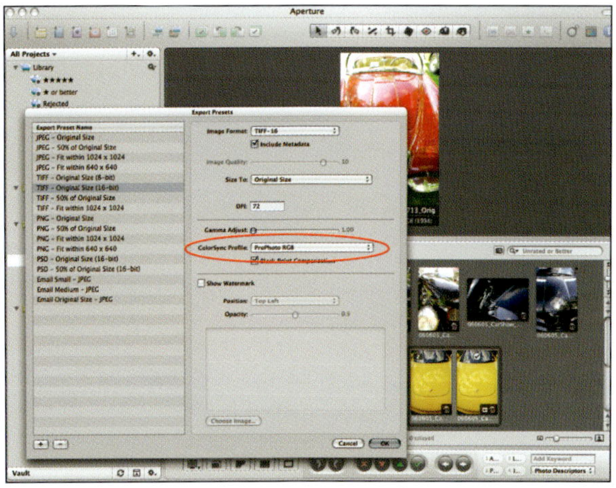

Figure 62 (above)—Apple Aperture provides custom export presets. These include the option to assign a working space that a version of the RAW file is saved to after processing. Figure 63 (right)—C1 is one of a number of RAW processing applications that provide a list of camera input profiles. Like other programs, C1 outputs images into a standard working space. Similar to Aperture, custom output presets can be defined for different output needs. This includes a menu for selecting an output color space.

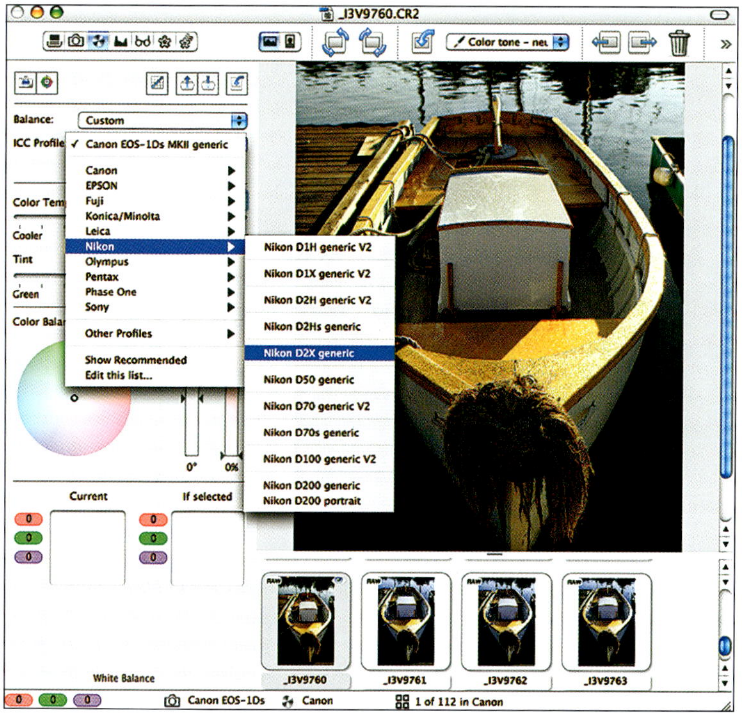

Figure 64—*GretagMacbeth's ColorChecker White Balance Card is one of the best tools available for setting a custom white balance in-camera. Place the card in the light that you will be photographing and take a picture of it filling the entire frame. It does not matter whether the card is in focus or not. Most digital SLRs will use the image of the photographed card to custom white balance the camera. Using the camera's menu system, find the custom white balance setting. This setting will allow you to choose the image of the white card. If you are unsure of how to do this with your camera, check the camera's documentation.*

Do not set the white balance to Auto. It is very important that you set a custom white balance prior to shooting the target. To do this you will need a truly neutral white or gray card (figure 64). Be careful using an 18-percent gray card because they tend to have a slight color cast. Shoot the white card and set the custom white balance on your camera.

If you set your camera to these zero settings and create a custom white balance prior to every shoot, the camera profile you make from this single photograph of the target will work for all kinds of lighting conditions. Remember that the objective of camera profiling is to correct any color aberrations inherent in your camera and to minimize the time necessary to correct for them in your editing software.

With these camera settings made, we can move on to shooting the color checker (target). Many digital cameras save JPEG or TIFF images in either sRGB or Adobe RGB working spaces. If the camera is converting the color of your image into one of these color spaces after it processes it, it makes sense to convert into the larger of the two, which is Adobe RGB. This will retain more color data than converting the image into sRGB. Make sure your camera is set to Adobe RGB before shooting the target.

Adjust the angle to make sure that the lights do not create a glare on any of the target's color swatches.

Lighting the target evenly is critical. If you are shooting the target outside, take the photograph in noon daylight in direct sunlight. Set up the target on an easel away from any structure that might cast color onto it. Do not set the target on a colored surface. If you are photographing the target with studio lights, set up two lights at 45-degree angles. Adjust the angle to make sure that the lights do not create a glare on any of the target's color swatches. If possible, try to use lighting modifiers, like a softbox, to even out the light.

Take light meter readings all the way around the periphery of the target, as well as in the center. Adjust your lighting to keep the exposure within .2 stops over the entire face of the color checker. Once this is achieved, you are ready to take the photograph.

Set the picture quality of the camera to the largest JPEG or TIFF setting and take the picture. After you have photographed the target, copy the image onto your computer.

Before loading the image of the test chart into your profile-building software, open it in Photoshop. If you have set your default RGB working space in Photoshop's Color Settings to something other than Adobe RGB (1998) and the color mismatch warnings are turned on, then a color mismatch dialog will appear asking you what you want to do. Tell it to preserve the embedded profile, click OK, and the test chart image will open. At this point we can check to see if the test chart has been exposed properly.

Using Photoshop's Eyedropper tool and Info palette, take RGB measurements of the black, gray, and white patches in the test chart image. First check to see if the gray, black, and white patches are neutral. Hover the Eyedropper over a gray patch and check its RGB value in the Info palette. The R, G, and B values should be equal (or within one or two levels of one another). Do the same with the white and gray swatches. You want to make sure that the target does not have a color cast or the profile-making software will reject it. This is why it is important to custom white balance your camera before photographing the target.

You want to make sure that the target does not have a color cast or the profile-making software will reject it.

Compare the RGB values of a black patch on the left to a black patch on the right. If any of the black swatches has picked up some glare, the swatch will appear more gray. Avoid glare at all costs. If the difference between one black swatch and another is greater than fifteen levels, then the target has not been lit evenly (figure 65).

Check the white swatches around the outer edge of the target as well as in the middle. The RGB values of the white patches should be within a range of RGB 210 to 245. If there are white swatches below this range, the target is underexposed; if there are white swatches above this range, the target is overexposed.

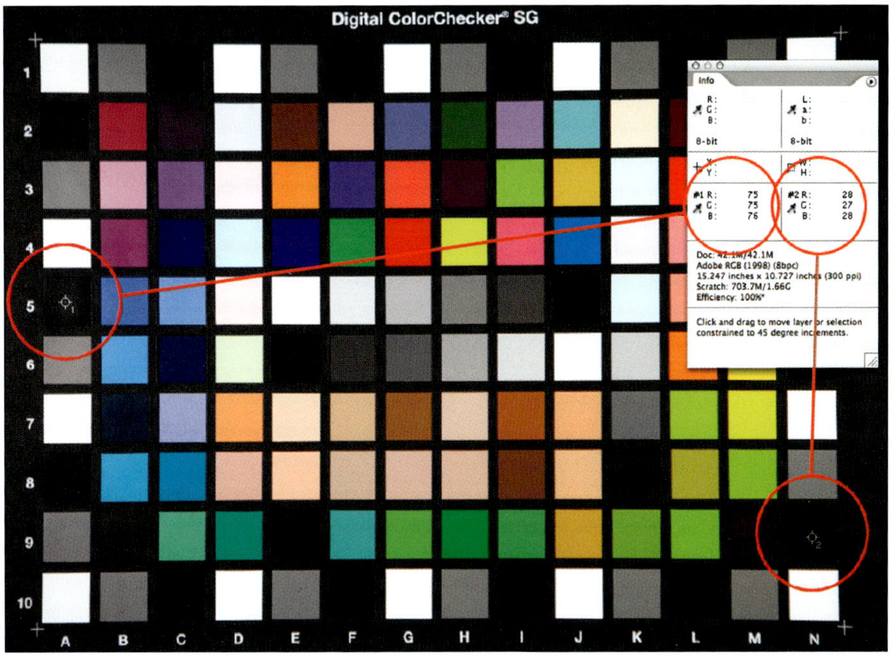

Figure 65—This is an example of the Digital ColorChecker SG photographed incorrectly. The black swatches on the left have picked up some glare. The glare lightens their value. Making a comparison between the black swatch on the left and the black swatch on the right shows that their RGB values are considerably different, far exceeding the maximum difference of fifteen levels (in RGB values). An application like Eye-One Match will display a warning when this target is imported indicating that the image has a glare problem and needs to be photographed again.

After confirming that the target image is exposed properly, it can be loaded into Eye-One Match and used to build a profile. Eye-One Match will only accept the Digital ColorChecker SG target. However, some of the other profile-building packages, like ProfileMaker, will give you a choice to use whichever target you prefer, like the standard 24-patch Macbeth ColorChecker or the universal IT-8 target made by Kodak and many of the film manufacturers. Whichever target you use, it is necessary to have the digital reference file that is an exact match to the physical target.

Prior to building a profile from the imported image, Eye-One Match will check to make sure that the image was photographed properly.

The profiling process is initiated by launching Eye-One Match, selecting the camera module, a mode (easy or advanced), and clicking the right arrow in the lower-right corner (figure 66). Eye-One Match guides the user step by step, giving on-line instructions and displaying graphics that make the application easy to understand.

Eye-One Match will ask the user to import the photographed image of the Digital ColorChecker SG and crop the image so that the software knows where to find the color swatches (figure 67). Prior to building a profile from the imported image, Eye-One Match will check to make sure that the image was photographed properly. If there is a problem, Match will give the user a specific warning, like the image is overexposed or not white balanced correctly.

If the target is accepted, then Match will proceed and will build an ICC profile for the camera, comparing the RGB color swatches in the photographed image to the LAB reference data of the same colors. This color data for the Digital ColorChecker SG is built into Eye-One Match. By comparing the camera color to the reference color, it is possible for the profile-building software to determine whether the camera records color accurately. Suppose that your camera records white with a slightly blue cast. When the profile-building software constructs the camera profile, it will map the RGB value of the camera's bluish white to the LAB value for pure white that is in the reference. It is as though the profile is saying, "Anytime the camera records an image with bluish white, it really means pure white, so tell any other device that is receiving an image from this camera that it really meant white, not bluish white."

After generating the profile, Eye-One Match also provides tools for modifying the profile before completing. Adjustments for exposure, contrast, saturation, shadow, and highlights make it possible to customize the profile so that it will generate very specific results. The first profile you build from the target should be aimed at generating accurate color with neutral grays. This profile can be considered the baseline. Every time that you zero

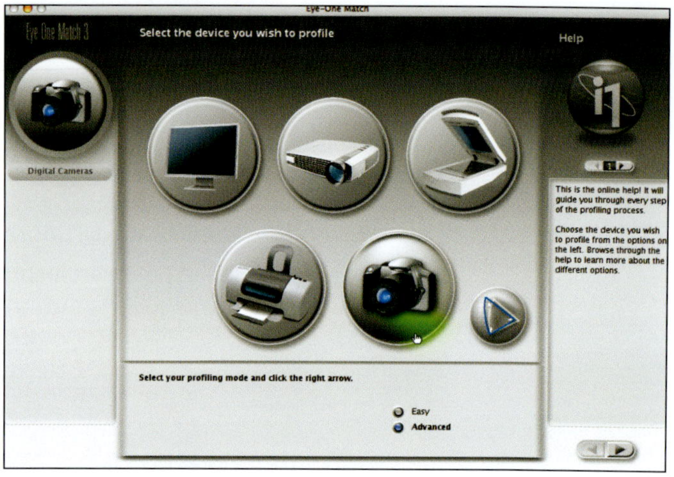

Figure 66—*GretagMacbeth's Eye-One Match provides modules for calibrating and profiling displays, projectors, scanners, printers, and cameras.* **Figure**

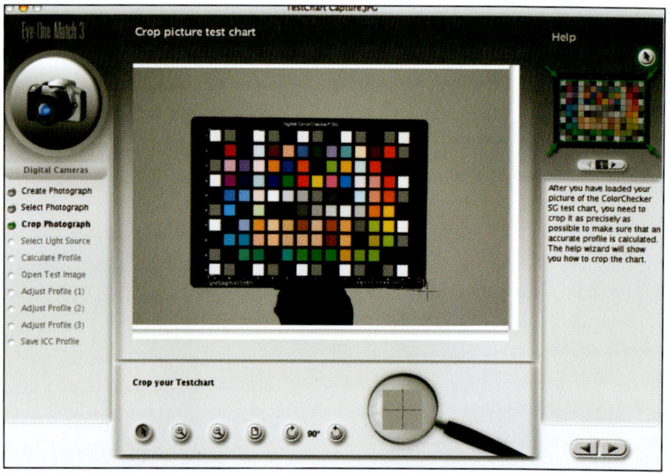

67 (right)—*After importing the photograph of the Digital ColorChecker SG it is necessary to tell Eye-One Match where the color swatches are in the photograph. This is accomplished by positioning the four corners of the cropping marquee at the corners of the color swatches. Target photograph by Mark Gundlach, GretagMacbeth Global Services.*

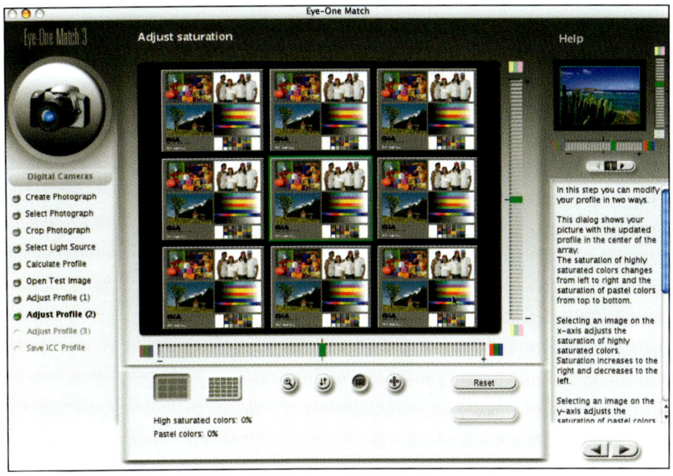

Figure 68—Eye-One Match provides features for modifying a camera profile. Working with a test picture allows the user to see how the adjustments will impact an image when the profile is assigned. Adjustments for exposure, contrast, saturation, shadow, and highlight can be made prior to building the profile.

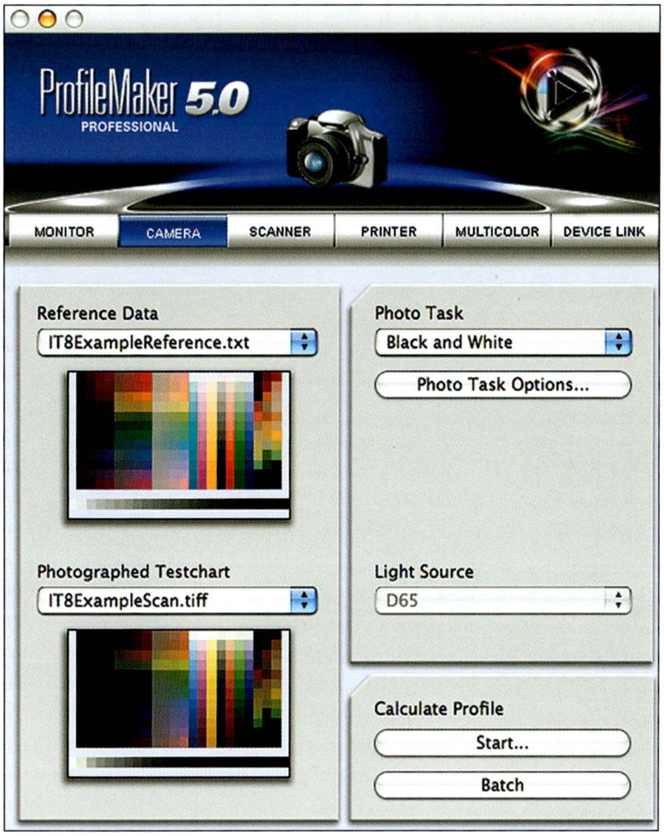

Figure 69—ProfileMaker Pro provides access to different testcharts for creating a camera profile. Both the reference data and the photographed testchart can be seen together. The profile can be modified using different Photo Tasks and can be matched to a defined lighting condition with the Light Source setting.

your camera and set a custom white balance and then use this profile, you will achieve very accurate color reproduction. This is great for reproduction work, but suppose that you also take photographs outdoors. In this case you may want the profile to favor a slight warm cast and maybe a little more saturation. Using the same target image and the tools in Eye-One Match, you can build a profile that produces a warmer, more saturated image (figure 68).

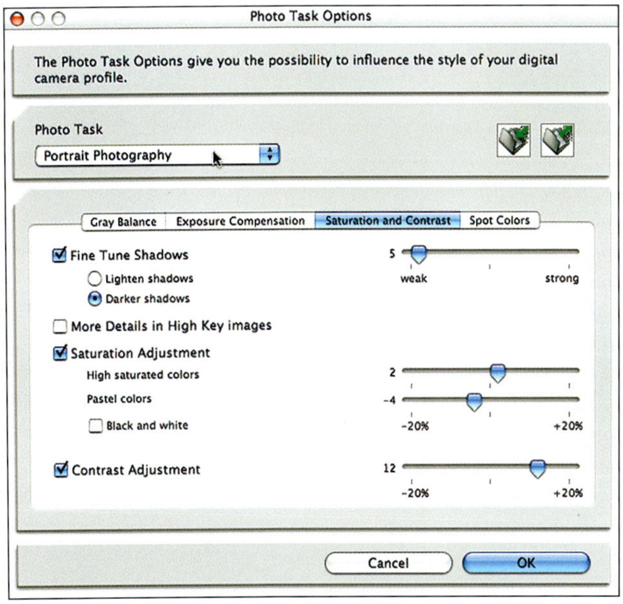

Figure 70—ProfileMaker Pro's Photo Task Options dialog box provide control over gray balance, exposure compensation, saturation and contrast, and spot colors. Custom settings can be saved.

For the most part, the process of creating a camera profile is the same in many profile-building applications.

GretagMacbeth's ProfileMaker Pro provides a bit more control when customizing a profile for specific types of photography. Figure 69 shows the standard ProfileMaker Pro screen for building a profile. With ProfileMaker, the user can choose from a number of different "testcharts" (the term used for color targets in this software). This example shows an industry standard IT8.

Prior to loading the photographed testchart, the user selects the reference chart that the photographed target will be compared to. The photographed image of the testchart is loaded next. Before generating a profile, the user can select a

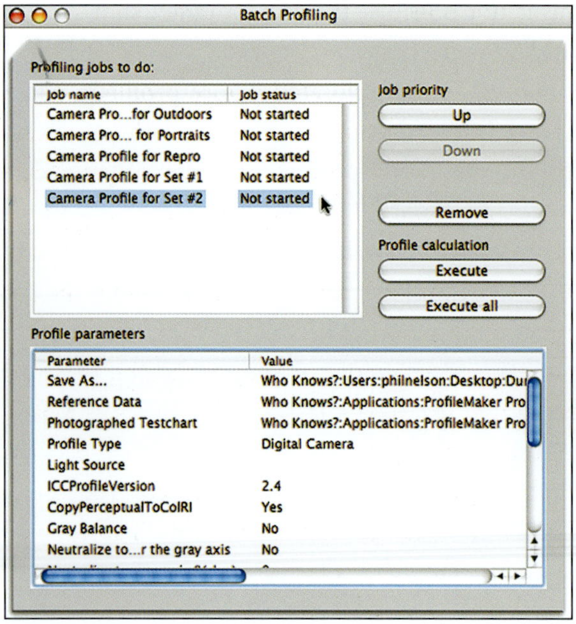

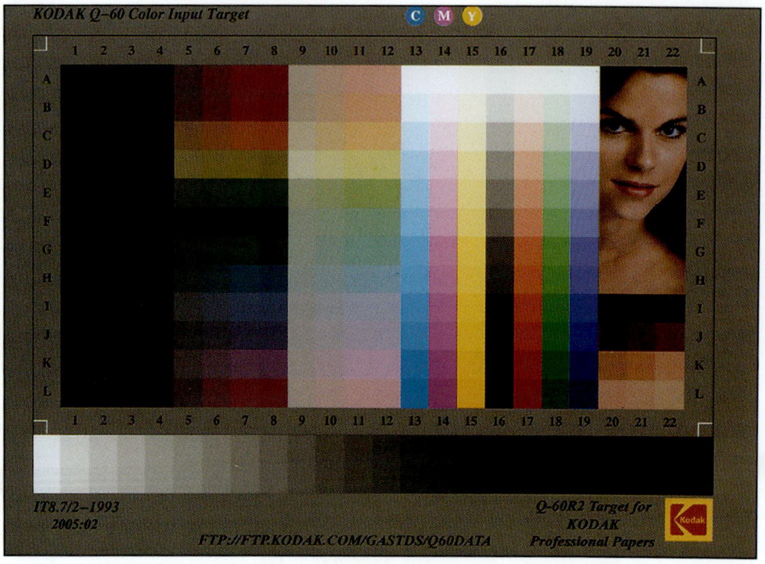

Figure 71 (left)—*ProfileMaker Pro's Batch Profile function helps save time by building profiles with different Photo Task settings in batch. From a single testchart (target) photograph, it is possible to generate multiple profiles for different lighting conditions.* *Figure 72 (right)*—*Kodak is one of several companies that produces IT8 scanning targets. They are made for both reflective (flatbed) and transparency scanners.*

Photo Task setting that identifies the type of image that the profile will be used for. Options include general purpose, outdoor, portrait, product, black and white, and reproduction (figure 70, previous page). These presets were created to provide the user with a simple way to modify a profile (or group of profiles) for certain types of photography.

If the user wants to create a custom setting, selecting Photo Task Options will open up all the controls for modifying a profile. These include settings for gray balance, exposure compensation, saturation and contrast, and spot colors. Similar to Eye-One Match, individual profiles can be made for different shooting conditions, but ProfileMaker allows the user to generate the profiles in a batch mode. Different Photo Task Options can be set for each profile and then saved to the batch list. When the user has completed setting up multiple profiles, ProfileMaker will build all the profiles in batch (figure 71).

Like profiling a camera, a scanned target is loaded into profile-building software and compared to a reference chart.

When the camera profile has been made, save it into the proper folder on your computer's hard drive (see the previous chapter). Be sure to give the profile a descriptive name so that you can recognize it later.

Scanners. Creating a profile for a scanner, for transparencies or reflective art, is very similar to profiling a digital camera. By scanning a target it is possible to characterize the color capabilities of the scanning device. Like profiling a camera, a scanned target is loaded into profile-building software and compared to a reference test chart. The results of this comparison are used to build the profile.

Targets are available for both flatbed scanners and film scanners, either as transparencies or as reflective art. IT8 targets are available from film manufacturers mounted in 35mm slide sleeves or in standard sheet-film sizes (figure 72). If you are using a particular film, try purchasing an IT8 transparency target for that film. If this is not possible, try using a target shot on film with the largest color gamut, like Fuji Velvia.

If it is possible, the scanner should be calibrated before profiling. Many scanners do not have calibrating features. If that is the case with your scanner, then you can simply skip the calibration process. However, if your scanner can be calibrated, then do this before scanning the target. If you are unsure, check your scanner's operation manual.

Like cameras, scanners need to be properly set up before scanning the target. It is critical that all color settings are zeroed. Make sure that if your scan driver or scanning software has automatic color-correction features, these are turned off. Set any contrast, brightness, color tone, and saturation adjustments to off or to their default setting (figure 73). If there are Levels or Curves controls, set these to their default state. Set the Levels control so that the scanner records the maximum tonal range—0 to 255. And, finally, if your scan driver or scanning application supports color management, make sure

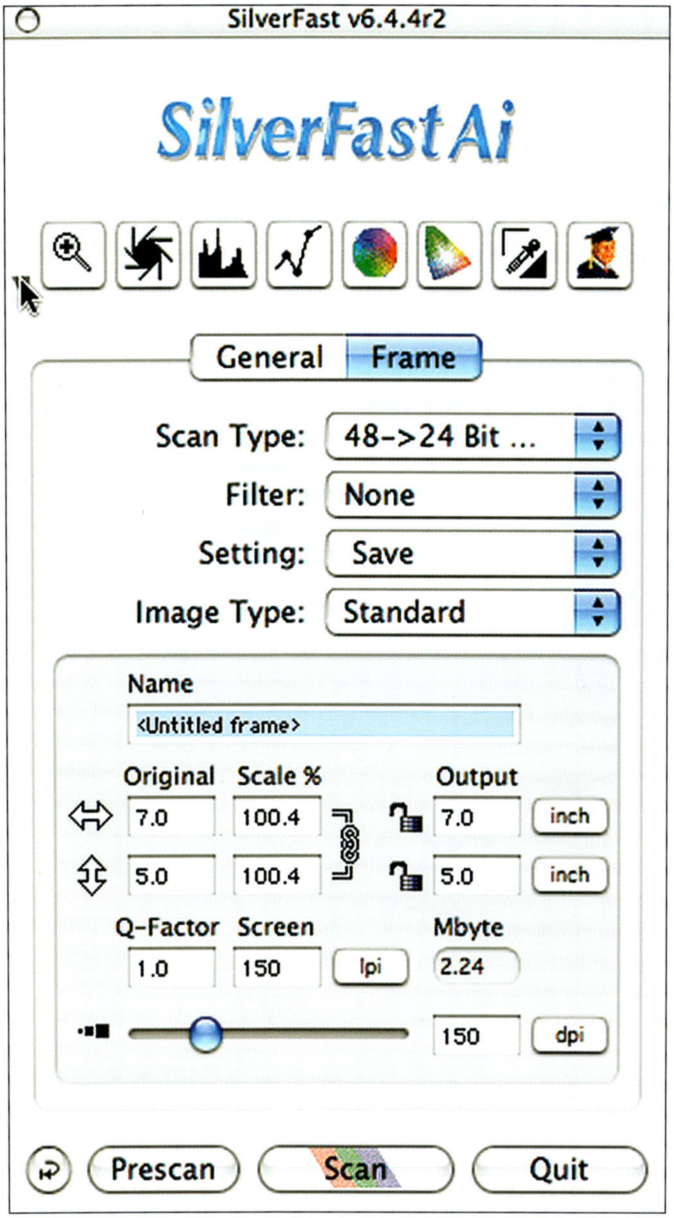

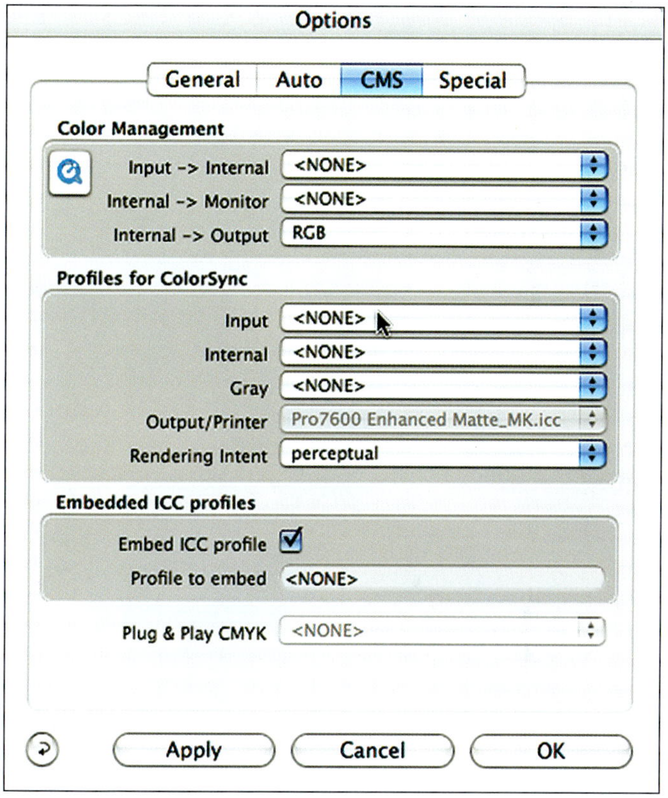

Figure 73 (left)—LaserSoft Imaging's SilverFast Ai scanning software provides controls for modifying the image as it is being scanned. When scanning a target that will be used to create a scanner profile, it is critical that all of these settings are turned off—especially any controls that perform automatic tonal or color correction. Figure 74 (above)—The color-management screen in SilverFast Ai provides menus for choosing the color engine, the source (or scanner) profile, and the destination profile. When scanning a target for building an ICC profile for the scanner, it is very important that color-management settings are turned off. In order to build an accurate profile, the raw scan of the target needs to be imported into the profile-building software. If the scanning software alters the color of the target in any way, the profile will not accurately characterize the scanner.

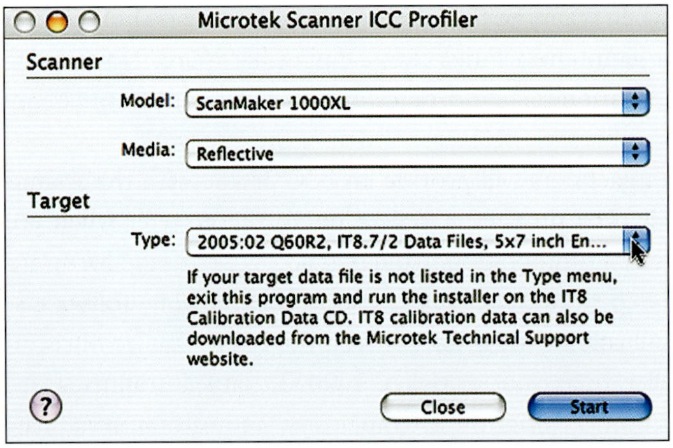

Figure 75—The Microtek Scanner ICC Profiler requests that the user identify the reference file for the target being scanned. This is a text file that accompanies that profile-building software and is an exact match to the physical target that is also included with the Microtek software.

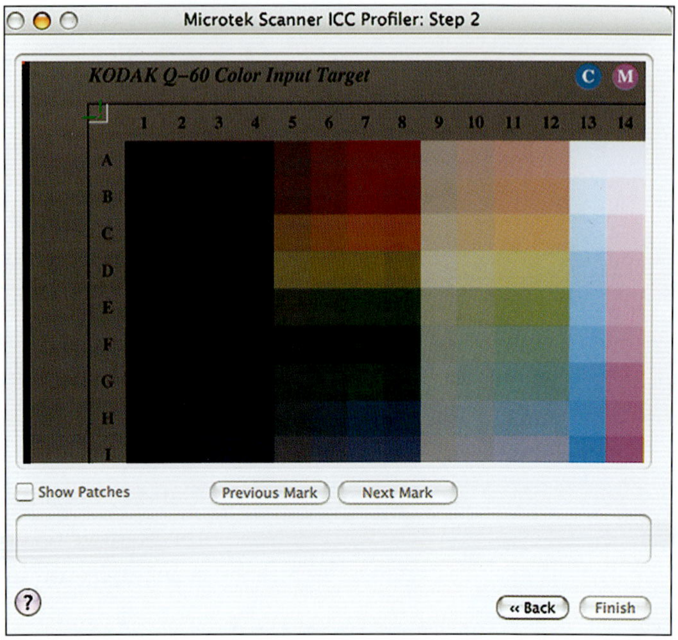

Figure 76—After the target is scanned, it is opened in the Microtek Scanner ICC Profiler. The scanned target is then compared to the reference data for the target and an ICC profile is constructed for the scanner.

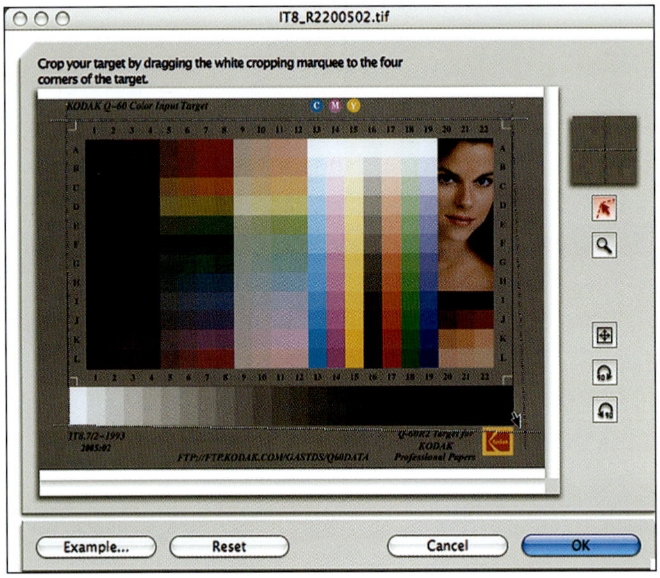

Figure 77—GretagMacbeth's ProfileMaker can use an IT8 target (shown here), the Macbeth ColorChecker 24, the Macbeth Digital ColorChecker SG, or a custom target imported by the user as long as the target has accurate matching reference data. When importing the scanned image of the target, the image needs to be cropped so that ProfileMaker knows exactly where to find the color patches.

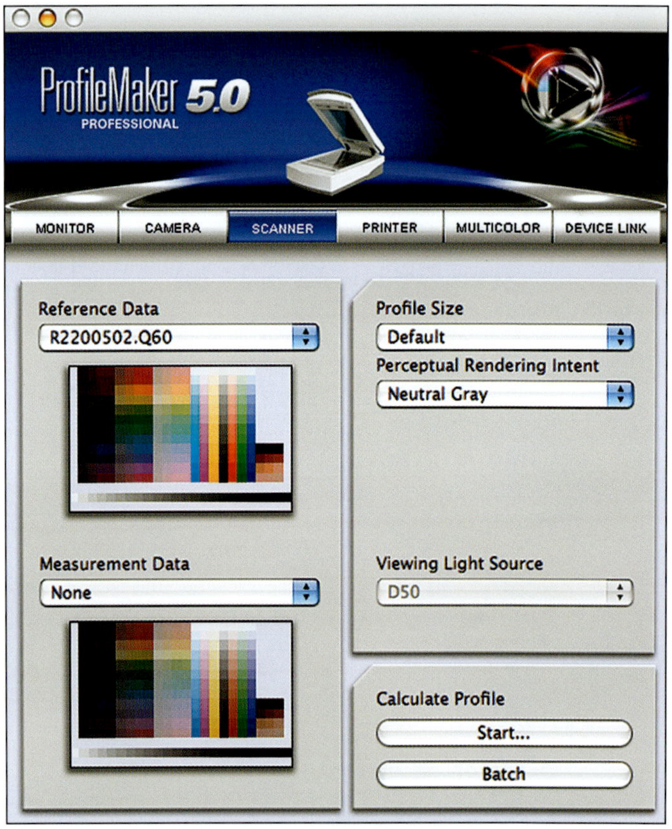

Figure 78—GretagMacbeth's ProfileMaker scanner module shows the reference data (top) and the image of the scanned IT8 target. ProfileMaker provides several settings that will modify the profile prior to building it.

that it is turned off when scanning the target (figure 74; page 66). Again, the objective of profiling is to characterize the scanning hardware. If your software alters the scan of the target, the profile you build will not be an accurate characterization.

Most scanner manufacturers will provide an ICC profile with the scanner when you purchase it. The profile is installed on your computer when you install the scan driver or scanning application that accompanies the hardware. Some scanners also ship with a scan target and profile-building software so that you can make a custom profile for the scanner. For example, Microtek includes an IT8 target with its ScanMaker 1000XL flatbed scanner and a program, Microtek Scanner ICC Profiler, for building a custom profile (figure 75). This application takes the scanned image of the target straight from the scanner and does not require that you turn off color-adjustment or color-management settings.

After scanning and saving the target as a TIFF file, open your profiling software. Identify the target reference data and then import the scanned image of the target. The profiling software will make a comparison of the reference and the scanned image and build a profile based on its findings (figure 76). The profile will accurately characterize the scanner and make the necessary color conversions when translating the scanner's color to a different color space, like your preferred working space.

Once the profile has been created and saved in the proper directory on your computer, it is a good idea to put it to the test.

Once the profile has been created and saved in the proper directory on your computer, it is a good idea to put it to the test. Since a typical workflow involves translating the scanner's color to a standard working space, you will need to set up your software to make this conversion. The conversion can happen in several places, either in the scan driver or in an application like Photoshop that is capable of making color conversions. It is important that the color conversion only happen once, either in the driver or an application, but never in both places. Where and how to correctly make these settings is described in the next chapter.

Creating Output Profiles

As you have hopefully figured out by now, building a device-dependent profile involves scanning, photographing, or displaying a target. To build an output profile it should stand to reason that a target will need to be printed in order to characterize a printing device, whether it is a Fuji Frontier, a LightJet, or an Epson inkjet printer.

Today, most photographers who are making their own prints are using sophisticated inkjet printers from Epson, Hewlett Packard, or Canon. These printers are capable of delivering output that rivals the photographic prints from older wet processes. They are capable of printing on all kinds of media from vinyl to canvas to matte and glossy paper stocks. They all provide inks that they claim will not fade for over a hundred years. These devices can produce images with a very large color gamut, and black & white prints that are absent of color altogether (this has been a problem for inkjet printers in the past).

Depending on how you work, you can send your job to an inkjet through the print driver that is provided with the printer or through a software RIP (Raster Image Processor), an application that facilitates the printing process and typically offers greater control over the printer. However, RIPs require more work to set up than installing a print driver and, depending on how you work, may not be worth the additional expense.

Your first consideration prior to making a printer profile is to determine what paper stock you will be profiling. Because every paper has its own unique characteristics and will react differently to the ink from your inkjet, it is necessary to make a profile for the printer and paper in combination. When you print to a glossy stock, your output looks quite different than when you print to a stock with a matte finish. It will look different still when you print to a semigloss paper. It only stands to reason that a profile will be needed for each paper that you print to.

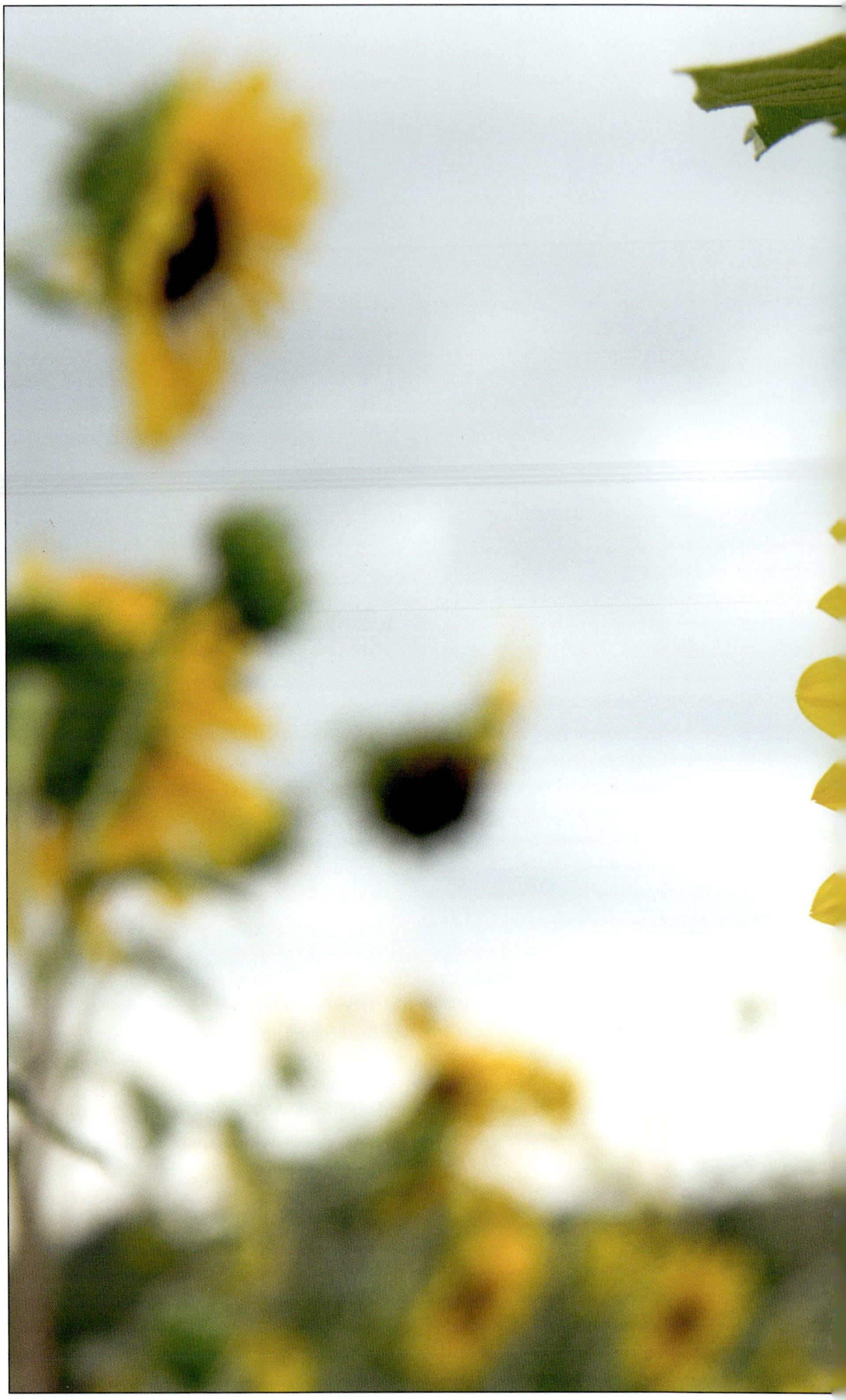

Figure 79—Sunflower, Tuscany.

Most printer manufacturers today will install a healthy variety of ICC printer profiles when installing the print driver. These profiles will work with the different paper stocks that the manufacturer provides for their printer. If you decide that you want to use paper not provided by the manufacturer of your printer, you will either have to search the Internet for a profile that supports the paper you are using, or you will have to build your own. Many paper manufacturers provide ICC profiles for their paper in combination with many of the most popular inkjet printers. Typically, these can be found on the paper company's web site.

Keep in mind that generic profiles from a manufacturer are built to support every printer of the same model that is sold into the marketplace.

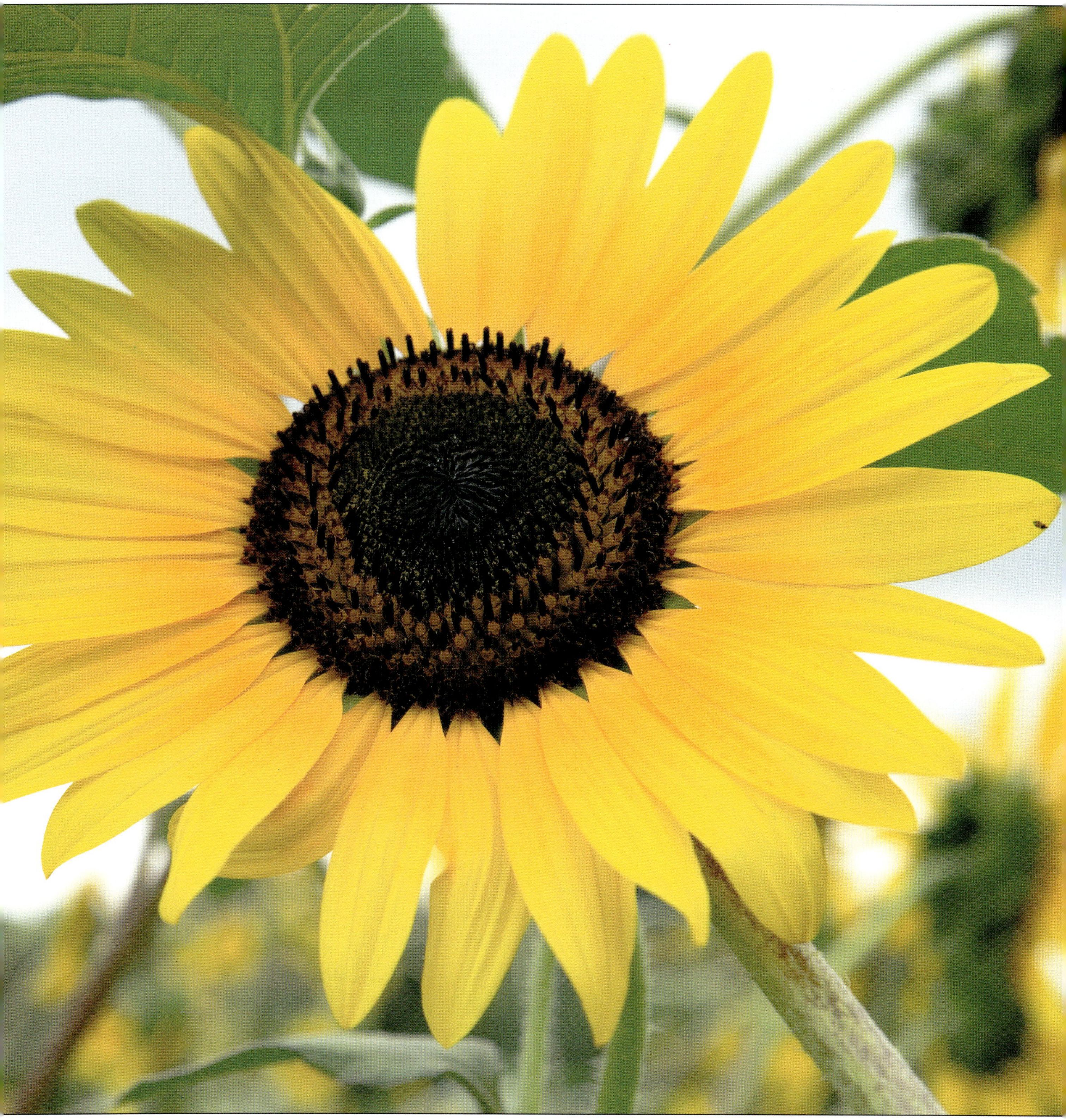

Building a custom profile for your own printer will provide you with a unique characterization of the device that you own. While many of the generic profiles provided by manufacturers are very good, they are never as good as having a custom profile for your printer. Since inkjet printing technology is the most widely used by photographers today, the following describes how to create an ICC profile for an inkjet printer.

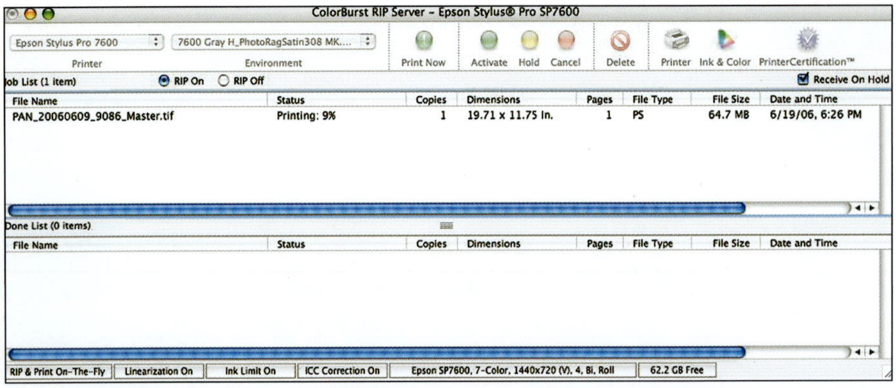

Figure 80—The ColorBurst X-Photo RIP provides a user interface for controlling print output. The RIP can be chosen like a printer in the standard print dialog box. Print jobs are sent to the RIP in the same fashion that they are sent to the print driver. However, most RIPs will provide advanced features for controlling the print output.

Inkjet Printer. Your next consideration prior to profiling your printer is whether to make a CMYK or RGB profile. If you are using the standard print driver that came with your printer, then you will need to build an RGB profile—and you can skip the following section on RIP calibration.

If you are using a RIP, more than likely you will need to build a CMYK profile. (There are a few RGB RIPs that are built for photographic output, like ColorByte's ImagePrint, but these are few and far between.) If your RIP provides calibration features, then you will want to calibrate your RIP in conjunction with the printer and paper you will be using.

RIP/Printer/Paper Calibration. RIPs are available from numerous developers for all kinds of printing applications, like sign printing, offset prepress, and proofing. They come as software only or as a software/hardware combination, typically to be utilized as a centralized printing resource for a workgroup. They also provide features that go beyond what is usually found in a print driver. Some work well for photography, like ColorBurst X-Photo (figure 80), EFI's Designer Edition RIP, or ColorByte ImagePrint. Features include color management, proofing capabilities, and the ability to nest print jobs, which maximizes paper and ink usage on large-format printers. In addition, many RIPs provide features for calibrating a printer. This is something that typically cannot be done with a printer driver and provides a higher level of control over the print quality.

This is something that typically cannot be done with a printer driver and provides a higher level of control over the print quality.

There are three common parameters that are established during the calibration process. First is the ink limit per color channel. This ensures that the printer is outputting the proper amount of ink for the paper on which it is printing. This is set for each CMYK ink channel. The next calibration step involves linearizing the printer. This ensures that the printer is distributing the ink in a linear (or even) fashion across the entire tonal range. Lastly, since many printers will layer inks over one another, it is important that a total ink limit is set.

Setting per-channel ink limits typically involves printing a test chart made up of values for each color channel. Values can range incrementally from 0% ink to 100%. A setting is identified for each channel based on the density of

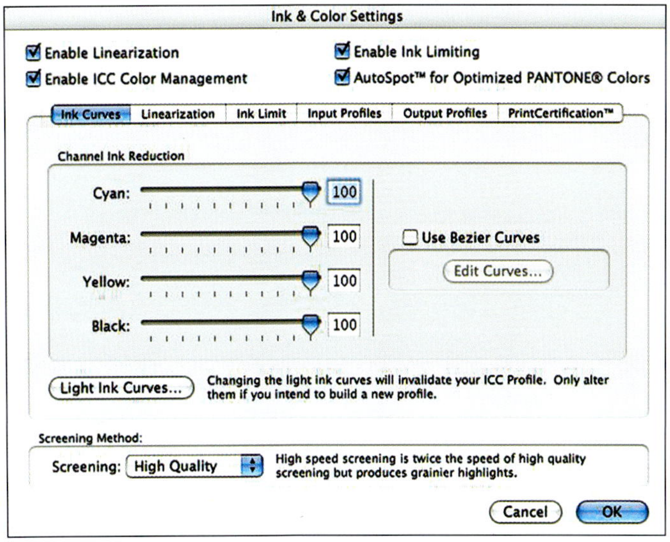

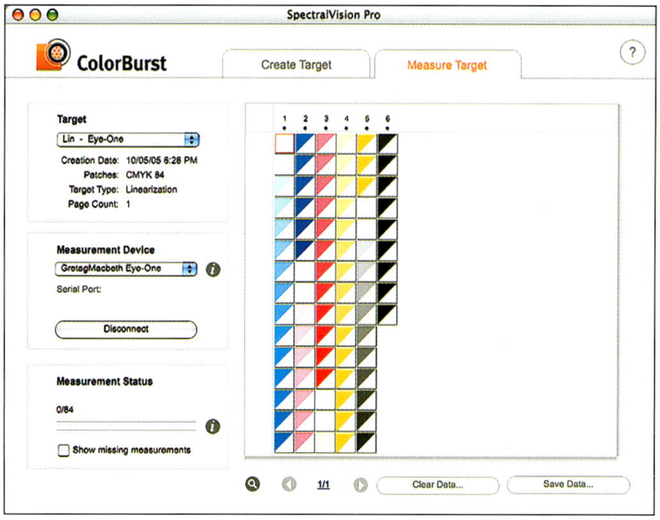

Figure 81 (left)—*ColorBurst provides access to setting ink limits for each CMYK channel. The ink limit for most inkjets is 100%.* *Figure 82 (right)*—*ColorBurst uses a utility application, SpectralVision Pro, to calibrate and create profiles for the printers it supports. This screen shows one of SpectralVision's linearization charts. Scanning the chart with a spectrophotometer generates a curve that will linearize the printer. The curve data is entered into ColorBurst's Ink & Color Settings.*

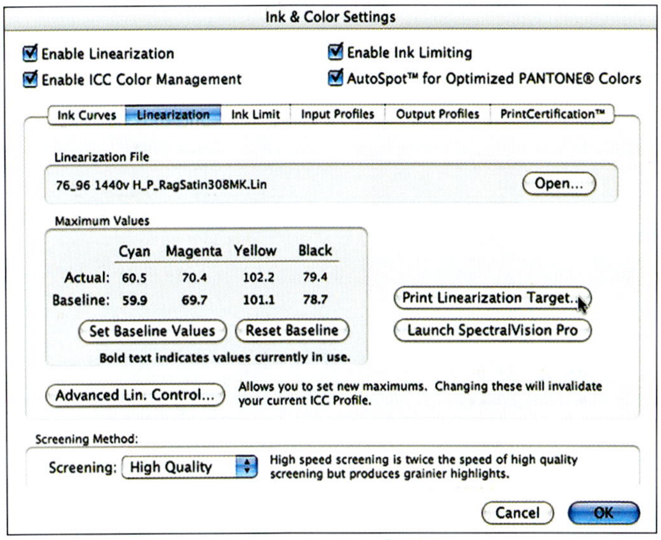

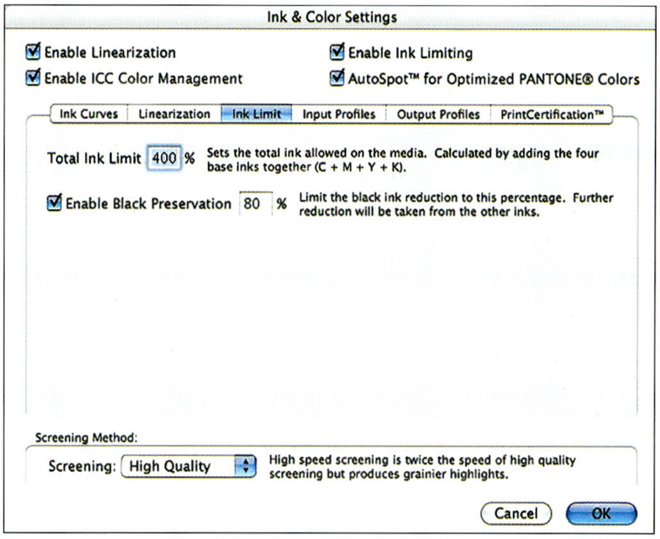

Figure 83 (left)—*A linearization file created by SpectralVision Pro can be opened into ColorBurst's Ink & Color Settings. The data curve will ensure that the printer is distributing all colors evenly over the entire tonal range.* *Figure 84 (right)*—*ColorBurst provides settings for defining total ink limits.*

the ink values. For example, if 100% magenta ink on the paper being calibrated is too dense, sticky, or creating a puddle, then the 100% value is too high and needs to be cut back. The proper density value for each channel can be identified simply by looking at the test chart. The value for each channel can then be set in the RIP (figure 81).

Linearization also involves printing a test chart or linearization chart (figures 82 and 83). Linearization charts are read with a spectrophotometer and will create a curve that corrects nonlinear output. Because printer calibration can drift, it is possible that the input value for any ink channel will not match the value that is printed. In other words, the printer might be told to print 40% cyan but in actuality print 30% cyan. The linearization process calibrates all the ink channels over the entire tonal range so that when the printer is told

Figure 85—Water Color.

to print 40% cyan, it prints 40% cyan. The process of relinearizing is a means for ensuring that the printer stays calibrated and linearized.

Setting the total ink limit controls all of the ink channels. By printing a test chart it is possible to determine whether the printer is outputting the proper amount of total ink. The printed chart shows all four CMYK color channels printed over one another. It is not uncommon to see puddles of black ink on the printout. The objective when printing this chart is to determine the maximum amount of overall ink that should be printed (figure 84, previous page).

Once the RIP/printer/paper combination has been calibrated, then an ICC output profile can be created. Because the profile is created directly after the printer is calibrated, it works its best when the printer is in this calibrated state. If the printer drifts out of calibration over time, the profile loses its effectiveness and will not produce as accurate a print. By relinearizing the RIP/printer/paper, it can be calibrated back to the linear state it was in when the profile was made, renewing the effectiveness of the profile.

Printers that Calibrate. A trend that has been growing in the inkjet industry is the inclusion of automatic printer calibration, as evidenced by the HP Designjet 130, a printer popular with photographers, and several other HP inkjet and laser printers. HP provides functionality that can be accessed from within their print driver that initiates automatic closed-loop color calibration. The printer prints a target with color swatches and, before ejecting the print, pulls it back into the printer so that the swatches can be scanned by a sensor attached to the print carriage. This process measures ink limits for individual papers, takes into consideration temperature and humidity, and saves the results back to the driver so that the printer can produce consistent color over time.

Building RGB and CMYK Output Profiles. Whether you are building a CMYK or RGB pro-

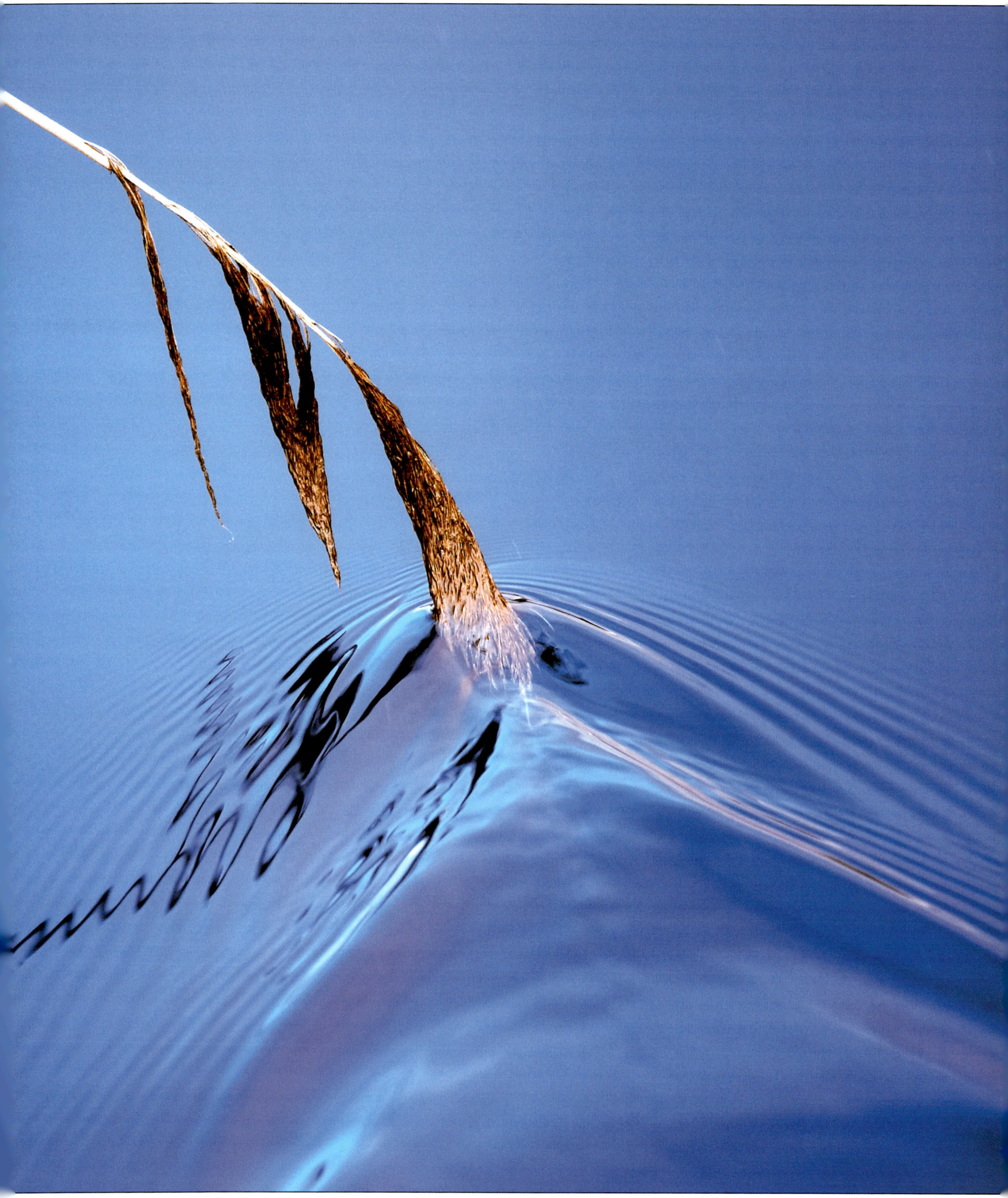

file, you will need a profiling target. The printer profiling target is a file, provided with your profile-building application, that is made up of hundreds of color patches—many targets even exceed a thousand patches. You will print this target, then scan it with a spectrophotometer. This data is then compared to a matching reference file, and an ICC profile is built that maps the printer's color to the actual color in the reference file. When used to convert color to the printer's color space, the profile will accurately translate the source color, typically coming from a working space, to the destination color space of the printer.

The target that you print and use to build a printer profile is dependent on the profile-building software and hardware that you choose to work with. Targets come in all shapes and sizes and are designed to accommodate the spectrophotometer that is used when the target is scanned. Some spectrophotometers, like the X-Rite Pulse or the GretagMacbeth i1, are handheld devices and can be used to scan targets of varying sizes. Others, like the X-Rite DTP70, a full-sheet, high-speed, strip-reading spectrophotometer, scans targets from 3.5 inches wide up to 9 inches wide. Because the target is fed through the strip reader it has to be a specific width. Additionally, there is software like GretagMacbeth's ProfileMaker Pro that supports a number of different spectrophotometers and provides a variety of profiles for the devices that it supports.

Whatever package you choose to work with will provide at least one target for either a CMYK or RGB profile. If the software provides you with a choice of targets, choose one that has approximately one thousand color patches. The number of patches scanned will have an impact on the quality of the profile. This might lead you to believe that the more patches that you scan the better the profile. While this might be true to some extent, there is a point of diminishing return. Scanning thousands and thousands of patches with a handheld spectrophotometer could take a considerable amount of time, and when compared to the gain in quality, will not be worth it. Scanning a thousand-patch target by hand takes around ten minutes and is worth the effort compared to the five minutes you might save scanning a 250-patch target.

Before printing the target, it is critical that all color management in the printing software be turned off. Otherwise, the target will not produce an accurate profile. Many packages will provide a means for printing a target right from within the profile-building software. While we can assume that profile-building applications that allow for printing targets are smart enough not to color convert the target when printing, this is *not* a safe assumption to make of your print driver or RIP. Therefore, if you are printing from your profile-building application, make sure that you turn off all color management in the print driver or RIP. Sometimes it takes some digging to find these controls. If you are having difficulty, consult the manual that came with your printer or RIP.

Before printing the target, it is critical that all color management in the printing software be turned off.

In some cases, you may decide that you want to print the target from Photoshop. Applications like GretagMacbeth's Eye-One Match install a fold-

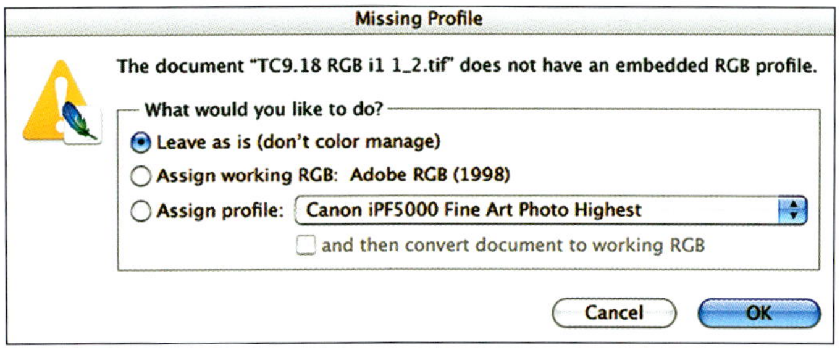

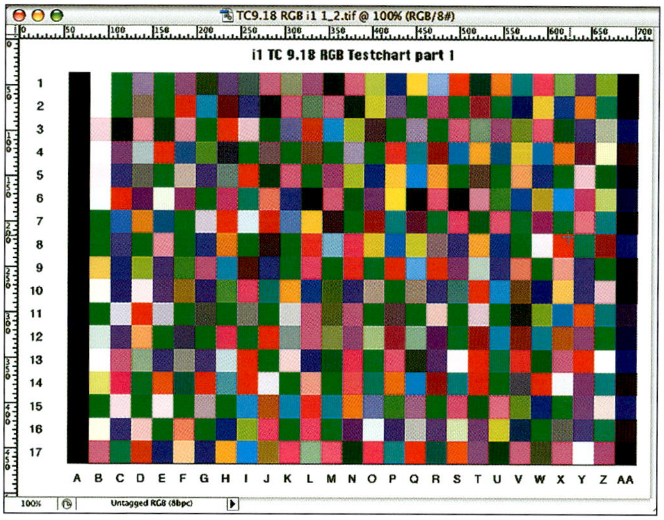

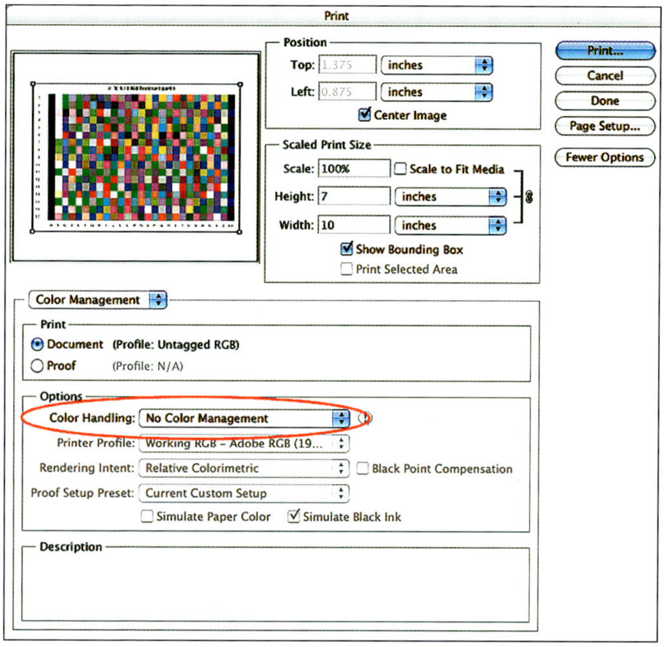

Figure 86 (above)—When opening a printer target in Photoshop, it is important not to color manage the image. If Photoshop's Color Settings are set to warn you when opening a file that does not have an embedded profile, then the Missing Profile dialog box will open when you attempt to open a printer target. Make sure to select Leave As Is (Don't Color Manage). *Figure 87 (top right)*—An i1 TC 9.18 target opened in Photoshop should be opened untagged. If Photoshop is set to show the Document Profile label in its document window (lower left-hand corner), it should read Untagged RGB or Untagged CMYK. Note that the TC 9.18 has approximately a thousand color patches. This version of the target is separated into three pages so that it can be printed on a small-format printer. *Figure 88 (bottom right)*—When printing the profiling target, it is very important that all color management is turned off. This screen shot shows the document's color space (or source color) is untagged, the required state when printing a profiling target. Photoshop CS2 has the option to set color handling to No Color Management. This tells Photoshop to simply send the image unaltered to the printer. Later, once the printer profile has been made, you can tell Photoshop to convert the source color, which will be a working space like Adobe RGB, to your printer's color space. This color conversion happens automatically on output without changing the image file. The image file can always remain in its source color space.

er of printer targets inside the program folder. These can be easily opened from Photoshop. Again, it is critical that nothing alters the target's colors when printing (figure 86). If you open a target in Photoshop and see a dialog box warning you that the file is untagged, select Leave As Is (Don't Color Manage). These files are not tagged with an ICC profile and should remain that way when you open them (figures 87 and 88).

Once the file is open, choose File > Print with Preview. The source color space in the Print with Preview dialog should indicate that the image is untagged. If you are printing with Photoshop CS2, then you will want to select No Color Management under the color handling options. This tells Photoshop that it should simply pass the target's color data to the printer without converting it.

Before the print job is passed to the print driver or RIP, make sure that the driver or RIP is also set to perform no color management (figure 89; next page). Not only is it important to turn off color management in the print driver or RIP, but it is also important to remember the settings that you

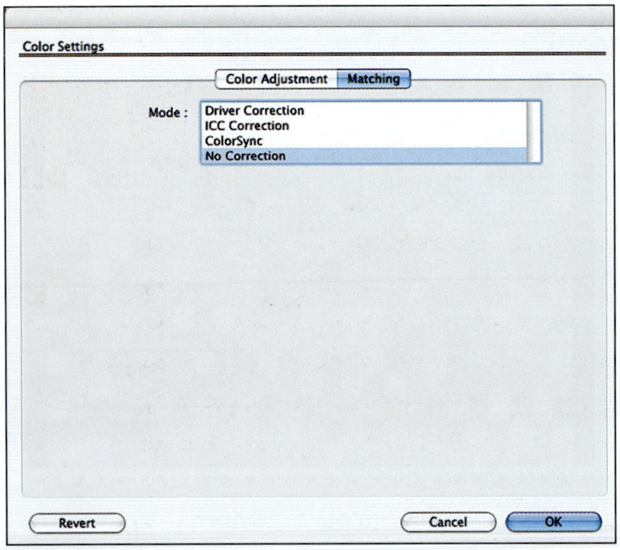

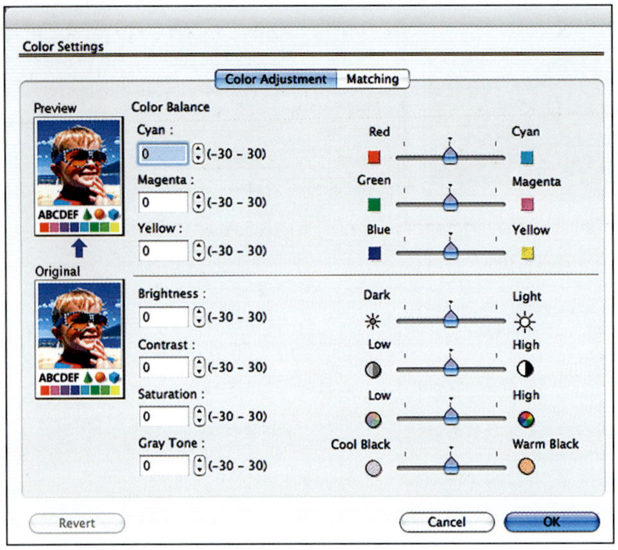

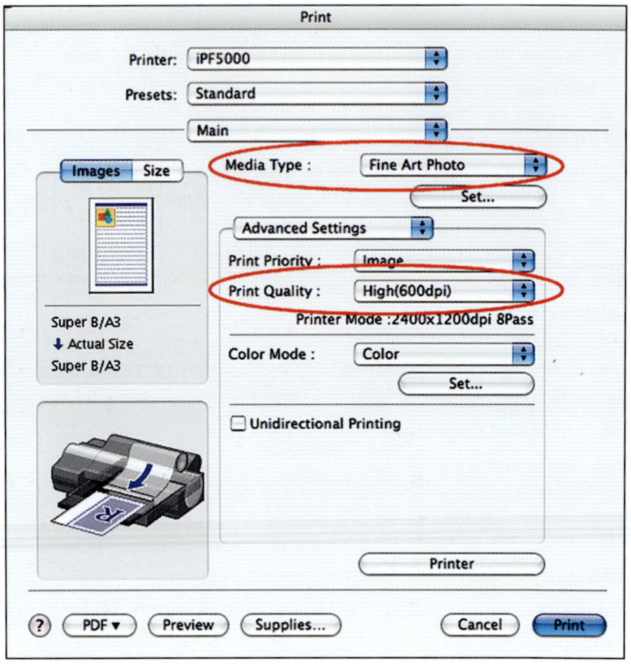

Figure 89 (top left)—When printing the printer target, it is critical that any color correction or color-management settings in the print driver or RIP are turned off. Sometimes these settings are buried deep in the driver. Check the printer's documentation if you are having a difficult time finding this setting. ***Figure 90 (bottom left)****—Many printer manufacturers provide access to extended color controls within their print drivers. It is very important when creating a profile for a printer that these settings are left alone and remain at the manufacturer's default settings.* ***Figure 91 (above)****—The Mac OS X printer driver for the Canon IPF 5000, like most print drivers, provides settings for Media Type, Print Quality, and Color Mode. Make sure to write down the settings that you choose when printing the print target. Later when you use the profile generated from the target, it is important to match these settings.*

choose for paper stock, print quality, and print resolution, and to avoid settings that might alter the target's color in any way. Many printer manufacturers like to include color features in their print drivers. These typically come in the form of color control sliders for each color channel. If you see these in your print driver, leave them alone (figure 90). Write down the settings that you choose when printing the target. You will want to use these exact settings after your printer profile has been made (figure 91).

Double check all your settings and print the target. After printing the target, handle it carefully and avoid touching the printed area. Inspect the printout for flaws. If the printer has a clogged inkjet head, you may see banding and it will be necessary to perform a head cleaning, then reprint the target.

The reaction that occurs between the ink and the paper coating takes at least a half hour to settle down.

Even though most inkjet manufacturers claim that their printers output dry prints, this does not mean that the inks have stabilized and that the colors will not continue to shift after printing. The chemical reaction that occurs between the ink and the paper coating takes at least a half hour to settle down. During this time, the color in your print will shift. It is very important that you let the print of your target "cure" for at least a half hour. For the best results, consider printing the target and putting in a safe place overnight. Don't let the cat walk on it.

Once the print has set up, it can be scanned with a spectrophotometer. If you own a handheld spectrophotometer, you will need to place the target on a flat surface with enough room to easily scan every patch.

Prior to scanning, put three or four sheets of the same paper you printed the target on under the target. If you are scanning on a colored tabletop, there is a chance that the color could be picked up by the spectrophotometer through the paper. This will affect the quality of the profile. Placing additional sheets under your target will eliminate this potential problem.

Using the ruler or guide that came with your spectrophotometer, carefully scan all the patches. The software that came with the device will guide you through the process. When you have completed the scanning, the software will build your output profile and save it in the proper directory on your computer.

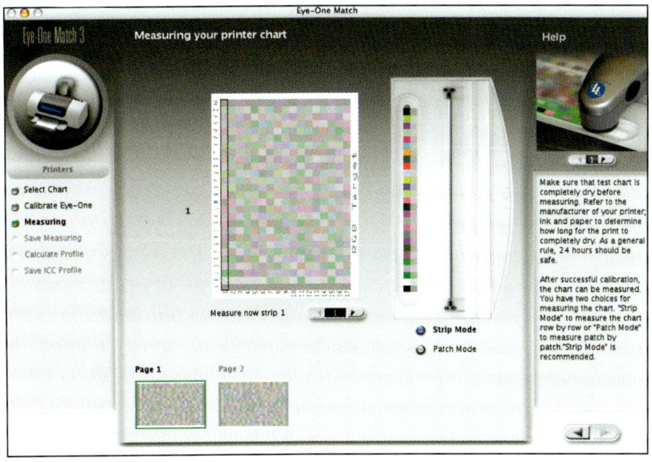

Figure 92—Scanning a target with a hand-held spectrophotometer involves passing the spectrophotometer over each row of the printed target. Eye-One Match shows the status of each row that is scanned, provides direct feedback if a row has not been scanned properly, and gives the flexibility to back up and scan a row again.

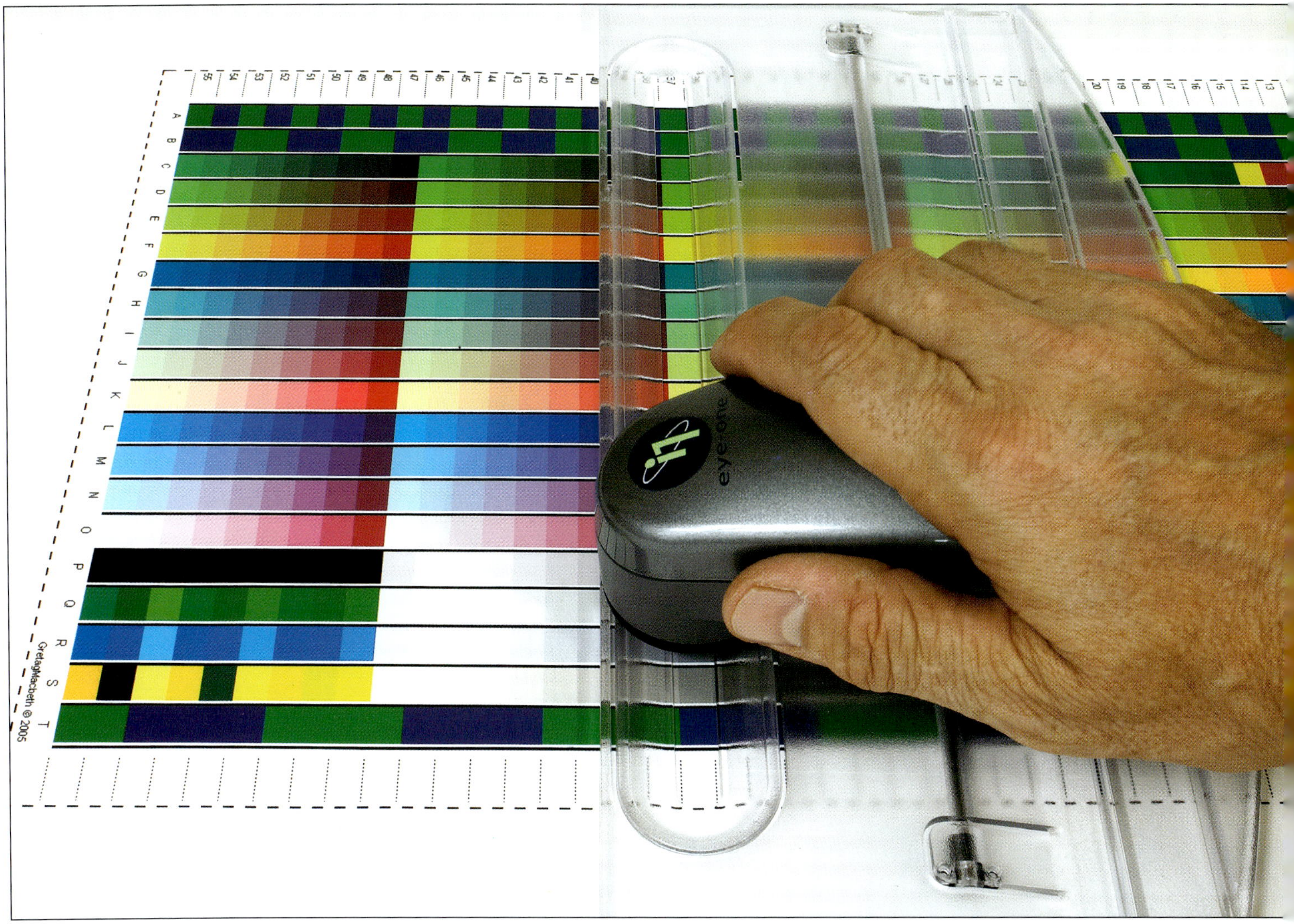

Figure 93—Scanning a TC 9.18 RGB TestChart with a GretagMacbeth i1 spectrophotometer.

Media Type. Manufacturers cannot possibly provide a profile for every available paper/printer combination. Therefore, at some point, you will want to use a paper for which no profile is provided by the manufacturer of your printer, like printing Hahnemühle Photo Rag on a Canon ImagePROGRAF 5000.

When this occurs, begin by checking the paper manufacturer's literature. Some paper providers include instructions that indicate the media type that should be selected with different popular printers. For example, Hahnemühle Photo Rag can be printed on Epson printers using Epson's Enhanced Matte media type. The same paper printed on the Canon IPF 5000 can be printed using Canon's Fine Art Photo media type. If you are unsure of which media type to use and the paper manufacturer provides no instructions, make a logical guess. If the paper has a semi-gloss finish, try a semi-gloss media type. If it's a matte finish, try a matte media type.

Some paper providers indicate the media type that should be selected with different popular printers.

Experiment until you find the best match. You can tell when you have a good match by checking a test print's ink coverage. If there is too much ink, it will smear or puddle. If there is too little ink, your test print will look washed out.

6. Walking Through the Color-Management Workflow

If setting up a color-managed workflow is like working on a car engine, then applying color management is like driving the car. Once you have spent a little bit of time with it, knowing which settings to make as your images move through the workflow becomes second nature. The following will help you learn how to avoid some of the common pitfalls.

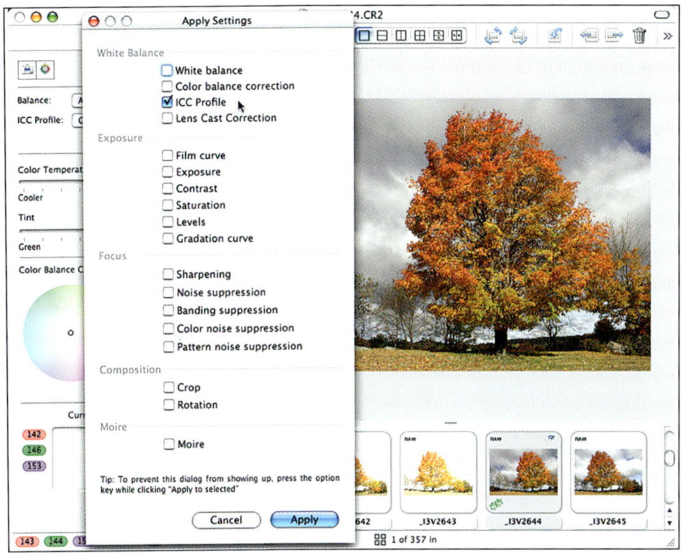

Figure 94—C1 can apply RAW conversion settings to selected images in a batch process. Included is a check box for assigning an ICC profile.

Inputting Images

The Digital Camera Workflow. *RAW Files.* From a color-management standpoint, working with RAW files is probably the easiest. Because many RAW conversion applications provide their own flavor of color "profiles" internally, these converters do not need a custom ICC profile for a camera. On the other hand, some RAW converters utilize ICC profiles and *can* take advantage of a custom camera profile created by the user.

Input your RAW images using whatever method is required by your RAW conversion software. Some, like Aperture, will require that the images are imported. Others, like Adobe Camera Raw with Adobe Bridge, can "browse" a folder where the images reside. If your RAW converter supports ICC profiles, then make sure that the correct profile is assigned to the image you are working on. Perform standard operations in the RAW converter for optimizing everything from white balance to sharpness.

When this is completed, the conversion settings can be assigned to all of the images in a photo shoot—this includes assigning an ICC profile, if your converter supports it. The RAW files can then be converted either individually or in batch to standard image files (figure 94).

Prior to RAW conversion, a working-space profile can be assigned. Then, when the RAW conversion is complete, the image(s) will be in your desired color space.

JPEG/TIFF Files. If your camera is set to RAW + JPEG, or to one of its JPEG (or TIFF) settings, then the camera will be processing the images that you take. Make sure that the camera's color settings are zeroed (see pages 63–64), then photograph a neutral white card to create your custom white balance. Decide whether you want your images tagged with sRGB or Adobe RGB (if your camera supports it). With these settings, you will be able to accurately convert the color in the images that you take using your camera's custom profile(s).

You will be able to accurately convert the color in the images that you take using your camera's custom profile(s).

Take some photographs, then save them in a folder on your computer. Using Photoshop, open one of them. If the file that you open has a profile embedded that does not match your default RGB working space (and Color Settings is set to warn you; see page 45), the Embedded Profile Mismatch dialog box will appear before the image is opened. Choose Discard the Embedded Profile (Don't Color Manage) and click OK. Since the next step will be to assign the camera's profile, there is no need for the embedded profile.

After the image opens, select Edit > Assign Profile and choose the custom profile that you created for your camera. This will change the appearance of the image on your display. Next, select Edit > Convert to Profile and choose the destination color space. In most cases, this should be your standard working space. You will also have the opportunity to set conversion options. Choose the color engine and rendering intent, then make sure that Black Point Compensation is checked. Click OK.

Whether shooting and processing RAW images or having the camera process the images for you, you have the opportunity to take advantage of color management to color correct your images before they are converted to your standard working space. Now that they are converted to the working space, they should not need a lot of color correction and you should have an accurate color rendering of the image that you photographed. At this stage, you should be able to move on to making creative adjustments in Photoshop, clean up any dust spots, sharpen the image, and prepare it for output.

The Scanning Workflow. Many scanning drivers and scanning applications, like LaserSoft Imaging's SilverFast Ai, provide color-management settings where you can define the source and destination color spaces (figure 95). Set the scanner's profile as the source. Set the destination color space to your working space profile. When the scanning software is set up to handle the color conversion, every time an image is scanned, it will be accurately converted. This workflow enhancement only needs to be set once, and then every time that you scan, the color will automatically be converted. The end result should be an accurate match between what you see on your calibrated and profiled display and the image that was scanned.

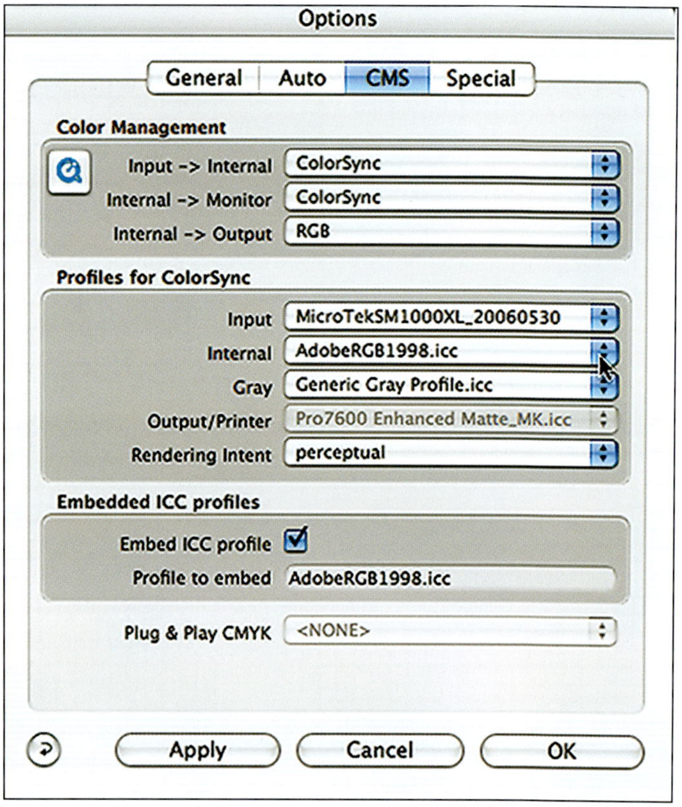

Figure 95—SilverFast's color-management dialog provides menus for assigning both the source and destination profiles and gives the user the choice of embedding the destination profile. The source (or input) profile is the custom profile built for the scanner. The destination (or internal) profile is the color space that the scanned image will be converted to, in this case Adobe RGB (1998).

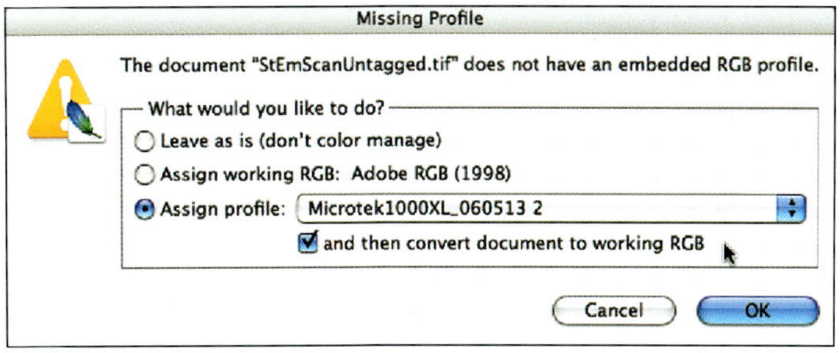

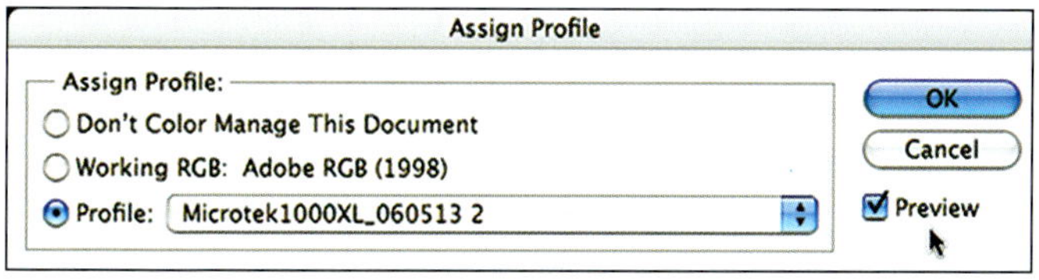

Figure 96 (left)—The Missing Profile dialog box opens if Color Settings in Photoshop have been set to present this type of warning. If you are opening an untagged scanned image, you have the opportunity to convert the color here. By assigning the scanner's profile and selecting the check box to convert to your defined working space, you can make the conversion in one step. ***Figure 97 (right)****—Photoshop's Assign Profile dialog box provides the means for assigning a scanner profile for an image. This does not alter the data in the image file but changes the appearance of the image on screen in accordance to the profile that is assigned. By assigning a profile, you can give an image source color definition so that it can be accurately converted to your standard working space.*

The alternative to having the scanning software handle the color conversion is to perform the conversion in a capable application like Photoshop CS2. If you are planning to color convert your scanned images in Photoshop, make sure that all color management is turned off in the scanning software. The file that you open in Photoshop should be the raw scan data—what Photoshop would define as an untagged file.

If you have set up Photoshop's color settings to warn you when opening a file that is not in your defined working space or is untagged, then Photoshop will present you with the warning dialog box when opening an untagged image from your scanner (figure 96). When presented with this dialog box, you have the option to leave the file alone, to convert it directly to your working space, or to assign a color profile and then convert the image to your working space.

The alternative to having the scanning software handle the color conversion is to perform the conversion in a capable application like Photoshop CS2.

Since you will need to tell Photoshop what the source color space is for this file before converting to your working space, the third option would be the recommended choice. Remember that the source color is defined by the profile for your scanner. By assigning this and then converting to your working space, you will let Photoshop know how to accurately convert the scanned image, and the result should match the image that you scanned. If you simply convert directly to your working space without first assigning your scanner's profile, then the result will be inaccurate and will look like an image that was not converted at all.

Photoshop is famous for having multiple ways of performing the same task. Another way of converting the scanned color is to open the untagged file and select Leave As Is (Don't Color Manage) in the Missing Profile dialog box. The image will then open as an untagged file.

In Photoshop CS2, you can select Edit > Assign Profile, then assign your scanner's ICC profile (figure 97). Make sure that the Preview check box is selected so that you can see the impact of assigning the profile. When you opened the untagged image, it probably did not look very good. This is how your scanner is recording color. By assigning the scanner's profile, you will then see what the colors are supposed to be. The scanner's profile is correcting the image, and Photoshop is showing you the appearance of the color on screen without actually changing the underlying data in the image file.

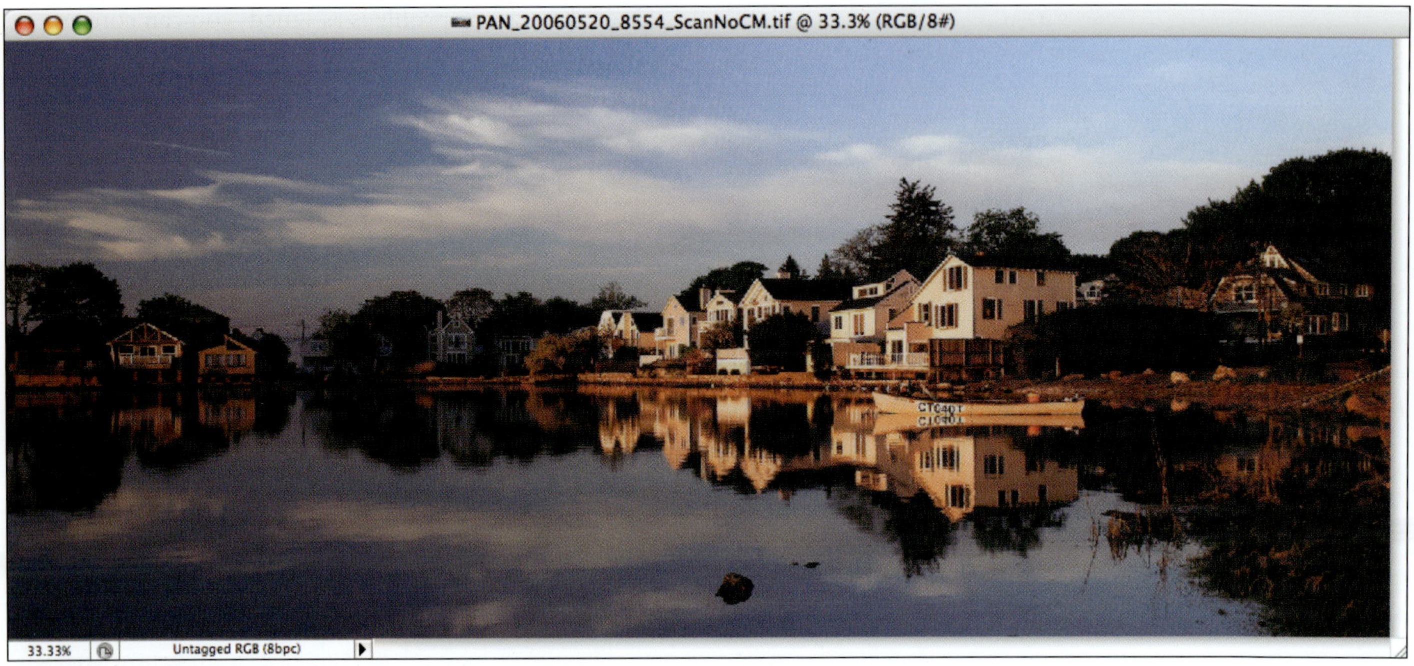

Figure 98—*This is an untagged image that was opened in Photoshop. Notice that in the lower-left corner of the image window there is label that indicates that the file is untagged. To show the document's color state, click on the triangle to the right of the label to reveal a pop-up menu. Select Document Profile from the menu.*

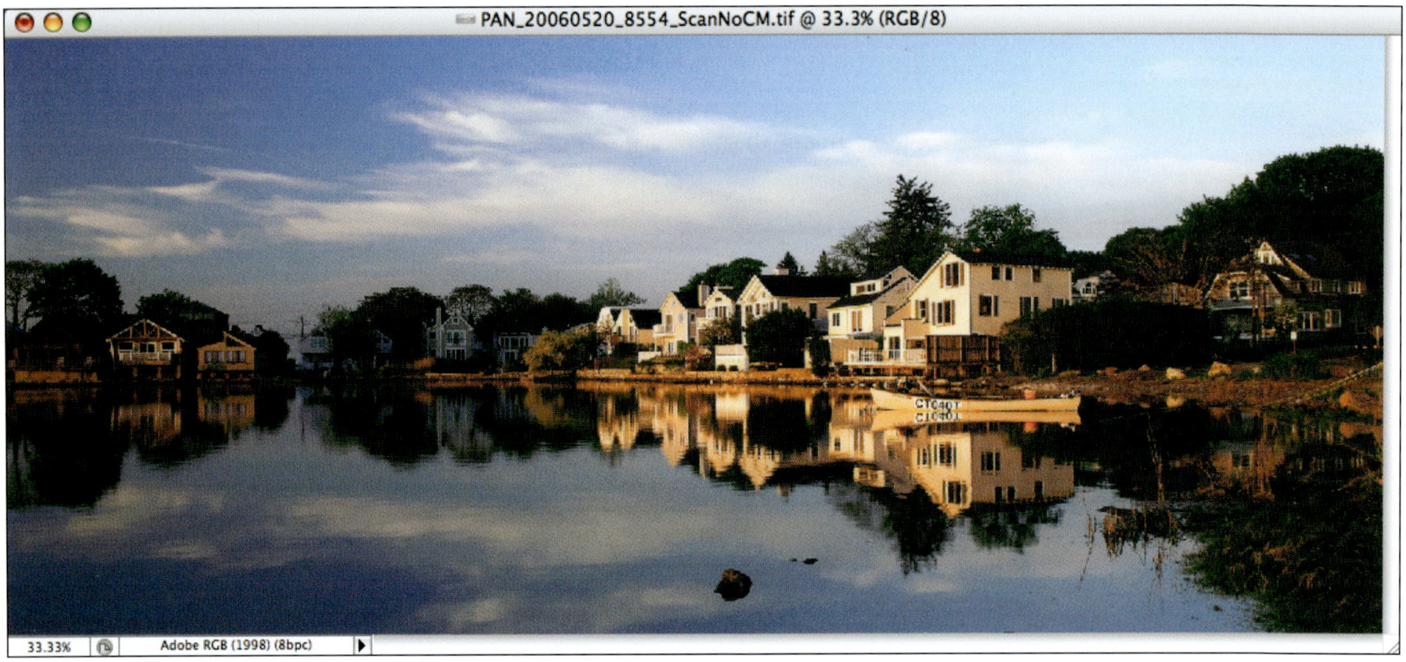

Figure 99—*This is the same scanned image after the scanner's profile was assigned and the file was converted to Adobe RGB (1998). Notice that the magenta cast in the untagged image has been removed. This image more accurately displays the color from the image that was scanned.*

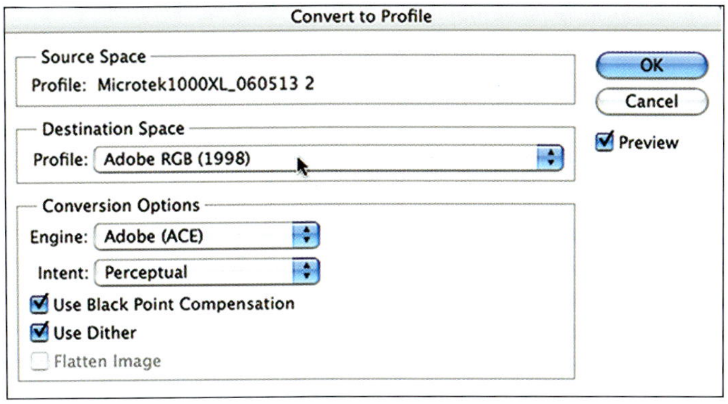

Figure 100—Photoshop's Convert to Profile dialog box shows the source color space—in this case, the color profile for a scanner. It also provides a menu for selecting a destination color space. This could be a working space like Adobe RGB (1998). Lastly, it provides options for running the conversion, like the color-management engine, the rendering intent, black point compensation, and dither.

Once the scanner profile is assigned, you can convert to your working space by going to Edit > Convert to Profile (figure 100). This dialog box will show you the source color space and will allow you to assign your destination working space. In addition, you will have the opportunity to select conversion options like the color engine and rendering intent.

Outputting Images

If you have converted and saved your images in an RGB working space, you will find that you will have the flexibility to output your images to a variety of destinations. When printing to a local printer, outputting digital images for the web, or preparing images for prepress, you will convert images from their working space to the color space of the output destination. When outputting, the working space becomes the source color space and the output color space becomes the destination. This is different from inputting an image into your computer, when the input device color is the source and the working space is the destination (figure 101).

When outputting from an image editing application, you will either export, save as, or print your image. Either during or prior to any of these processes, you will need to set up a color conversion. This may involve converting the image's color into the output color space prior to saving or printing the file. Or, it might involve making the proper settings so that the color conversion takes place during the export or printing process. If the conversion takes place while printing or exporting the photograph, then the image can always remain in its source color space. The printing or exporting process will handle the conversion at the time these operations are initiated. What you

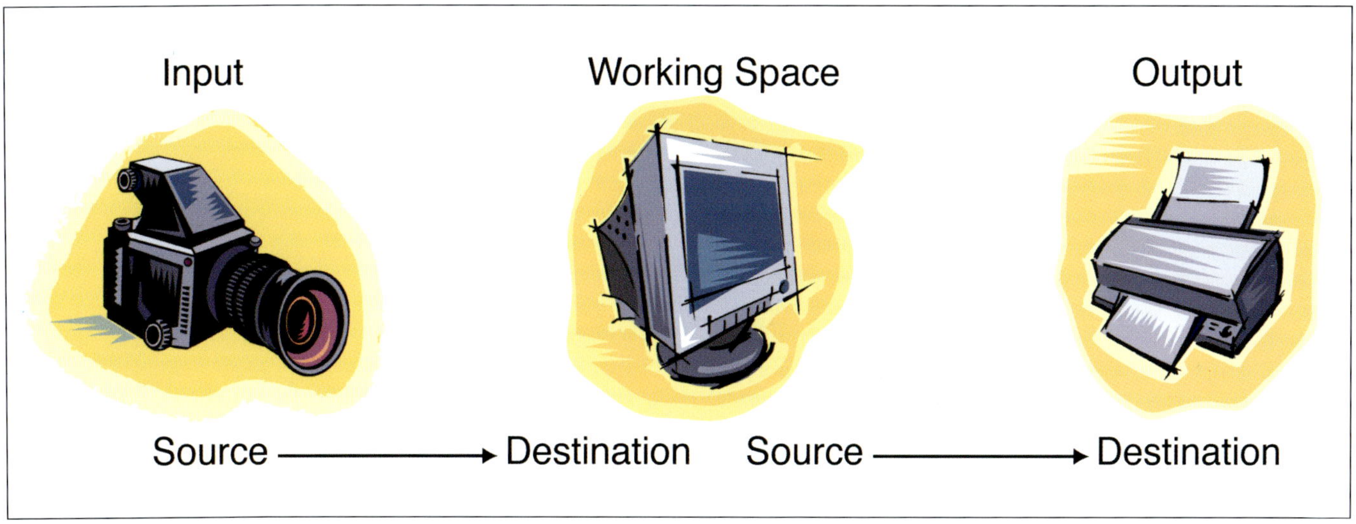

Figure 101—When inputting an image into your computer, the color space of the input device represents the source color. On many occasions you will translate the input color to the color of a working space. The working space color is the destination. When outputting to a printer or digital file, the working space then becomes the source color space and the output color space becomes the destination. The working space can be either the source or destination, depending on the type of color conversion that is taking place.

are trying to accomplish at the time of output, will help you determine which approach to take. For example, if you are preparing files for a client who requests your images in a CMYK color space, you may want to run this conversion, save the files, and send them to your client. If you are printing, there is no need to initiate a conversion; it can be handled as part of the printing process.

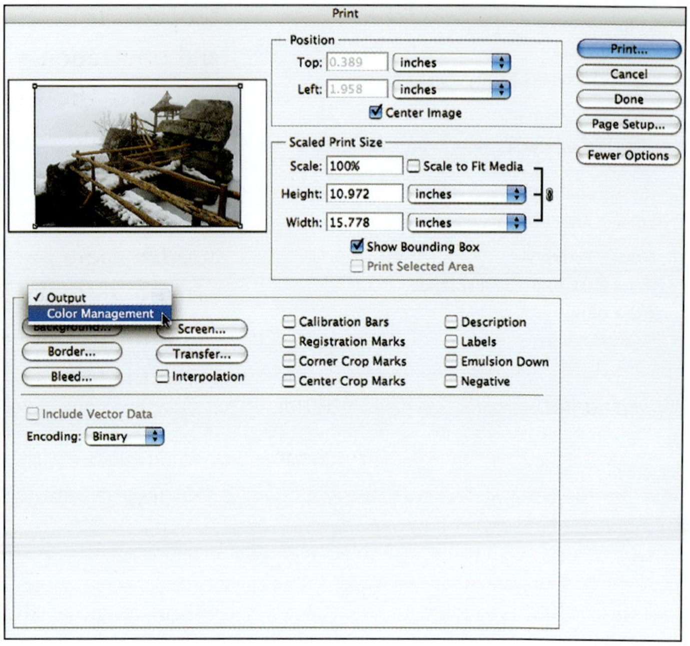

Figure 102—To reveal the color-management control options in the Print with Preview dialog box, select Color Management under Options from the pop-up menu located just below the image preview.

Converting your image's color to the output color space is a relatively simple matter. However, you need to know what color space to output to.

Graphic Design/Prepress. If you are converting to a CMYK color space for graphic design or prepress, refer to chapter 7.

Worldwide Web. If you are outputting an image for the worldwide web, there is one simple choice: your destination color space is sRGB. This color space was designed to provide color consistency across the web, and because it is supported in many of the commonly used web browsers, it is the logical choice for web output. To convert to sRGB using Photoshop CS2, select Edit > Convert to Profile. Choose sRGB from the profile menu, then click OK and Save As to save the file as a version of your original. The new image file is now in the sRGB color space.

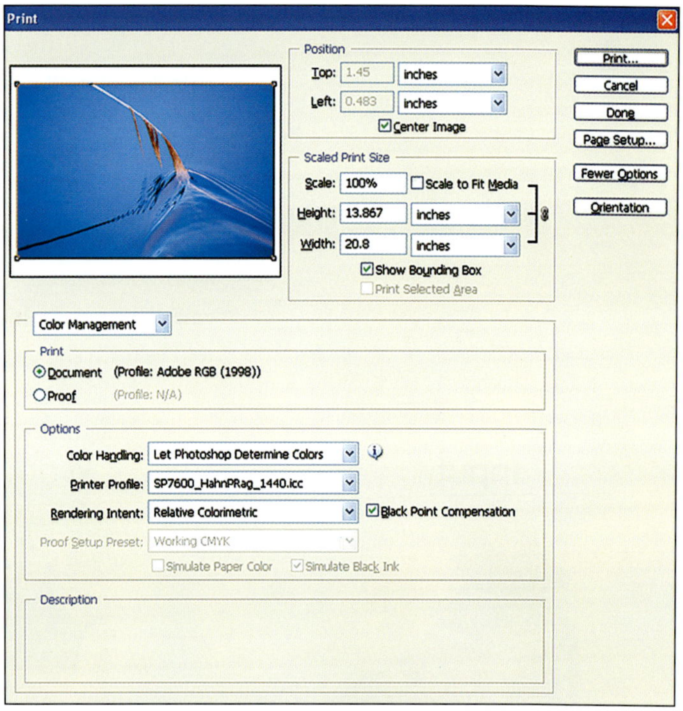

Figure 103—Photoshop CS2's Print with Preview dialog box fully expanded. When color handling is set to Let Photoshop Determine Colors, it is very important to make sure that the print driver is set to turn off all color management.

Inkjet Printer. If you are outputting to your inkjet printer, you will want to utilize one of the printer profiles that you have made or that was installed with the printer's driver. The profile that you use for printing should support both the printer and the paper you are printing on.

Selecting File > Print with Preview provides the necessary controls to properly convert your image's color when printing. If the Print with Preview dialog box is not fully expanded as shown in figure 102, then push the More Options button under the Page Setup button at the upper right. This will extend the Print with Preview dialog box by adding more printing options at the bottom. If you are doing this for the first time, you will see options for applying printer's marks to your printed output. To expose the color-management options, select Color Management from the Options pop-up menu located just below the image preview (figure 102).

Now that you have the Print with Preview dialog set with all of its color conversion features exposed, it should look like figure 103. Before making any color output assignments, make sure that the image orientation is set properly. If necessary, click the Page Setup button to change the paper size and orientation.

Under the Color Management menu, you'll find three sections: Print, Options, and Description (which provides a description of each setting as you position your cursor over it). The Print section shows the image's current color space next to the Document radio button. Just below Document is another radio button labeled Proof. For a standard print, leave these settings as they are. If you are planning to print a hard-proof, choose the Proof option. (Hard-proofing is described in the next chapter.)

Soft-proofing an image prior to printing will help you determine which rendering intent to choose.

In the Options section there are three pop-up menus that are used to designate how the image color conversion is to be handled by Photoshop before the print is made. The settings are Color Handling, Printer Profile, and Rendering Intent. Below these three menus is an additional menu and some check boxes that are disabled. When you print a hard-proof these options will be activated. For a standard print, focus on the three menus that are active.

The first menu provides choices for where the output color conversion will take place. Let Photoshop Determine Colors tells Photoshop to perform the color conversion. Let Printer Determine Colors tells Photoshop to pass the image to the printer driver or RIP without any conversion so that the driver or RIP can perform the conversion. As you would expect, No Color Management turns off any color conversion, and Photoshop will pass the unaltered image to the print driver or RIP. Select Let Photoshop Determine Colors.

The next menu, Printer Profile, lists the ICC color profiles that are installed on your computer. Here, you can choose the output profile for the printer and paper you are using. This is the destination color space for your image.

The third menu lists the four rendering intents. Soft-proofing an image prior to printing will help you determine which rendering intent to choose from (see chapter 3 for more on this). For now, select either Perceptual or Relative Colorimetric. Leave Black Point Compensation selected; this will help render the best blacks when printing.

When you have completed making the settings in the Print with Preview dialog box, push the Print button. This passes the print job from Photoshop to the printer's driver or to a RIP for additional handling and exits Photoshop.

If you are using a Macintosh with OS X, the standard print dialog will appear. This dialog is generic for every printer with the manufacturer's specific features appearing about halfway down the Copies & Pages menu. If you created your own printer profile, then you want to make sure that the print settings that you used when printing the color target are duplicated whenever you use the profile you generated. Make sure to select the same media, quality, and resolution settings. If you are using an ICC profile provided by the printer or paper manufacturer, then make sure to select the manufacturer's recommended media, quality, and resolution settings. If the manufacturer has not included this information with their documentation, then you will have to experiment with the profile. Make some logical assumptions. If you are printing on a glossy paper stock, select a media type for glossy paper. If you are printing on matte paper, select a media type for matte paper. For quality and resolution, again make some logical choices.

Because Photoshop has already been set up to manage the color conversion of your image, it is critical that the print driver is not set to convert the image again—so make sure that the driver's color-management setting is turned off. Look for a setting like "no color correction" or "no color management" and make sure it is selected. Double check all of your settings—especially if you are printing a large print. When you are confident that all the settings are correct, click the Print button.

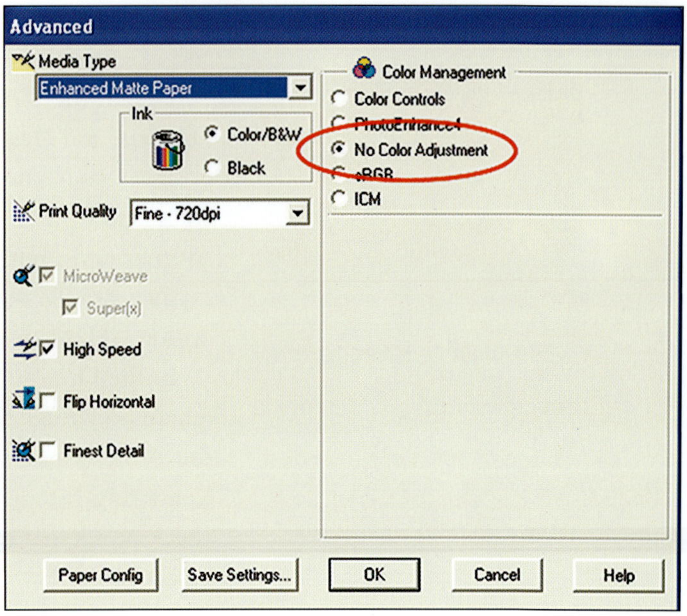

Figure 104—The Advanced section of the Epson 7600 print dialog box for Windows. Sometimes the settings for shutting off color management are buried deep in the printer driver settings. If you have difficulty finding these controls for your printer, check the printer's documentation for color-management settings.

If you are printing from Windows, the print driver's dialog will appear after you choose Print from Photoshop's Print with Preview dialog (figure 104). Even though the print driver for Windows may look entirely different than the Macintosh driver, the print settings are very similar, if not identical. Again, if you have built your own custom profile for your printer, make sure to set the media type, quality, and resolution so that they match the settings that you made when you printed the color-management target to create the profile. If you are using a profile created by the printer or paper manufacturer, follow the same procedures that are recommended for Macintosh users. Again, make absolutely sure that if Photoshop is performing the color conversion the color-management setting in the print driver is turned off.

Outputting to a RIP. Outputting to a RIP can be similar to outputting to a print driver. Many RIPs that are available today provide a mechanism for printing from within an application like Photoshop, making the integration of the RIP in the workflow very seamless. The usual methods for outputting through a RIP is to drop the image file into a watched folder where the RIP can pick it up, or to import images directly into the RIP using the RIP image-import feature. ColorByte's ImagePrint RIP provides a browser like Adobe's Bridge that gives direct access to the computer's file system and provides a thumbnail view of all the images in a selected folder. Images can be dragged from the browser and arranged on a page before printing.

Unlike most drivers today most RIPs can perform a color conversion using ICC profiles.

Just like a print driver, a RIP needs to be configured for color management. Unlike most drivers today, however, most RIPs can perform a color conversion using ICC profiles. This eliminates the need to set up the color conversion in an image-editing application when printing. With ImagePrint, the image file is opened and the RIP looks for an embedded profile as the source color space. If it doesn't find one, a source profile is assigned. The user assigns an output profile along with a rendering intent, and the RIP takes care of the output conversion. Most RIPs will handle color management in a similar fashion. They require the assignment of a source profile and a destination profile. Some, like ColorBurst, can save these settings along with settings for paper type, print resolution, etc., as "environments" that can be recalled whenever it is necessary to change the print process. Like a preset, this saves having to enter all the settings in the RIP every time the printing process is changed.

RAW Converters that Print. Software developers are bringing to market applications that better address the complete needs of the photographer. While Photoshop is the 800-pound gorilla in the digital imaging arena, it has features that are not needed by photographers. With the introduction of Apple's Aperture and Adobe Lightroom (still in beta as of this writing), the photo industry is seeing the first applications that provide most of the features that are needed for taking an image all the way through the workflow—from ingestion, to RAW conversion, to output. They provide features for applying metadata, for archiving, and creating electronic or printed output. These applications will convert a RAW image file and print it all in one step. It is not necessary to create a JPEG or TIFF to print (figure 107, next page).

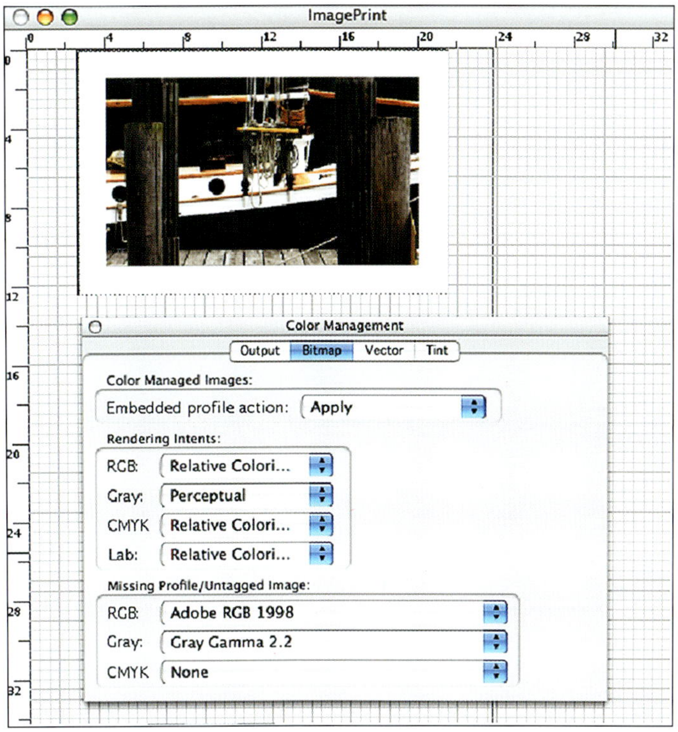

Figure 105—ColorByte's ImagePrint RIP can be set to always use an image's embedded profile as the source color space. If the image does not have an embedded profile, ImagePrint will default to the profile designated by the user.

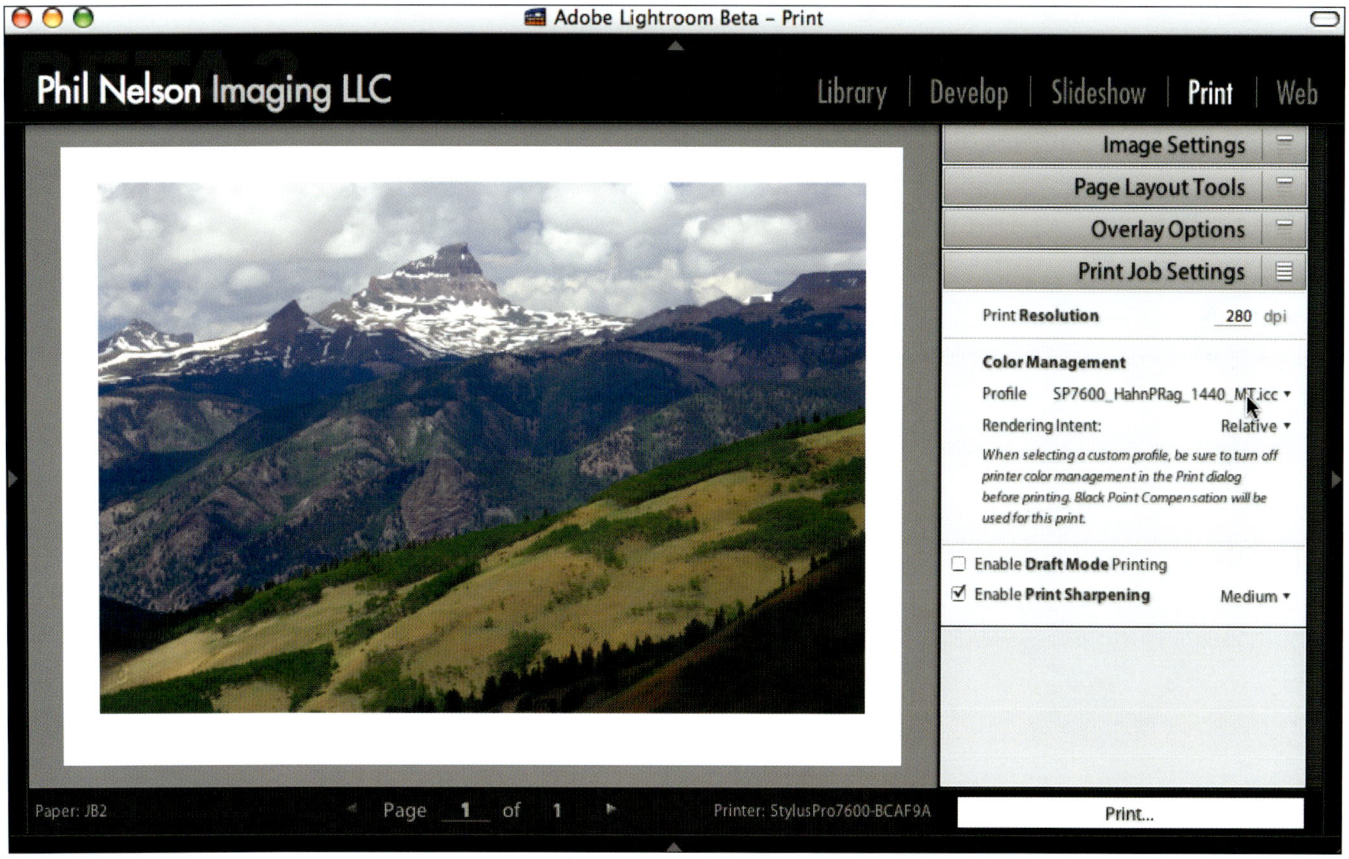

Figure 106—Adobe Lightroom can take an image all the way through the image-processing workflow. Its print capabilities are extensive, allowing the user to create output of individual images or complex contact sheets, all from RAW images.

Common Pitfalls

If you are finding that the color in your printed images is not meeting your expectations, double check your settings all the way through the printing process. Here are some of the most common problems:

Redundant Conversion. The most common error when applying color management when printing is converting an image's color twice, once in the

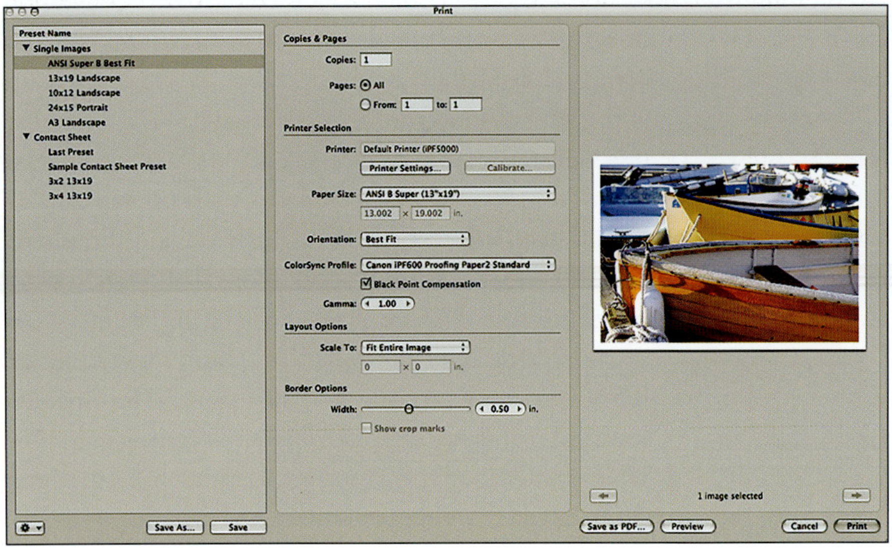

Figure 107 (left)—Aperture's Print dialog box gives the user the ability to create presets for printing both single images and contact sheets. Having the ability to save specific print settings as presets makes printing very quick. ***Figure 108 (below)****—Always double check your application and driver settings when printing to make sure that the image's color is being converted only once. Setting up print output that converts image color twice is one of the most common mistakes made when printing.*

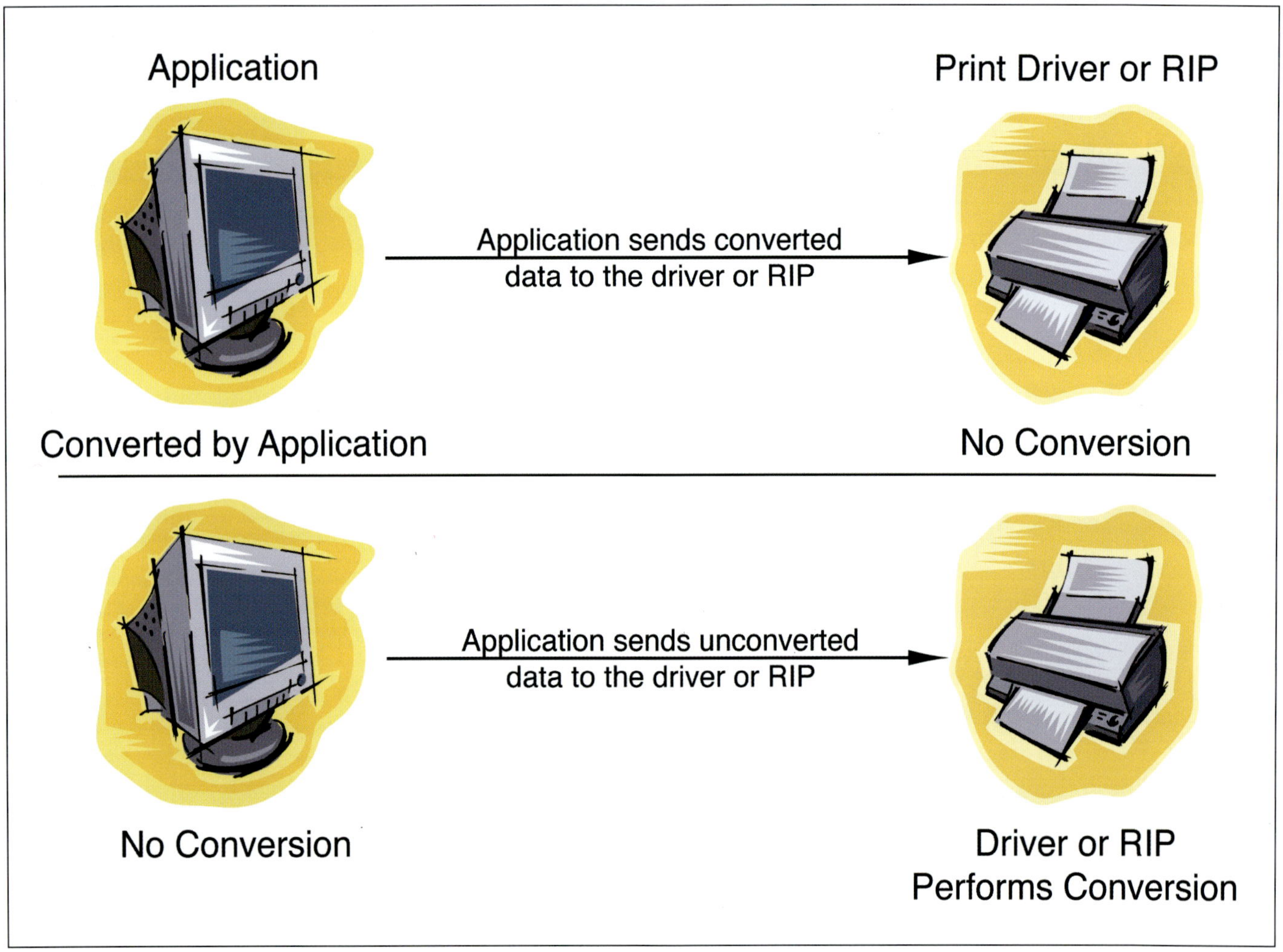

application and again in the print driver. When you set up an application like Photoshop, Lightroom, or Aperture to convert your image's color from its standard working space to the output color space of your printer, it is very important to turn off all color-management settings in the printer's driver or in the RIP that might be processing the job. If you set up the print driver or RIP to do the color conversion, then make sure that the application that you are printing from does not also convert the image's color. Color conversion when printing should take place *once,* either in the application that is printing, or in the printer driver or RIP (figure 108).

Printer Presets. Many print drivers will provide functionality for creating printing presets. Setting all the proper settings in the printer's dialog box oftentimes is a tedious process. Having the ability to capture all the driver's settings in a conveniently accessed preset can minimize the tedium. Be very careful when using presets. Even though you may think that the preset has captured your settings and is consistent when applying them, this is not always the case. Presets are not always consistently "sticky" and can make incorrect settings without you knowing it. It is highly recommended that you double check all of the driver's settings before pushing the Print button and that you not rely on printer presets (figure 109). This is especially important when printing to a large format printer when there is a high risk of wasting a lot of paper and ink.

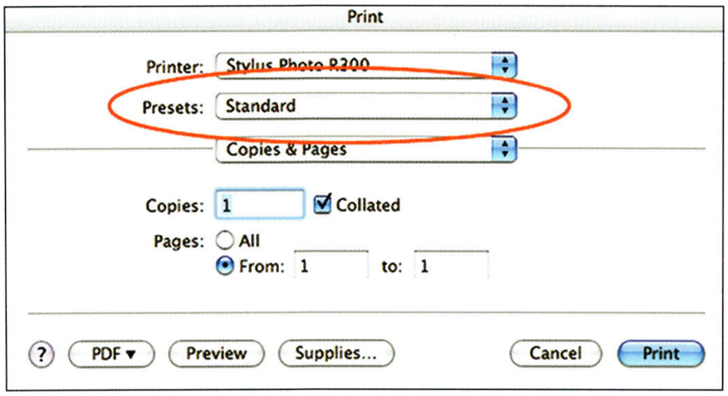

Figure 109—Be careful of printer presets. They are not always consistent and can make incorrect settings without you knowing it. It is always best to double check all of your print driver's settings before pushing the print button.

Assigning the Monitor's Profile. Back before the invention of working spaces, it was a common misconception that the monitor's color space was a good place to put image color. Since every monitor has a different color space, it did not take too long for anyone doing this to realize that their color was not matching when the image was moved from one computer to another. When you have successfully calibrated and profiled your display and made sure that the profile is correctly assigned to the display, leave it alone. Monitor profiles are for monitors. Do not assign your monitor's profile to a photograph. Do not convert your image's color to your monitor's color space.

7. Proofing

One of color management's greatest assets is its proofing capabilities. Proofing is the process of simulating, either on the computer display or on paper, how an image will look when output.

When proofing on a computer screen (soft-proofing), it is possible to see what the image will look like prior to actually printing. Because every printing process is different and every paper will render a different result, it is very helpful to know how the final output will look before wasting any media.

Proofing to paper (hard-proofing) is the process of simulating how a print job might look when printed to another printing device. This is valuable when it is critical to know how the final output of a job will look prior to spending large amounts of money to print the job. Imagine simulating how an image will look when printed on an offset press or to a costly large-format image printer like a LightJet 5000XL. The hard-proof is printed on a local printer or proofer, but only renders the colors that the final destination printer is capable of rendering.

Proofing helps set real expectations early in a job's workflow. By proofing, it is possible to find out early on in the process whether images will print properly. If a proof indicates that the image will look bad when output, it is possible to take corrective action before wasting time and money.

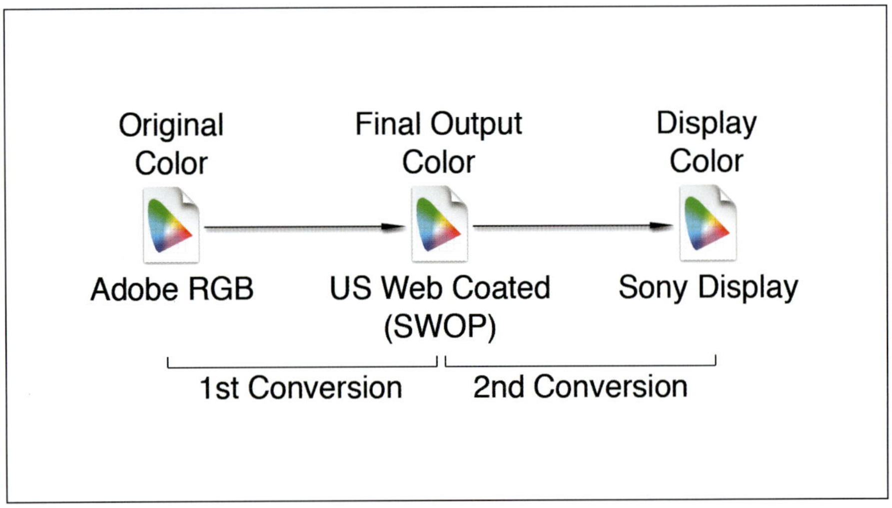

Figure 110—To simulate the color of a printed image on a monitor, it is first necessary to convert the original image color to the color space of the final output device and then convert the color again from the final output color space to the color space of the computer monitor. The color that is displayed on screen consists only of the colors that the final output device is able to reproduce. The process is very similar for hard-proofing. Instead of converting the color of the final output device to the screen's color space, the conversion would be made to the proofing printer's color space and then printed.

Final Output Device (FOD) Profile

Unlike running a standard output conversion, where an image's source color—typically a working space—is converted to the destination color space of the printer and media, proofing requires adding an additional color profile to the conversion process. This additional profile is the color space of the device that is being simulated: the final output device (FOD).

When soft-proofing, the source color is first converted to the color space of the FOD and then sent to the display using the display's profile. This two-step process ensures that the display is accurately showing only the color that the FOD is able to print. Imagine simulating the output capabilities of your local inkjet printer on the screen of your computer prior to printing. The soft-proof provides a preview of the final print without actually changing the original image file.

When hard-proofing, the original image is converted to the FOD's color space and then converted to the color space of the proofing device. The proofing device can be a local inkjet printer. When trying to simulate how an image will look when printed to an offset press, for example, it is necessary to have an ICC profile that characterizes the press. An image is first converted to the offset press color space (FOD) using the press profile and then converted again to the color space of the local proofing printer. By the time the image reaches the proofing printer, its color has been translated into the color space of the printing press. The proofer receives only the colors that the final output device, the press, is able to print, providing a simulation of the print job.

This two-step process ensures that the display is accurately showing only the color that the FOD is able to print.

Soft-Proofing

Today, many image-editing applications provide a means for simulating on screen how a photograph will look when it is printed. Of all the applications, Photoshop provides the greatest flexibility for soft-proofing. To soft-proof in Photoshop, it is necessary to utilize the output profile of the printer that is being simulated and a calibrated and profiled display.

Open an image in Photoshop CS2 that is in a common working space. Select View > Proof Setup > Custom (figure 111, next page). The dialog box that opens provides the tools for performing a soft-proof. After all the settings in the dialog have been made, it is possible to save them by pushing the Save button on the right. This creates a preset that can be recalled either from this dialog (under Custom Proof Conditions) or from the bottom of Photoshop's View > Proof Setup menu (figure 112, next page). It can also be accessed from the Print with Preview dialog box when printing a hard-proof—more on hard-proofing later.

The settings in the Customize Proof Condition dialog box define the color conversion for the soft-proof. The Device to Simulate menu gives access to the output profiles installed on your computer. Choose the profile of the output device that you want to simulate on screen. You can also choose a rendering intent. With the Preview button checked, it is possible to see the effects of the settings as they are made. Use the Preview check box to toggle the soft-proofing on and off and watch how the color in the image changes. This is also an excellent opportunity to determine which rendering intent to use prior to printing. As you change the setting in the Rendering Intent menu watch how your image is affected and choose the rendering intent that you think will yield the best result (figure 113).

Aside from controls for setting the output profile for Device to Simulate and selecting a rendering intent, Photoshop provides settings that control more precisely how the final output will be rendered. Soft-proofing involves transforming the color in an image twice—once from the source color space to the color space of the final output device and another transformation from the final output color space to the color space of the display. The controls in the Customize Proof Condition dialog box affect aspects of both of these conversions (figure 114).

Within the Customize Proof Condition dialog box are the main controls for setting up the soft-proof. At the bottom is a set of controls labeled Display Options (On-Screen). All of the controls above Display Options affect the first transformation from source color to the color space of the final output device. The Display Options settings affect aspects of the second transformation from the FOD's color space to the display.

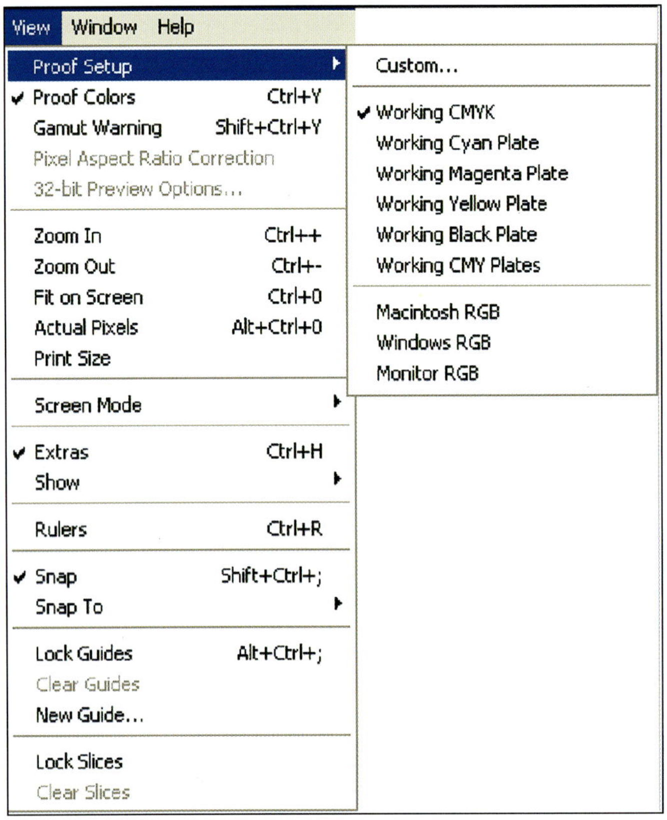

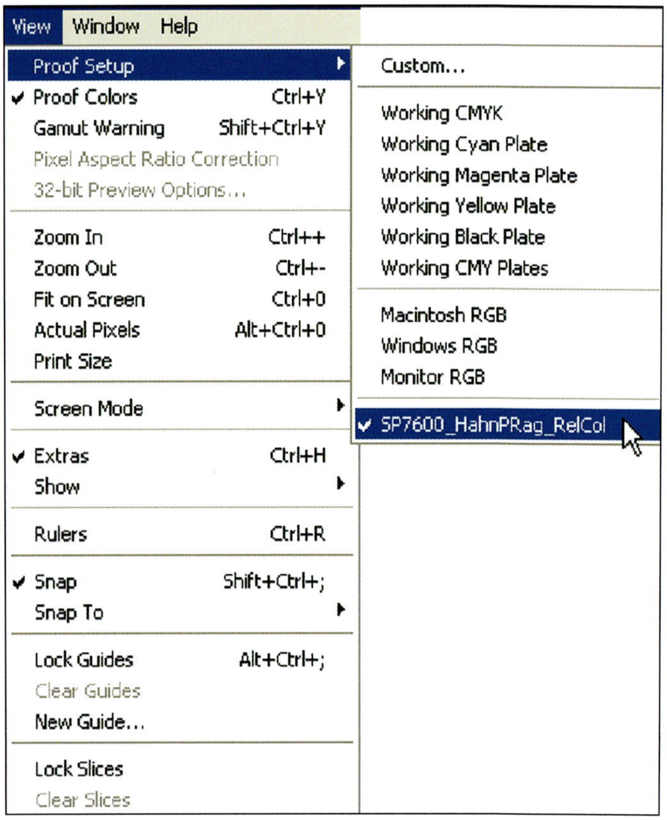

Figure 111 (left)*—Under View > Proof Setup in Photoshop CS2 is a list of menu items for soft-proofing to screen. Choose Working CMYK to display a proof of the image in the CMYK working space that was defined in Photoshop's Color Settings. The additional items under Working CMYK, down to the separator line, provide views of each of the CMYK color plates. The three RGB settings that follow provide a soft-proof of the image as it might appear in applications that do not support ICC color management. Macintosh RGB simulates how the image will look using a gamma of 1.8. The Windows RGB option displays the image using a gamma of 2.2. With Monitor RGB you see a proof of the image using the display's profile without the image's source color space. Again, the intent of these three RGB settings is to provide a simulation that shows how an image will look in applications that do not support ICC color management.*
Figure 112 (right)*—After saving the settings in the Customize Proof Condition dialog, they appear as a preset in the View > Proof Setup menu.*

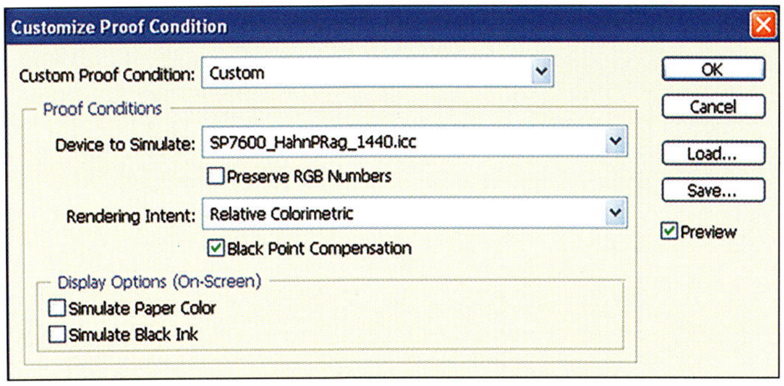

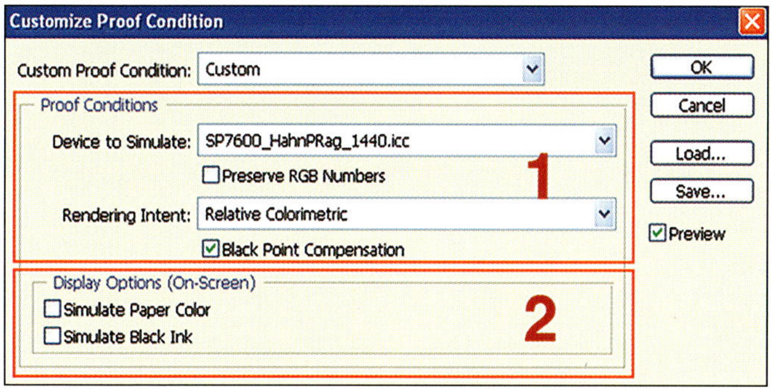

Figure 113 (left)—The Photoshop CS2 Customize Proof Condition dialog box. Figure 114 (right)—Behind-the-scenes soft-proofing conducts two color transformations. The controls in box 1 affect the transformation from the source color space to the color space of the device that is being proofed (or final output device). After the first transformation, the controls in box 2 affect the transformation from the color space of the final output device to the color space of the monitor that is displaying the soft-proof. The second set of controls further effects how the image might print by simulating black ink and paper color. In the background these two options control the rendering intent and Black Point Compensation that is used when the second color transformation takes place.

When Preserve RGB Numbers is selected, the soft-proof will show what the image would look like if no color conversion took place when outputting. This feature is only available when converting to the same color mode as the original—in other words, from RGB to RGB or CMYK to CMYK. Black Point Compensation, defined in chapter 4, maximizes the dynamic range of the image when converting. This setting should be left on.

Under Display Options, there are controls for simulating paper color and black ink. When these two settings are turned off, a relative colorimetric rendering intent and Black Point Compensation are used to send the color of the FOD to the display. With these settings turned off, the black ink and paper white values of the FOD are mapped to the black and white points of the display. Typically, this will render to the monitor a larger dynamic range than the FOD is capable of.

This will give a more accurate representation of the black that will be rendered on output.

Selecting Simulate Black Ink will turn off Black Point Compensation (not the BPC that takes place in the first transformation, but the one that happens behind the scenes during the second transformation). This maps the black point of the final output device to an equivalent value on the monitor and will give a more accurate representation of the black that will be rendered on output. Selecting Simulate Paper White changes the rendering intent from relative to absolute colorimetric and turns on and dims Simulate Black Ink. This sends the paper white value of the final output device to the display. Since Black Point Compensation is disabled when using an absolute colorimetric rendering intent, the setting cannot be changed. Choosing Simulate Paper White provides a preview of the compressed dynamic range that will result when outputting. This produces a more accurate soft-proof.

Prior to printing to a local printer, you may want to make some last-minute targeted edits that fine-tune the image for output. By duplicating the image window, it is possible to view the original and a soft-proof simultaneously. Seeing both views at the same time can help with the final edit.

With only your original image opened in Photoshop, select Image > Duplicate. This will open a copy of the original in a new window. Go to Window > Arrange > Tile Horizontally or Arrange > Tile Vertically. Then select Window > Arrange > Match Zoom and Location. This ensures that both

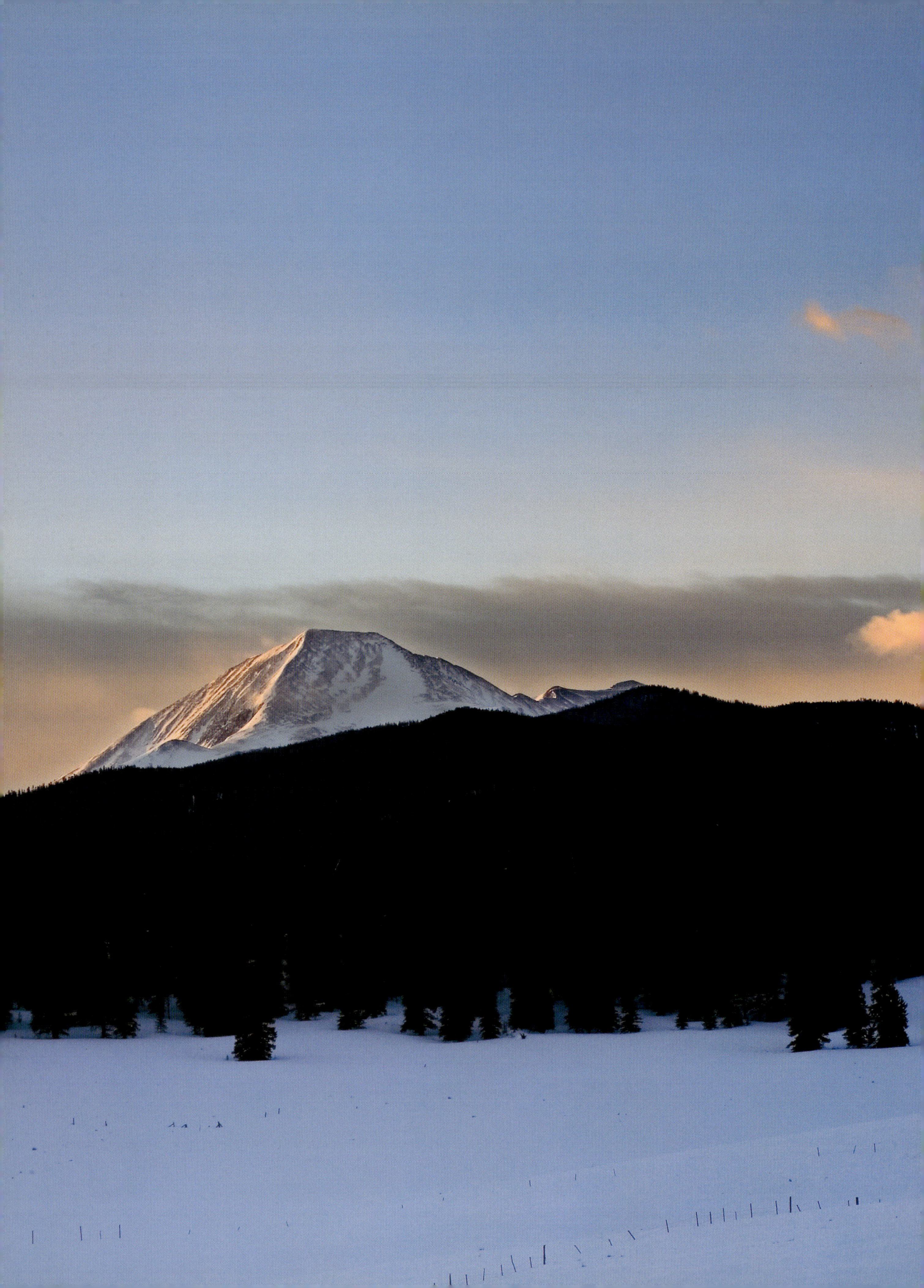

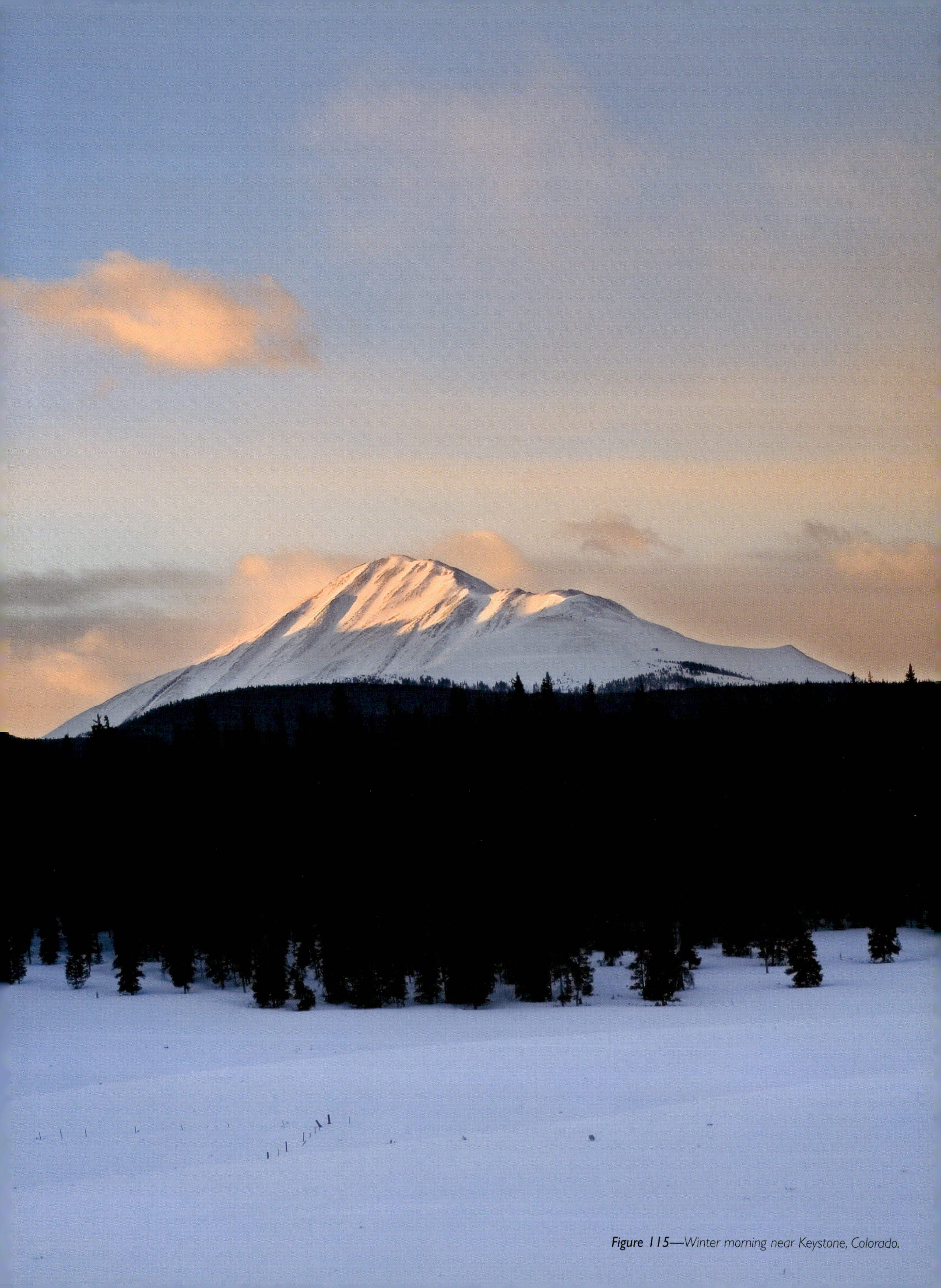

Figure 115—Winter morning near Keystone, Colorado.

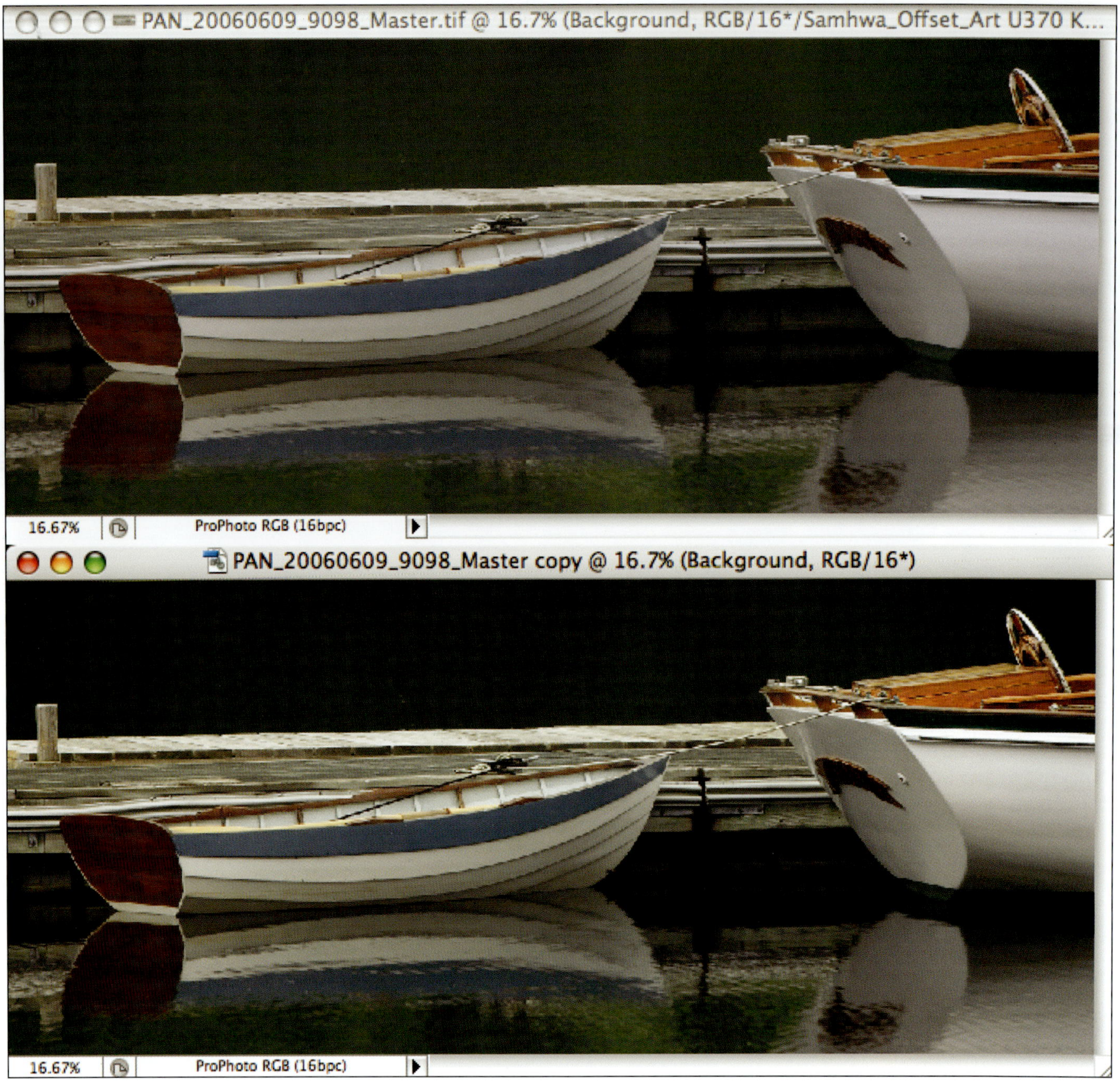

Figure 116—The same image is displayed in two separate windows in Photoshop. The top image is in soft-proof mode. This duplicate view provides a comparison between the original and a simulation of the printed image and can be used to make final targeted adjustments to the image before actually printing. It is always possible to tell which image is a soft-proof by looking at the window's title bar. The title of the soft-proof image has the name of the output profile appended to it.

images are displayed with equal magnification and at the same location (figure 116). Make the original image the active window and turn on a soft-proof. Having two views of the image can show how much the image will be impacted when printing.

It is also possible to zoom in and out and to move around both images simultaneously with shortcut keys. Holding down the Shift key in combination with the standard keyboard shortcuts for navigating an image will allow you to navigate all images displayed. Hold down the Shift key and using the standard key commands for zooming in (Command/Control + space bar), zoom in on both images. Holding down the Shift key and the space bar will allow you to move around both images as well.

Gamut Warning. Another powerful feature in Photoshop is its ability to show a gamut warning. When the gamut warning is invoked, Photoshop displays all of the colors that are outside the color space of the final output device that is being soft-proofed. It does this by painting all of the out-of-gamut pixels with a flat color. This warning defines all of the colors in an image that will be altered when converting to the output device's color space.

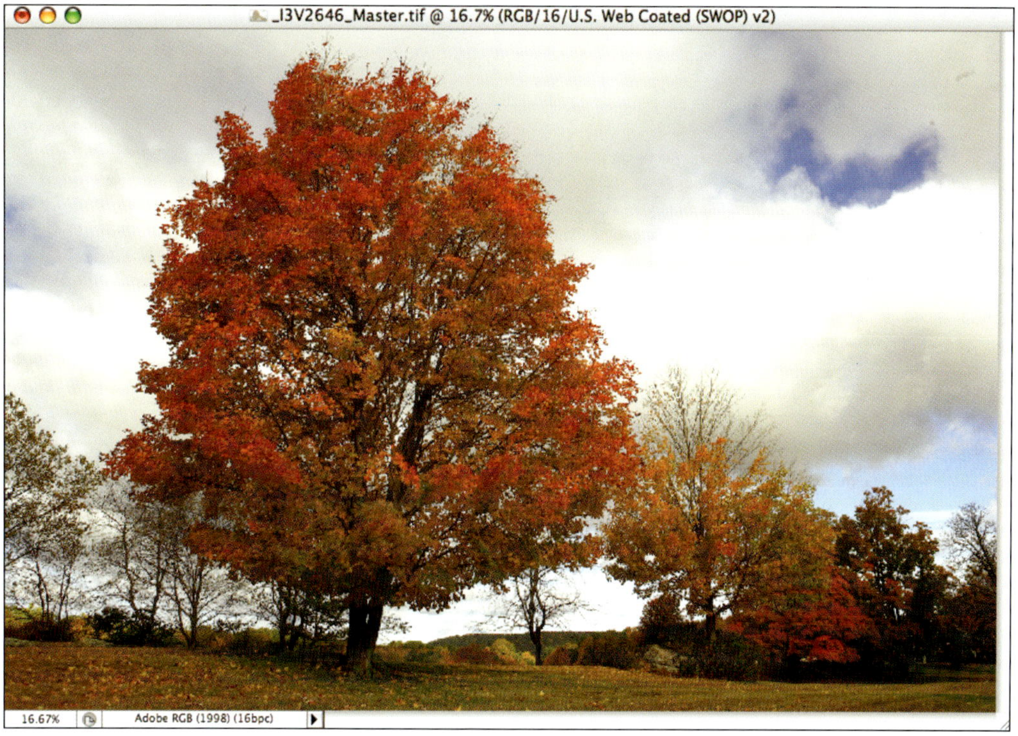

Figure 117—The highly saturated orange and red colors in this image are outside the color space of U.S. Web Coated (SWOP) v2, the profile that is being used to define the color capabilities of the final output device. The soft-proof has desaturated these colors.

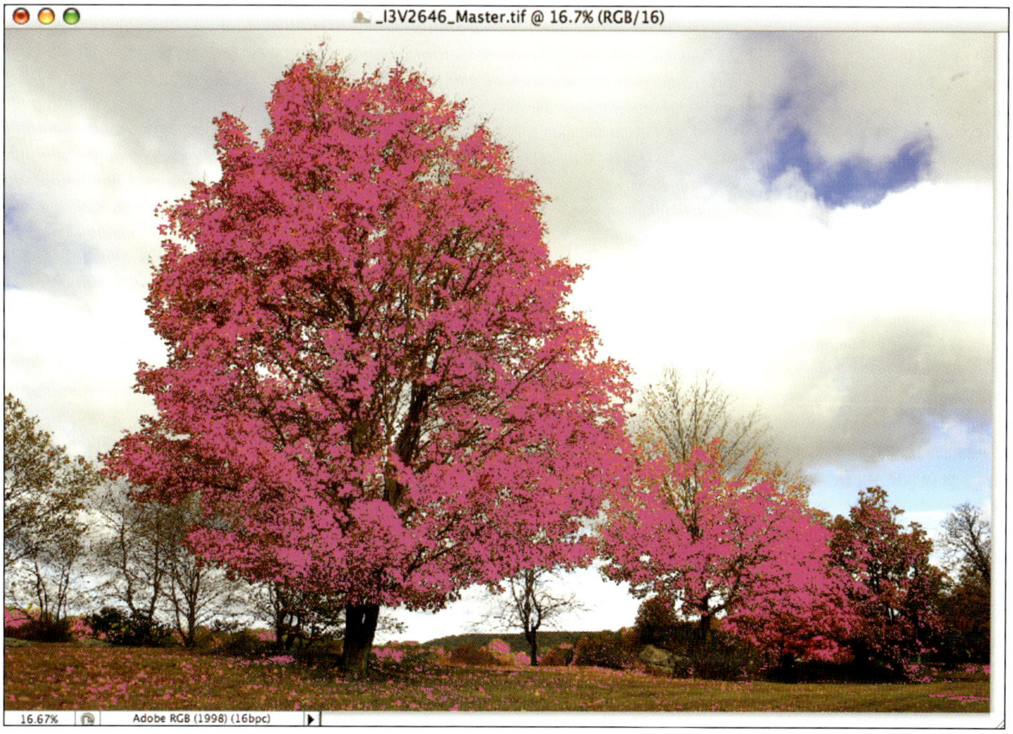

Figure 118—When Gamut Warning is invoked the colors that are outside the U.S. Web Coated (SWOP) v2 color space are painted with this flat magenta color. (The gamut warning color can be defined in Photoshop's preferences.) The colors painted by the gamut warning are too saturated and cannot be printed by a web press adhering to the SWOP specification.

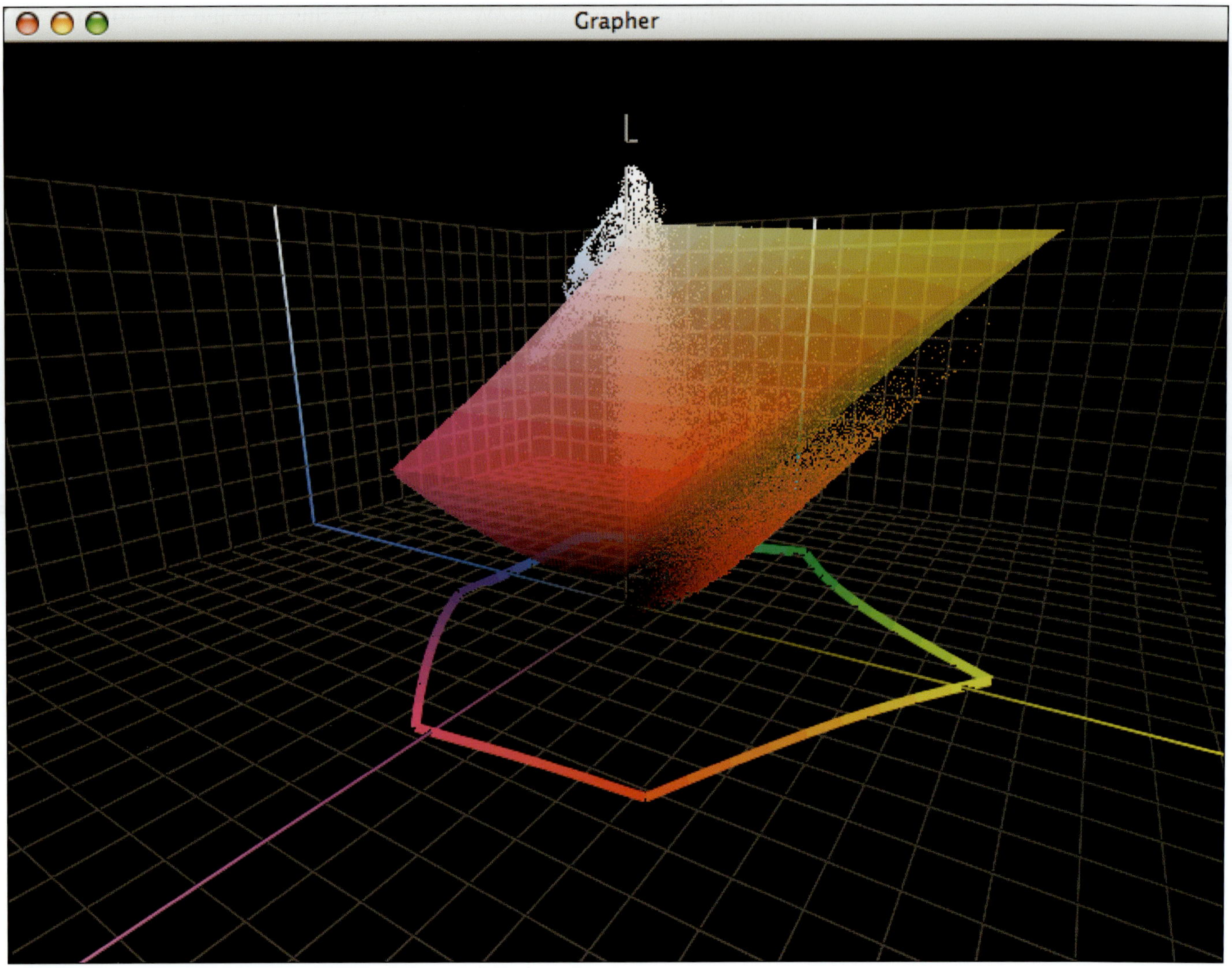

Figure 119—This three-dimensional chart shows the colors of the autumn tree image, plotted as dots, and the color space of U.S. Web Coated (SWOP) v2, plotted as a solid mass. It is clear that many of the colors of the image are plotted outside of the U.S. Web Coated color space. These colors are out of gamut, just as was indicated by Photoshop's gamut warning.

This provides the user an opportunity to make final adjustments in Photoshop before printing or simply to allow the output color conversion to handle the transformation. A method for dealing with these colors in Photoshop would be to target them with a Hue/Saturation adjustment layer and to desaturate them until the gamut warning disappears.

It helps sometimes to look at the same process from a different perspective. The image in figure 119 is a three-dimensional plot of the colors in the image of the autumn tree. The colors are plotted as dots. The more solid shape is a plot of the U.S. Web Coated (SWOP) v2 color space. The application that is making this diagram, Chromix ColorThink Pro, provides a mechanism for importing both images and ICC profiles, which it plots in three dimensions based on the LAB color model. It is clear that much of the red and orange colors of the image are plotted outside the U.S. Web Coated color space, just as was indicated by Photoshop's gamut warning.

Apple's Aperture is another application that provides soft-proofing. Since Aperture provides RAW conversion capabilities, it is possible to preview final output while adjusting the RAW image. With this capability, the adjustments that are made right from the beginning are targeted to the color capabilities of the output device. This is a very powerful feature that can save considerable time and frustration, because the user is always working within the color parameters of the output device. Also, Aperture is one of the few applications available that allows versioning from a single RAW file (figure 120). The combination of on-screen proofing and versioning provides the user an easy way to edit and accurately target a single image for multiple output destinations.

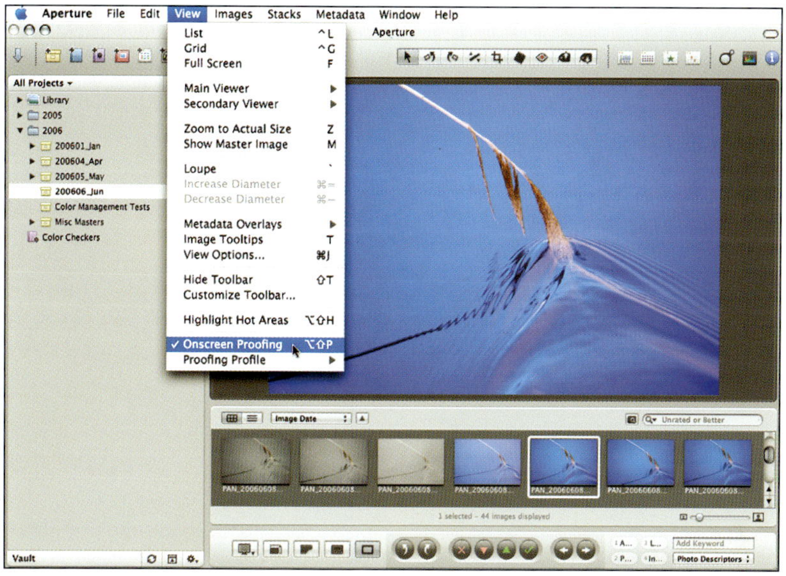

Figure 120 (right)—Apple Aperture's Onscreen Proofing provides an on-screen proof of the image's final output. This feature can be invoked prior to making edits to a RAW image ensuring that any RAW adjustments are targeting the color capabilities of the final output device.

Phase One's Capture One is another RAW conversion application that provides full access to ICC Color Management including the ability to soft-proof while editing for RAW conversion (figure 121). Like Aperture, Capture One can assign an output profile that will preview how the image will look when printed.

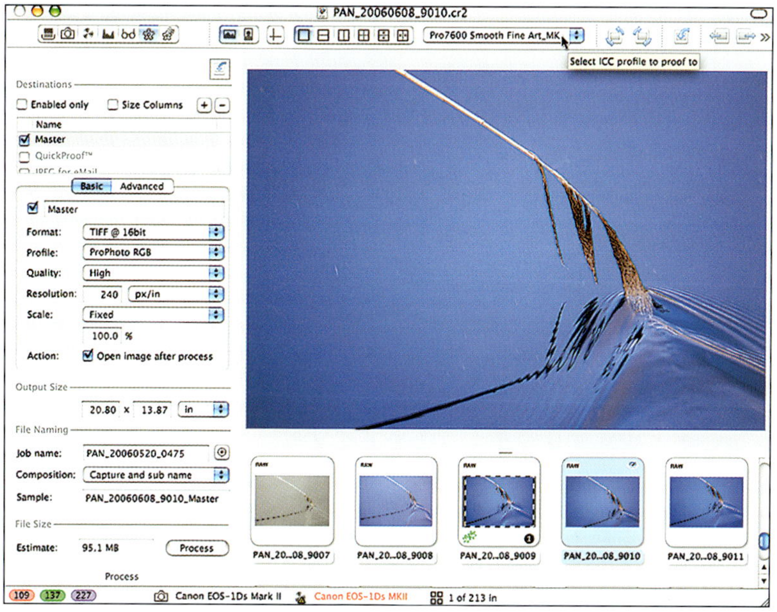

Figure 121 (below)—Phase One Capture One provides on-screen proofing while setting up an image for RAW conversion.

Hard-Proofing

If soft-proofing consists of creating an output simulation on a computer display, then hard-proofing is creating an output simulation on paper. Like soft-proofs, hard-proofs are intended to provide a preview on paper of how the image will reproduce when sent to the final output device.

Consider a LightJet 5000, for example. This is a costly and very large laser image processor. It is not the type of device that you would install in your studio to run off an occasional print. Some photographic service providers use LightJets to output large-format prints, say 50 x 50 inches. If you were producing large prints for a client, prior to sending the job to the LightJet service provider, you might want to show your client what the final image will look like. Using the service provider's ICC profile for the LightJet you create a hard-proof for your client on your inkjet printer. This print mimics how the LightJet will handle the color in your image.

Here is another scenario. Consider having to provide images to an ad agency for a brochure. The brochure will be printed in four-color process on a sheetfed offset press. The agency is asking that you provide proofs of your images that will give them an indication of how the photographs will look when inserted into the brochure and printed. They cannot provide you an output profile, so you decide to use the U.S. Sheetfed Coated profile that was installed with Photoshop to print some hard-proofs for the agency. This generic profile best matches the brochure printing process that the agency has described to you, and you believe it will render the best results.

The process that takes place behind the scenes when hard-proofing is very similar to what happens when soft-proofing. Instead of having one source and one destination color space, represented by their respective profiles the hard-proofing process uses three profiles. Color is transformed from the original source color space to the color space of the final output device, say an offset press. The color is then transformed again from the color space of the final output device to the color space of the device on which the proof will be printed, say a local inkjet printer.

As an example, imagine printing a proof of an image that will be printed in a magazine. You know that the highly saturated image color that you see on your computer display will undergo some changes when printed in CMYK on a four-color press. The proof will give a good indication of what will happen.

Adobe's Standard Profiles

When installing Adobe Creative Suite applications, Adobe also loads fourteen generic profiles. The four RGB profiles are standard working space profiles. More than likely you will recognize these. The ten CMYK profiles address standards that have been established for different types of printing in the United States, Japan, and Europe. These profiles, even though they are generic, provide color conversions that are close to the output gamut of the processes that they support. For example, U.S. Web Coated (SWOP) v2 was developed to support conversion of color to an output process that supports the publishing industry's standard print specifications for web offset publications (SWOP). Using this profile to prep output for web offset printing is a safe bet when you do not have the specific profile for the printer or proofer that is the final output device. To understand what each of the profiles is designed for, open Photoshop's Color Settings dialog box, select one of the profiles in the RGB or CMYK working space menus, hover your cursor over the menu, and read the description of the profile in the Description area at the bottom of the dialog box.

4 RGB PROFILES

Adobe RGB (1998)
Apple RGB
ColorMatch RGB
sRGB IEC61966-2.1

10 CMYK PROFILES

U.S. Web Coated (SWOP) v2
U.S. Web Uncoated v2
U.S. Sheetfed Coated v2
U.S. Sheetfed Uncoated v2
Europe ISO Coated FOGRA27
Euroscale Uncoated v2
Japan Web Coated (Ad)
Japan Color 2001 Coated
Japan Color 2001 Uncoated
Japan Color 2002 Newspaper

To print the proof, the application doing the printing will need to be able to assign three profiles for output.

The magazine adheres to the SWOP specifications for printing, so using the U.S. Web Coated (SWOP) profile will create a pretty accurate color simulation based on the capabilities of the final output device, a web offset press. Compared to the color space your image is currently in, Adobe RGB (1998), the web press's color space is pretty small. To print the proof you will use an Epson SP4800 inkjet printer. This printer has a very large color gamut, much larger than the offset press. Your objective when printing the hard-proof is to make sure that the Epson inkjet only prints colors that are reproducible on the web press. If the Epson 4800 prints colors that cannot be printed on the web press, the proof will be inaccurate and potentially misleading. The process of color transformation for this proof is one of "dumbing down" the color of the image to the small color space of the web press and then telling the inkjet to only print those specific colors—and in the process, make sure that the "dumb" colors are printed accurately.

To print the proof, the application doing the printing will need to perform two color conversions: one from the source color space to the color space of the output device, another from the color space of the final output device to the color space of the proofing device.

When using Photoshop's Print with Preview feature, there are controls for setting up a hard-proof. Open an image and select File > Print with Preview in Photoshop CS2. When the dialog opens, make sure that the bottom section of the dialog box is revealing the Color Management features (select Color Management from the pop-up menu just below the image preview).

In the Print section of the dialog box, there are two radio buttons. The default setting is Document with the name of the profile that is currently assigned. This is the source color space of the document being printed (typically, this profile is a working space). The other radio button, Proof, instructs Photoshop to generate a hard-proof. When selected, the name of the profile of the final destination output device will be displayed to the right. This is the profile of the device that is being simulated. You will notice that there is no option here for selecting a different profile. This is handled by the Proof Setup Preset menu, found in the Options section of the dialog (figure 122, next page).

If Photoshop CS2 is being used to control all of the color transformations for the hard-proof, then the Color Handling pop-up menu must be set to Let Photoshop Determine Colors. The menu just below this, labeled Printer Profile, defines the profile of the proofing device. The Proof Setup Preset menu provides access to the presets saved in the Proof Setup dialog in Photoshop (figure 123, next page). If you have saved a number of Proof Setup presets for soft-proofing, they will appear in this menu along with an option to choose the Working CMYK profile, defined in Photoshop's Color Settings, or the Current Custom Setup. If you soft-proof an image prior to printing using a custom setup, the last profile that was assigned for the soft-proof will accessible for a hard-proof when selecting Current Custom Setup. When one of these is chosen, the profile listed to the right of the Proof radio button changes to the profile that was selected in Proof Setup. If you set U.S. Web

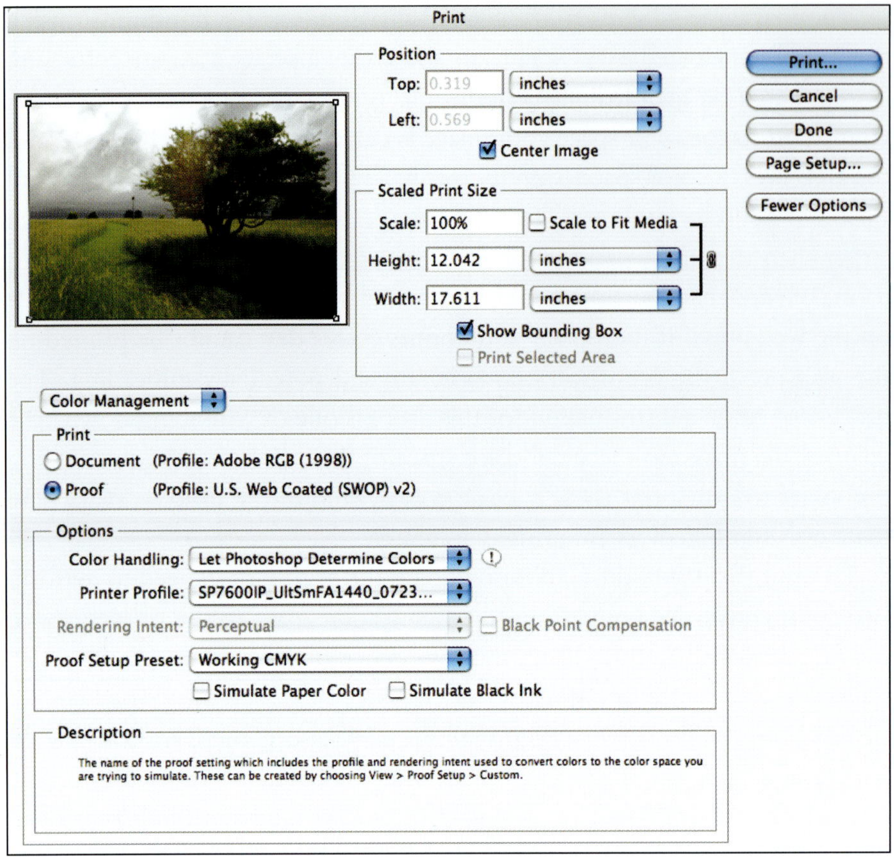

Figure 122—Photoshop CS2's Print with Preview dialog provides the necessary settings to output a hard-proof. Photoshop assumes that the source color space of the document being printed is the color space that is currently defined. The label to the right of the Document radio button shows the name of the source profile. Selecting the Proof radio button puts Photoshop in hard-proof mode. Settings in the Options section of the dialog specify the profile assignments for the device being simulated and the device that is printing the proof. The profile for the device printing the proof is set using the Printer Profile menu, and the profile for the device that is being simulated is set using the Proof Setup Preset menu.

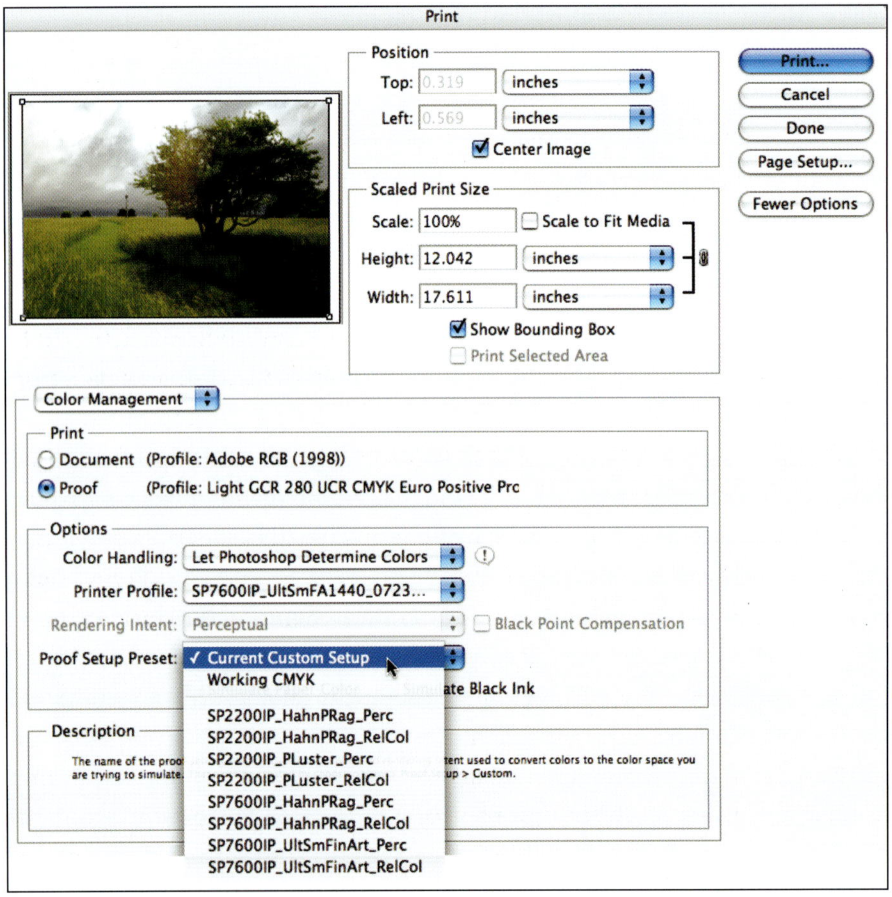

Figure 123—The Proof Setup Preset menu lists the presets that were saved in the Customize Proof Setup dialog in Photoshop CS2. Choosing any one of these will set the final output device profile that is to be used in the hard-proof. Selecting Working CMYK sets the profile that is defined in Photoshop's Color Settings dialog for CMYK working space. Current Custom Setup tells Photoshop to use the last output profile that was set in the Customize Proof Setup dialog.

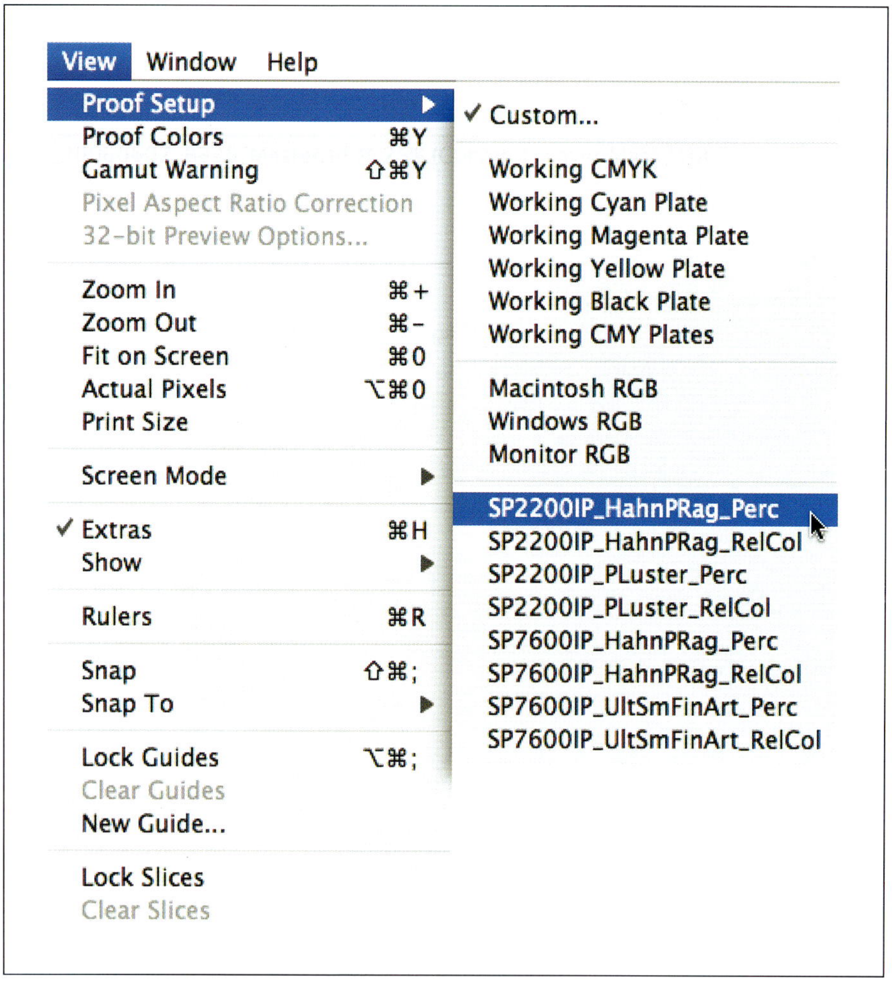

Figure 124—The View > Proof Setup menu in Photoshop CS2 lists the same proofing presets that are available in the Print with Preview dialog box. Selecting a preset from this menu will initiate a soft-proof. Selecting one of these presets in Print with Preview defines the final output device profile that is to be used when hard-proofing.

Coated (SWOP) as your standard CMYK working space in Color Settings, choosing Working CMYK will assign U.S. Web Coated (SWOP) as the final output device color space.

Rendering Intent and Black Point Compensation are dimmed when proofing, and relative colorimetric with black point compensation (BPC) is automatically assigned. The Simulate Paper Color and Simulate Black Ink check boxes control the use of BPC and determine whether an absolute or relative colorimetric rendering intent is assigned for the conversion.

Selecting Simulate Black Ink will turn off BPC for the transformation from the final destination color space to the proofer's color. Rather than mapping the black point of the printer that is being simulated to the black point of the proofer, this setting tells the proofer to print black the same way the final output device would print it. This renders a more accurate simulation of how black will be printed on the final output device.

This more accurately simulates what the final print will look like.

Selecting Simulate Paper Color changes the relative colorimetric rendering intent to absolute colorimetric for the conversion from final output color to the color space of the proofer. This also selects and dims Simulate Black Ink which, again, turns off BPC. Using an absolute colorimetric rendering intent will map the paper white of the device that is being proofed to the white point of the proofer. This more accurately simulates what the final print will look like. If the proof involves simulating newsprint, mapping the paper white of

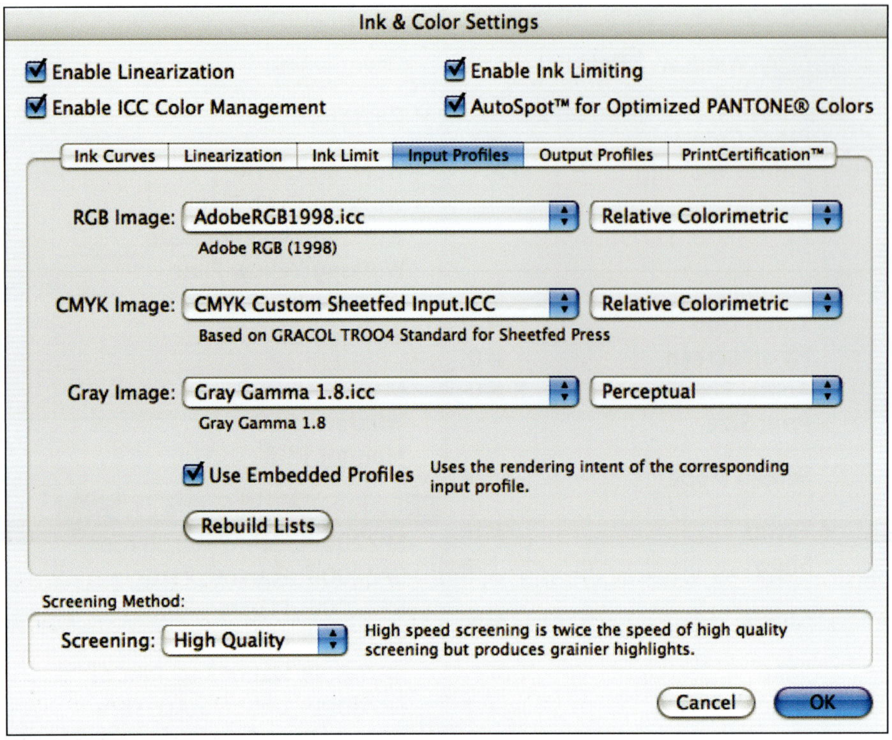

Figure 125—The Ink & Color Settings in the ColorBurst X-Photo RIP provide a tab for defining both the input profiles and the output profiles for printing. When setting up ColorBurst's color features, the RIP asks that a source profile be defined for RGB, CMYK, and Gray images. This profile is used to define the source color of the incoming image. If Use Embedded Profiles is checked, ColorBurst will ignore the source profiles defined in this dialog and use the embedded profile. This feature can be turned off, which will assign the profiles defined in this dialog as the source color space for all images that are opened.

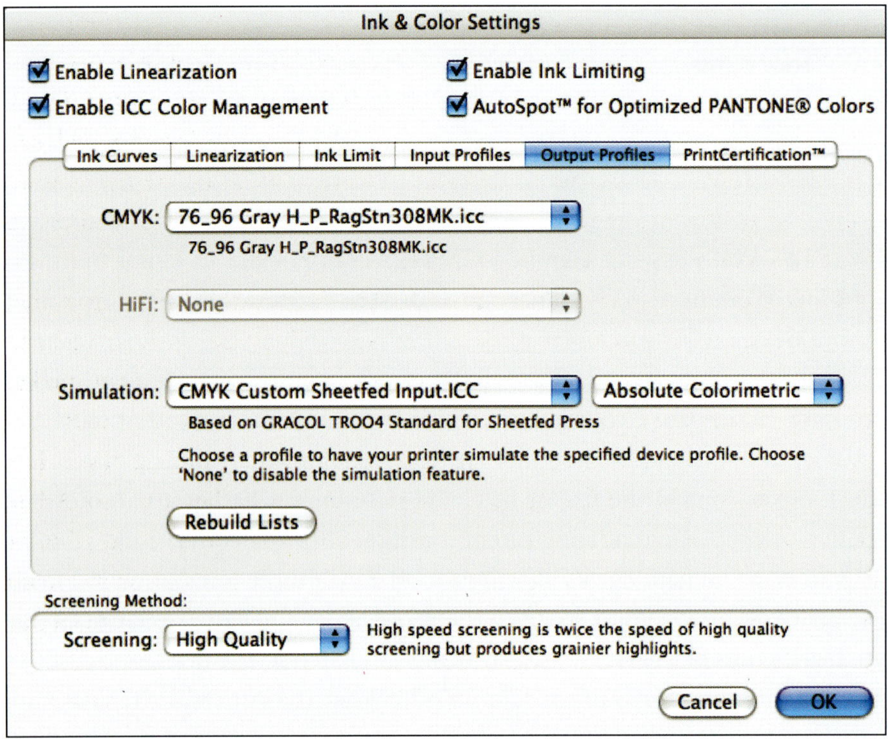

Figure 126—The Output Profiles tab of the Ink & Color Settings dialog in the ColorBurst RIP provides a Simulation menu for selecting a profile for a hard-proof. Setting this menu to None turns hard-proofing off.

the device that is being simulated to the white point of the proofer will tell the proofing device that white is really the color of newsprint. If necessary, the proofing device will print a gray tone to mimic the color of newsprint. The Simulate Paper Color setting will render the most accurate hard-proof. (It is perfectly understandable if you have to reread this paragraph a couple of times to get all this to sink in.)

When all the settings are made in Photoshop's Print with Preview dialog, it is very important to remember that Photoshop is performing the color con-

Figure 127—ColorByte's ImagePrint RIP provides similar functionality to the ColorBurst RIP. If an output profile is selected in the Proofer menu, ImagePrint will output a hard-proof. In this screen shot the proofer is set to None, which turns hard-proofing off.

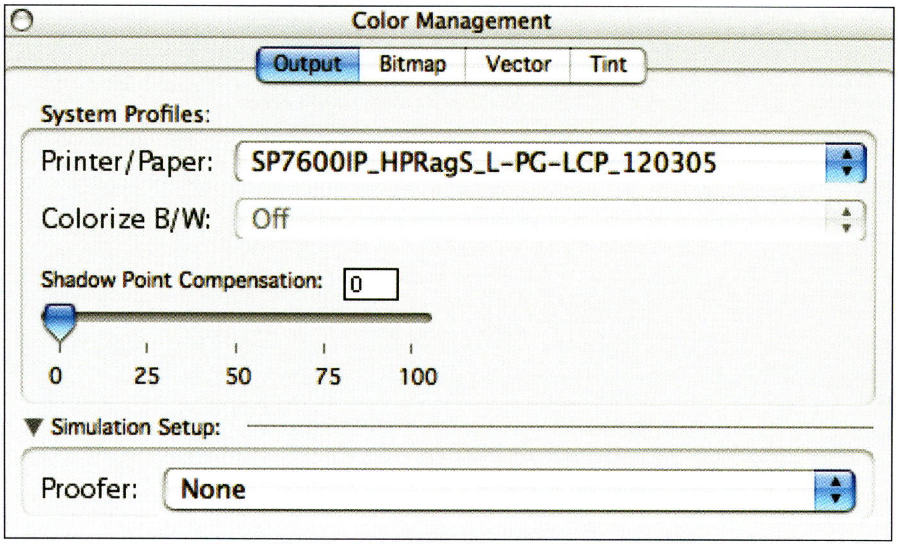

version for the hard-proof and that the print driver or RIP needs to be instructed to not convert the print job again. Make sure that all color-management features in the driver or RIP are disabled.

RIPs that Proof. Most RIPs can be set up to print a hard-proof. Similar to the settings in Photoshop, the RIP's settings will ask for source, final output device, and proofer profiles in order to perform the proofing color conversion. Unlike Photoshop, which assumes the source color space of the document being printed is the one that is currently assigned, most RIPs will ask for the source color space to be explicitly defined. Many RIPs today will also support the use of embedded profiles as an option. If an image that has an embedded profile is opened in the RIP, the source profile that is defined in the RIP is ignored and the embedded profile is used.

Paper and ink are not cheap. For this reason alone, running a soft-proof before printing makes great sense.

If you have bought an inkjet printer in the last ten years and marveled at how seemingly inexpensive they are, it wasn't long before you realized that the printer manufacturer is making most of their money on print media. Paper and ink are not cheap. For this reason alone, running a soft-proof before printing makes great sense. Why waste paper and ink running test prints when you can run the test print up on your computer display at no cost? The ability to proof, whether to screen or paper, is only possible because of color management. If you are going to take the time to set up a color-managed workflow, then, by all means, take advantage of proofing. Its benefits will pay off the first time that you make a proof.

8. The Work Environment

Much of the setup process for building a color-managed workflow is focused on camera, scanning, computer, and printing equipment—making sure that these devices are properly calibrated and profiled. It is easy to forget that the environment in which one works also plays an influential role in color management. A color-managed work environment can make a huge difference in how color is perceived, either on paper or on a computer display.

ISO 3664

Believe it or not, there is an ISO standard for Viewing Conditions in Graphic Technology and Photography. ISO 3664, available for download from www .iso.org, describes in detail how to create an environment that fully supports the photography or graphic-design workflow. This can be of considerable value to photographers who are particularly concerned with accurate color matching. Photographing packaging, for example, where matching logo or brand colors is critical to the success of a job, is rife with challenges. Being able to neutralize a color-managed work environment can have a big impact on one's ability to accurately compare colors and to make color-critical decisions. While creating an environment that adheres to all the aspects of ISO 3664 may seem extreme for most photographers, it might not seem so extreme for the ad agency that holds the Revlon account where color accuracy can make or break a job. Most photographers can benefit from understanding how to set up a work environment, even if it means implementing a small percentage of what is described in ISO 3664.

Being able to neutralize a color-managed work environment can have a big impact on one's ability to accurately compare colors.

Room Lighting

The color and relative brightness of the ambient light in a photographic work environment needs close scrutiny. Consider the color temperature of the light near the computer display on which you work. Is the light warm or cool? What kind of lighting are you working under? Is it incandescent, florescent, daylight, or something else? How bright is the light in your office or studio? These characteristics have a direct effect on how you perceive color and tonal values on your computer's monitor.

The ambient light level in the work environment should be much lower than the luminance level of the white point of the display. If the monitor's white point is set to D65, the level of ambient light should be less than 64 lux. A setting much lower than 64 lux, even as low as 32 lux, is preferable.

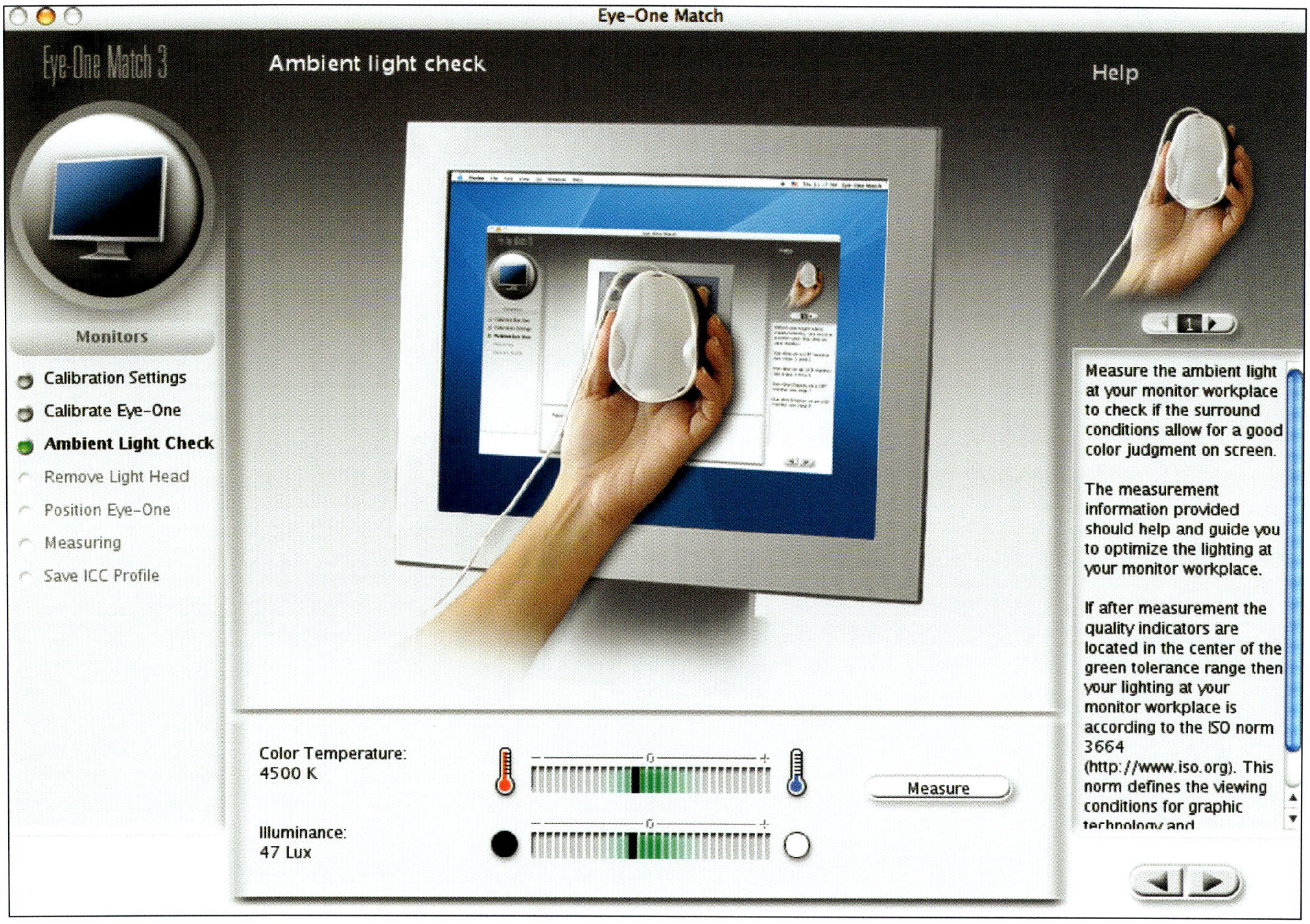

Figure 128—GretagMacbeth's Eye-One Display 2 can read ambient light values in a work environment. By attaching the white cap included with the Eye-One Display 2 colorimeter, and choosing Perform Ambient Light Check in i1 Match, it is possible to read both the brightness and color temperature of the ambient light around your computer display. If the black lines on each scale align with the zero position, the ambient light in your work area conforms to the ISO 3664 standard. In this illustration, the black lines are slightly below the zero mark and adjustments in room lighting would be necessary to make the light slightly cooler and slightly brighter.

Furnishings and the position of a display in a work environment can play a role in color perception.

Measuring the color and brightness of room lighting is possible with some of the colorimeters that are available for display calibration. Some spectrophotometers can make these measurements as well. GretagMacbeth's Eye-One Display 2 colorimeter comes with the added functionality of measuring ambient light values. The device has a white translucent cap that snaps into place, and together with the software that is used to calibrate and profile a display, i1Match, it is possible to take an ambient light reading during the calibration/profiling process. i1Match uses ISO 3664 as its gauge for optimum lighting conditions. Ambient light measurements will indicate how close the lighting around a computer display is to the ISO standard and will indicate the necessary steps for correcting bad lighting conditions.

Furnishings and the position of a display in a work environment can play a role in color perception as well. Imagine the impact of facing a computer display near a south-facing window. Unless the window is curtained off, there is a good chance that the display will pick up glare all day long. Some higher-end displays come with a hood that will help minimize veiling glare, but even a hood might not help if the display is placed near a window. Also, be

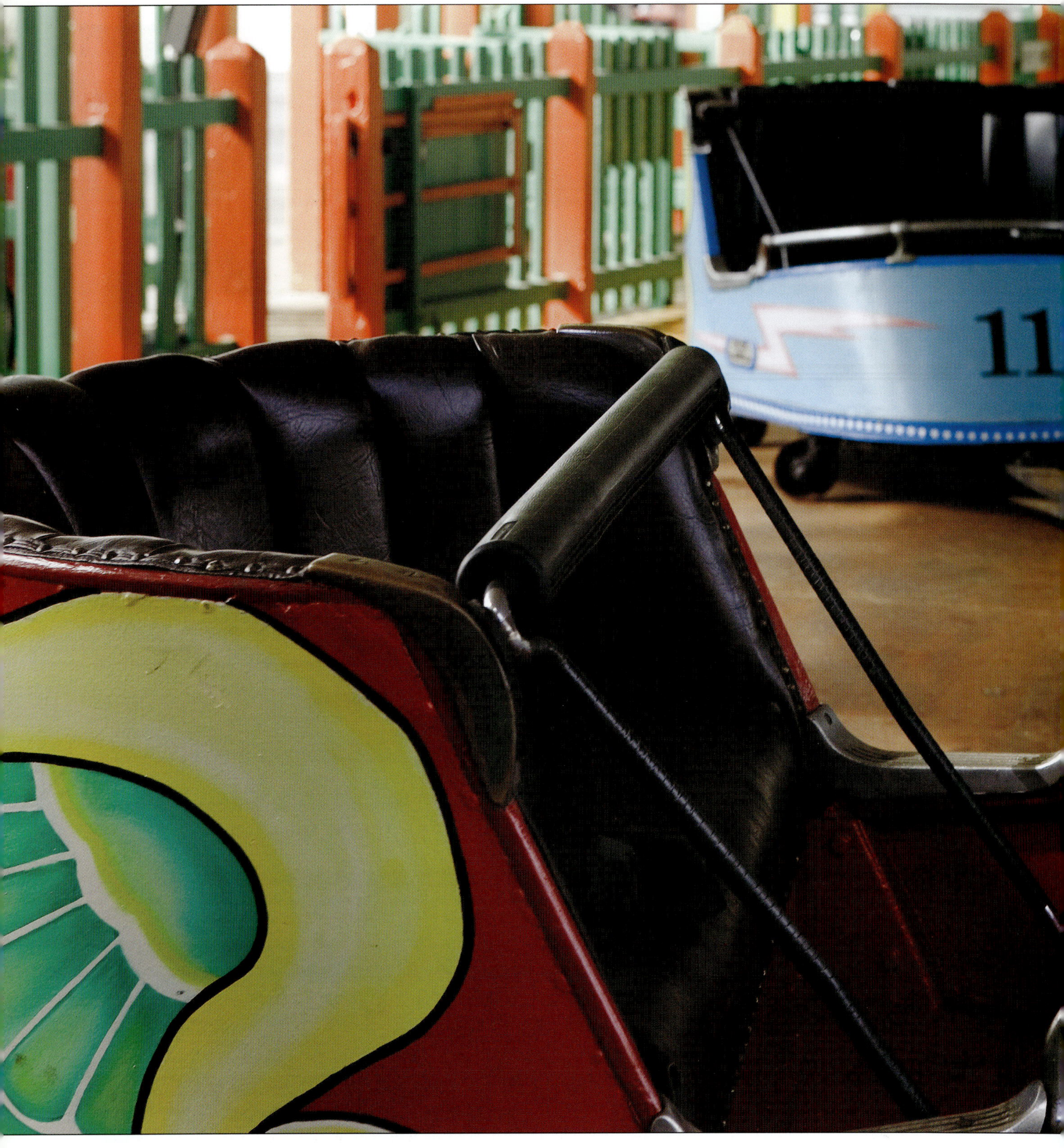

Figure 129—Twirl-a-Whirl, Playland.

mindful of the surface color of the desktop that the display is sitting on. If it is brightly colored, it could be reflected in the display and affect your color perception. A gray or neutrally colored surface is recommended. Try to avoid having windows or unshielded lamps directly in your field of view or casting a reflection or glare on the display's surface.

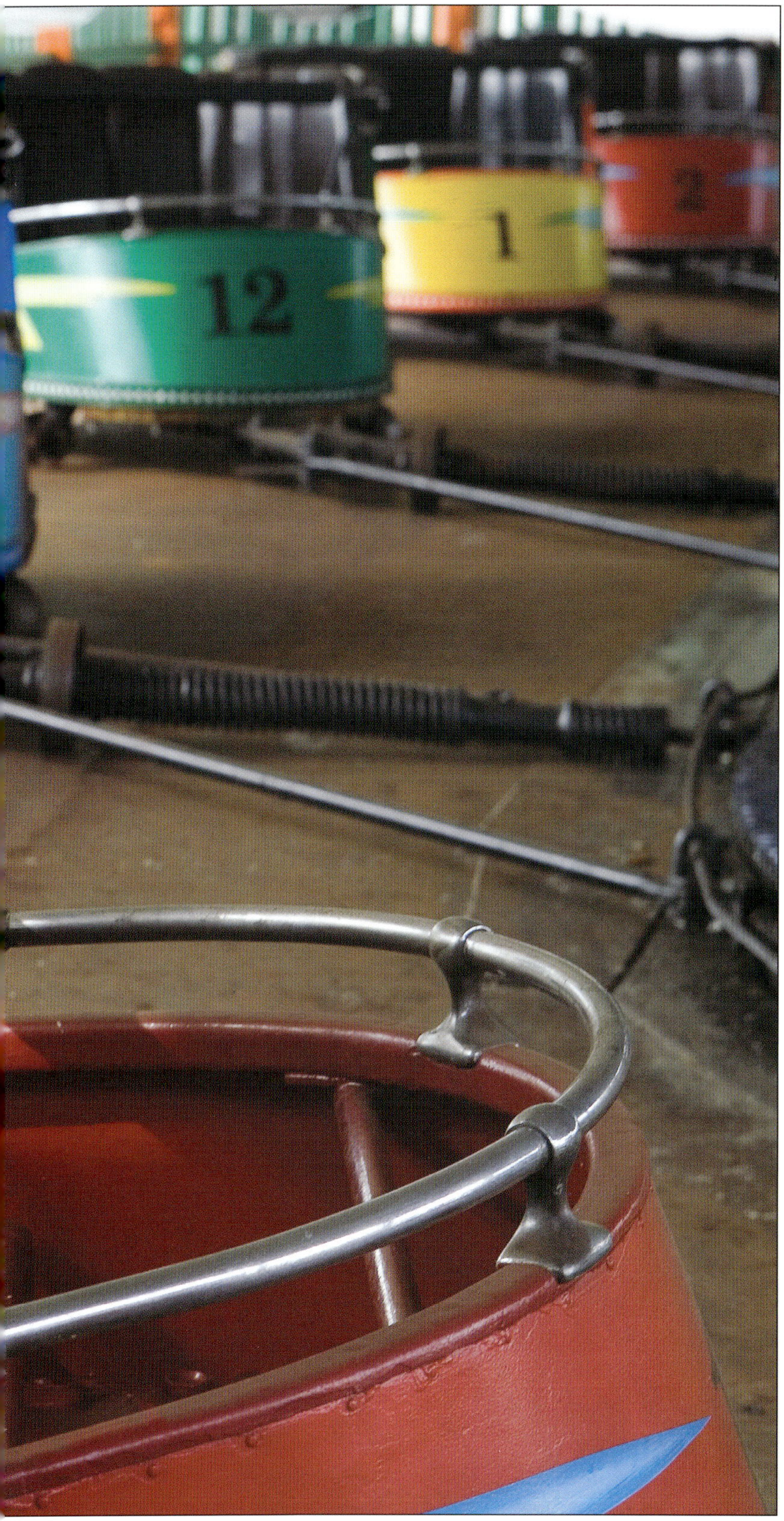

Evaluating Prints

While general room lighting can influence how colors are interpreted on your computer's display, lighting for making an accurate evaluation of print output is also critical. The lighting for evaluating a print should match the conditions under which a print will be displayed. Because lighting conditions under which a print will be displayed are frequently different and often difficult to mimic, it is more practical to create viewing conditions that are based on the ISO standard.

Practical Appraisal. Imagine viewing a print under incandescent lights, like a desk lamp with a common household lightbulb. It could be compared to shooting daylight-balanced film indoors. Incandescent light is very warm and will cast an orange light on the print, influencing how you perceive its color. The brightness of room lighting can also have an impact on how color is perceived. To make accurate and consistent evaluations of printed output it is necessary to stabilize the light under which prints are viewed. The standard lighting color temperature for viewing prints is around 5000° Kelvin (or often described as the CIE illuminant D50), the equivalent of daylight. The light level for making a practical assessment of a print is 500 lux (±125).

Lighting systems are available that are balanced to D50. Light bulbs, desk lamps, track lights, and fluorescent bulbs can be purchased that match the color temperature of daylight. Solux (www.solux.com), for example, provides a relatively inexpensive desk lamp with a D50 bulb.

A light booth is one of the better tools that can be used to evaluate prints. They are available in varying shapes and sizes and with various levels of lighting control. These devices are built to provide very controlled viewing conditions with balanced color temperature and consistent illumination. Placing a printed image under a light booth can make color evaluation much easier. Depending on the model, some provide controls for changing color temperature and brightness. Having a light booth near a calibrated and profiled display is a very good way to compare the color in a print to the image on a computer display.

Critical Color Matching. When comparing prints side by side, it is necessary to view the images in very bright lighting conditions in order to make an accurate assessment of the photographs' color. The illuminance should be 2,000 lux (±250). Keep in mind that this is not room lighting, but the light under which you make a print-to-print comparison to determine color matching. This level of light will be too bright to assess how the colors in your images will look when making a practical appraisal.

The Color-Critical Workstation

If you work in a studio environment with numerous workstations, you may have attempted to calibrate and profile of all of your displays with the intention of making them all match. You may have discovered that this is not as easy as you originally hoped. If the age and manufacturer of your displays varies, it only stands to reason that making them all match can be very difficult. Also, if they are placed in different areas of your studio under different lighting, that can have an impact as well.

If you are finding this effort to be far more time-consuming than it is worth, try setting up a single workstation where you evaluate all of your color work. Be sure to calibrate and profile all of your other displays, but don't be overly concerned if they do not exactly match one another. Set up the color-critical workstation, and take particular care to make certain that this system is located away from windows in an area where it is not affected by glare. Even though all the workstations in your studio may be used to process photographs in one way or another, it is this single system where color will be critically evaluated.

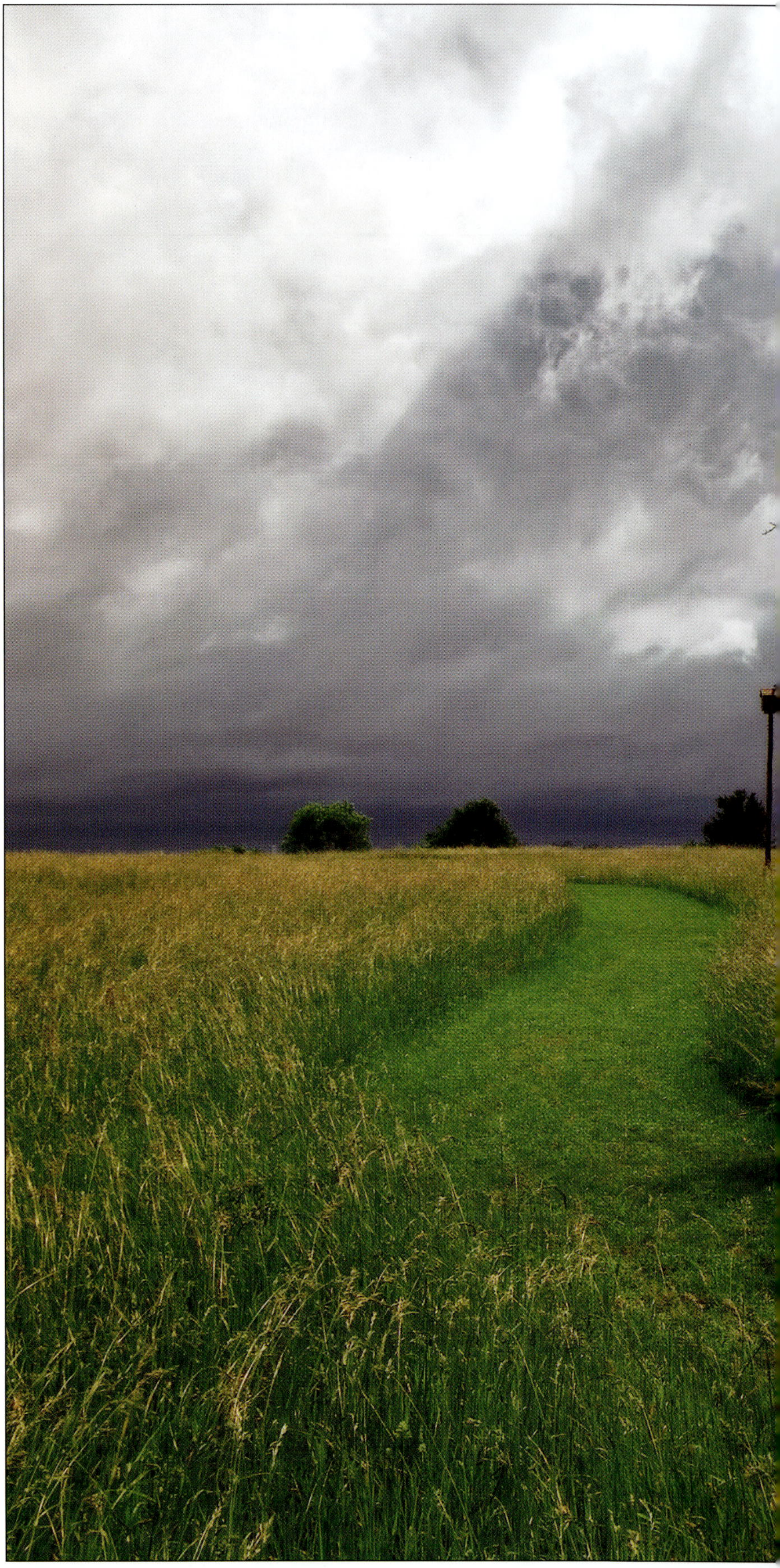

***Figure 130**—Griswold Point, Connecticut Coast.*

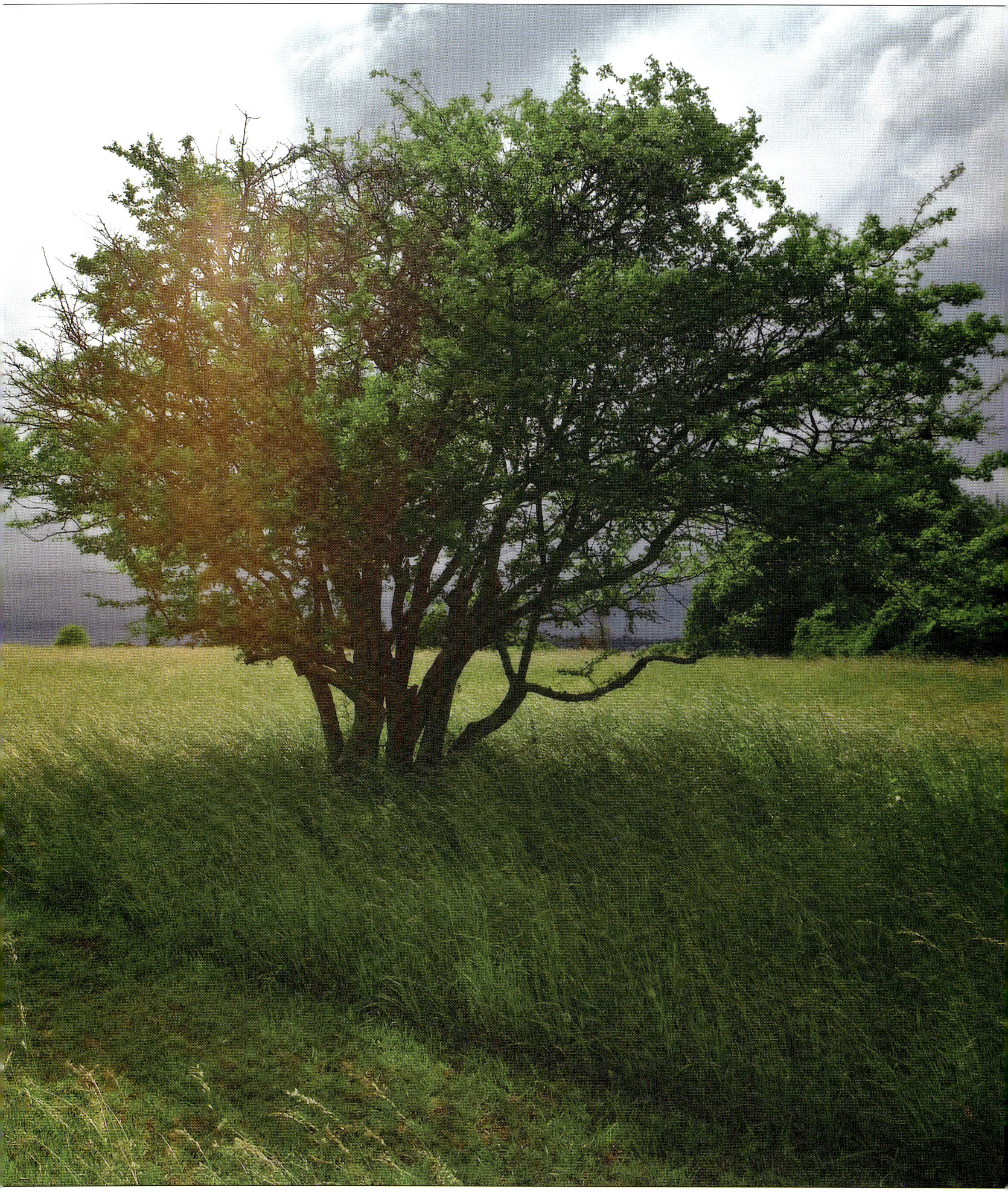

9. The Extended Workflow

Having direct control of the entire photographic workflow, from image capture to final printed output, is a luxury that many photographers do not have. At some point, images need to be handed over to members of the extended workflow, such as service providers, graphic designers, prepress shops, printers, or someone who will take responsibility for them—responsibility that is out of your immediate control.

What happens to your images at this point depends very much on your relationship with the person (or organization) to whom you have handed them. Clearly communicating your needs and expectations up-front is just as important as understanding the needs and expectations of the third party that you are depending on to provide the best-possible reproduction of your images. Knowing the color-management capabilities of a lab or service provider and clearly understanding how they need you to prepare your image

Figure 131—Tuscan hillside.

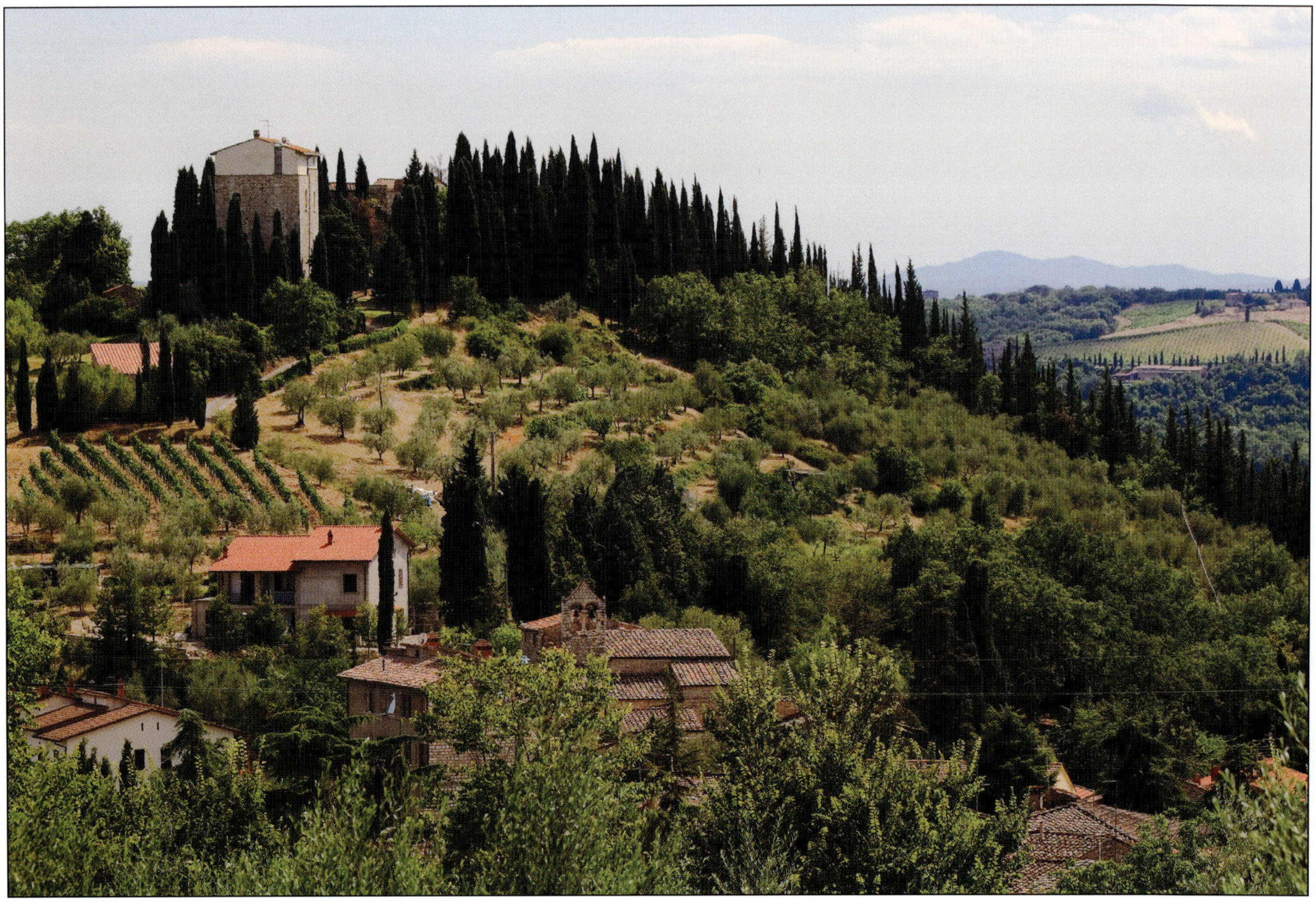

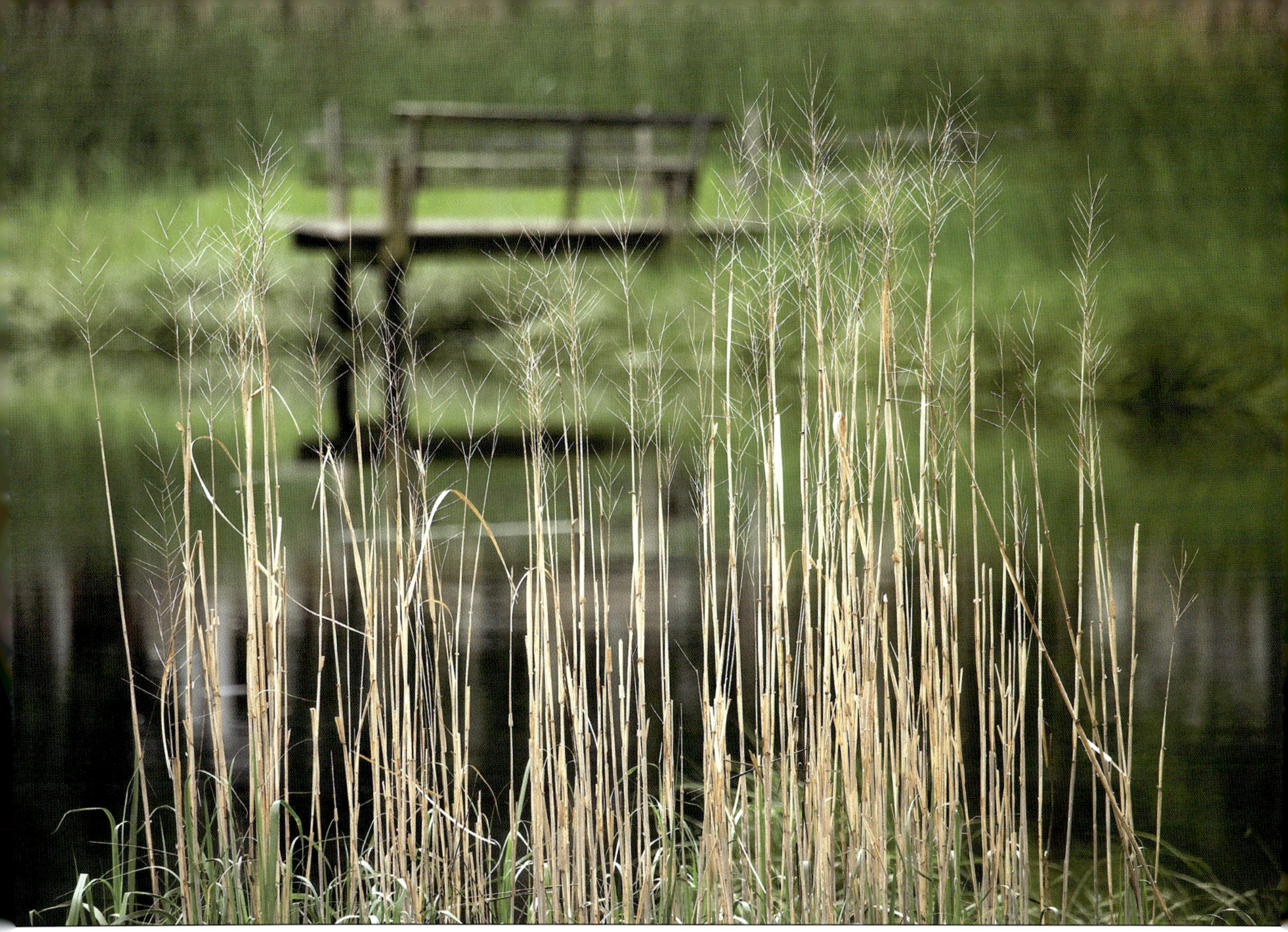

Figure 132—Riverbank. Old Lyme, CT.

files before delivery will help you ensure that they give you the best-possible results. Here is an example.

A wedding photographer, having just moved her business to a new location, decides to research digital labs where she can have her photographs printed. Usually her jobs require that she print hundreds of 4 x 6- or 5 x 7-inch prints for her clients. She processes her images on her computer to ensure that color and tone, among other things, are correct prior to turning the job over to the digital lab for final output. Accurate color is very important to her.

When interviewing the owner of the first lab she visits, she asks if they color manage their Fuji Frontier digital printer. The owner says that, yes, they do. All images are inspected by Frank, the Frontier operator, prior to being printed, and Frank makes the necessary color enhancements if needed. The photographer says that this is not exactly what she had in mind. She is wondering if they have an ICC color profile for the Frontier. The owner tells her not to worry—if she provides them with all of her images in sRGB, Frank will make sure that her printed images will look great. She tells him that she is going to interview a couple more labs and will get back to him.

The photographer's expectations are that the lab will support an extended color-managed workflow, one that will provide her an ICC color profile

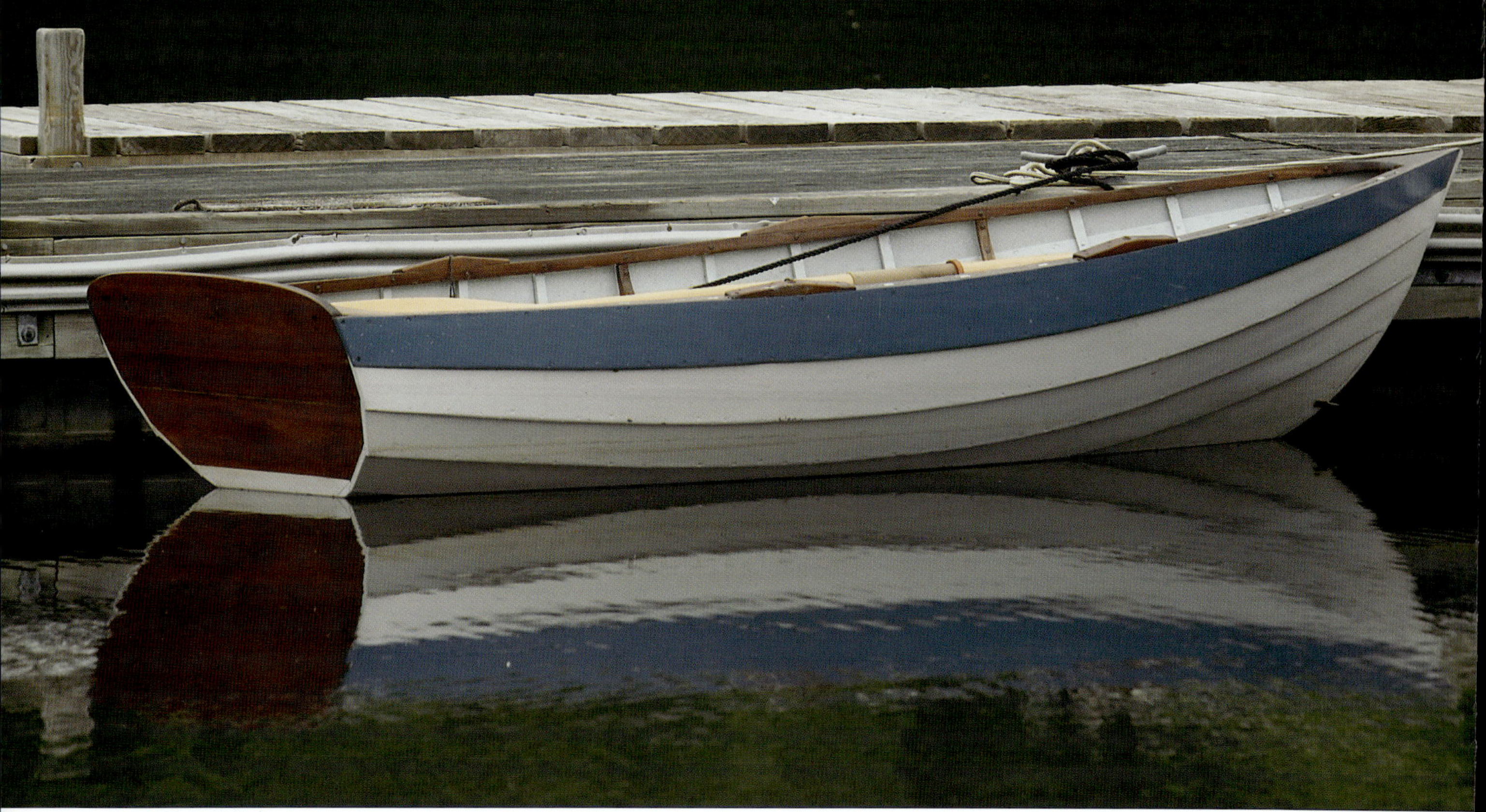

Figure 132—Dockside. Hamburg, CT.

for the device the lab will be outputting her images from. Even though Frank, the Fuji operator may have incredible color sense, she cannot rely on him to consistently deliver the color that she sees in her files on her studio computer. Having a color profile will allow her to soft-proof her photographs before delivery to the lab, which will give her a high level of confidence that the lab will match the color in her image files. She can run the color conversion in Photoshop, and when she delivers her files to the lab, they simply need to print them without anyone having to "color manage" them. She decides to look further until she finds a lab that provides this level of service, a lab that clearly understands her needs.

Working with Photo Labs

More and more labs are providing ICC profiles for their printing devices to better support the needs of photographers who are color-management savvy. Many of the labs providing large-format prints will post their profiles on their web site. Some, like Calypso Imaging (www.calypsoinc.com), will give a discount on prints if the photographer converts the photograph's color using their output profile prior to delivering the image to them. Calypso posts their ICC profiles on their web site for anyone to download.

Other services, like Dry Creek Photo (www.drycreekphoto.com), have created profiles for many labs across the United States, including hundreds of

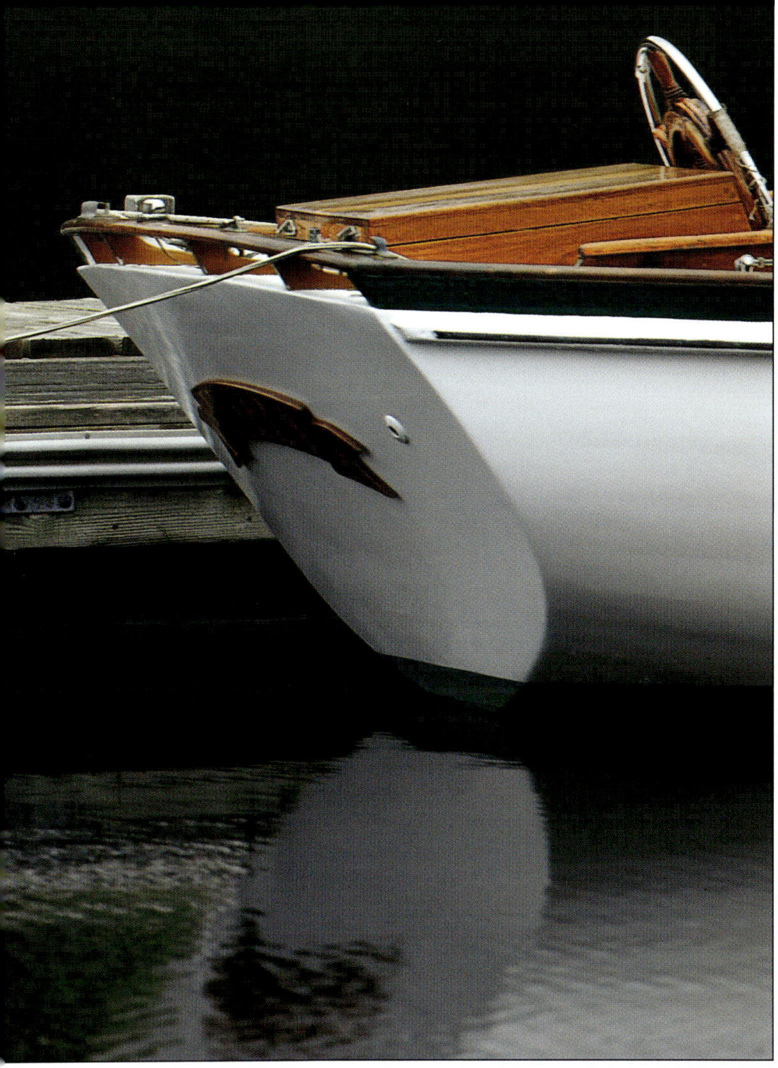

Costco stores. Downloading the ICC profile of the lab's output device makes it possible to soft-proof and to see how the output device will handle your photograph's color before you ever send your image to the lab.

Once the lab receives your converted file, they can send it straight to the printer without having to do a color conversion themselves. This saves them considerable time and helps them deliver color-accurate prints to their customers—it's a win–win situation for both the photographer and the lab.

Preparing Images for Clients

The need to clearly understand the expectations of a client when starting a project goes without saying. One aspect of the job that sometimes is overlooked when delivering digital files, however, is color handling. These days, it is necessary to ask what color space the client prefers and who is responsible for performing the color conversion—especially if the image is being printed using some form of CMYK output, which is typical. In some cases, the client will ask the photographer to deliver RGB files, and in others to convert the files to CMYK. Here are some rules of thumb that will help ensure that you meet your client's needs.

There is a low level of likelihood that the color they see in your RGB images will match on press.

Clarify the RGB Color Space. If the client asks for files in RGB, clarify what RGB color space you intend to deliver the file in. Adobe RGB (1998) is a safe haven if the client cannot specifically tell you what RGB color space they prefer. If the client (graphic designer, prepress shop, or printer) is intending to convert the image color for CMYK press output, make absolutely sure that they understand that there is a low level of likelihood that the color they see in your RGB images will match on press. Simply because most presses have a much smaller CMYK color space, they are not able to reproduce the highly saturated color that might exist in an RGB image. If the client does not understand this, they may think that the RGB images that you deliver represent what they will get out of the printing press. If this is the case, it would be safer to convince them to let you do the CMYK conversion and not let them see the RGB file at all. If this is not possible, provide some hard-proofs with the images output to a CMYK color space like U.S. Web Coated (SWOP) v2, or a space close to the color space of the press the job will be run on, so that the client can clearly see in advance that the color will be transformed on press.

Get an ICC Profile. If the client is intending to use your images solely for print, ask if they can provide you an ICC profile for the final output device that the job will be printed on. If the job is being printed on an offset press, there is a chance that they may be able to provide a profile. If the client does not understand color management, ask if they can put you in touch with the designer, prepress shop, or printer.

If the client is planning to use your images solely for print, and they cannot provide you a profile, but want you to convert your images to CMYK, convert to U.S. Web Coated (SWOP) v2. Just like Adobe RGB is a safe destination for RGB files, U.S. Web Coated (SWOP) v2 is a safe destination for CMYK files.

Web Images. If the client is intending to use your images solely for the web, provide your photographs in sRGB.

File Format. Deliver the image files as flattened, uncompressed TIFFs. Make sure you embed the profile when you save.

Converting and Embedding

Prior to delivering image files, make absolutely sure that each file has color definition, either by assigning a profile or by converting the image to a defined color space. If the recipient of the images is going to be converting the files, provide them in a source color space that is clearly defined. The best way to clearly define the color space of an image file is to embed the source ICC profile.

No matter who you might be delivering an image file to, it is always a good idea to embed the ICC color profile with the image prior to delivering it. The embedded profile defines the color space of the image so that whoever receives the file can accurately convert your image color for output. Whether you deliver the file in RGB or CMYK, make sure that the Embed Color Profile check box is selected in the Save As dialog box.

Figure 132—Morning Reservoir, Westport, CT.

Above all, the number-one priority when working with anyone who is a member of the extended workflow is good communication. Understanding their needs and making sure that they understand yours is the best way to ensure that your images will be reproduced with the best-possible quality.

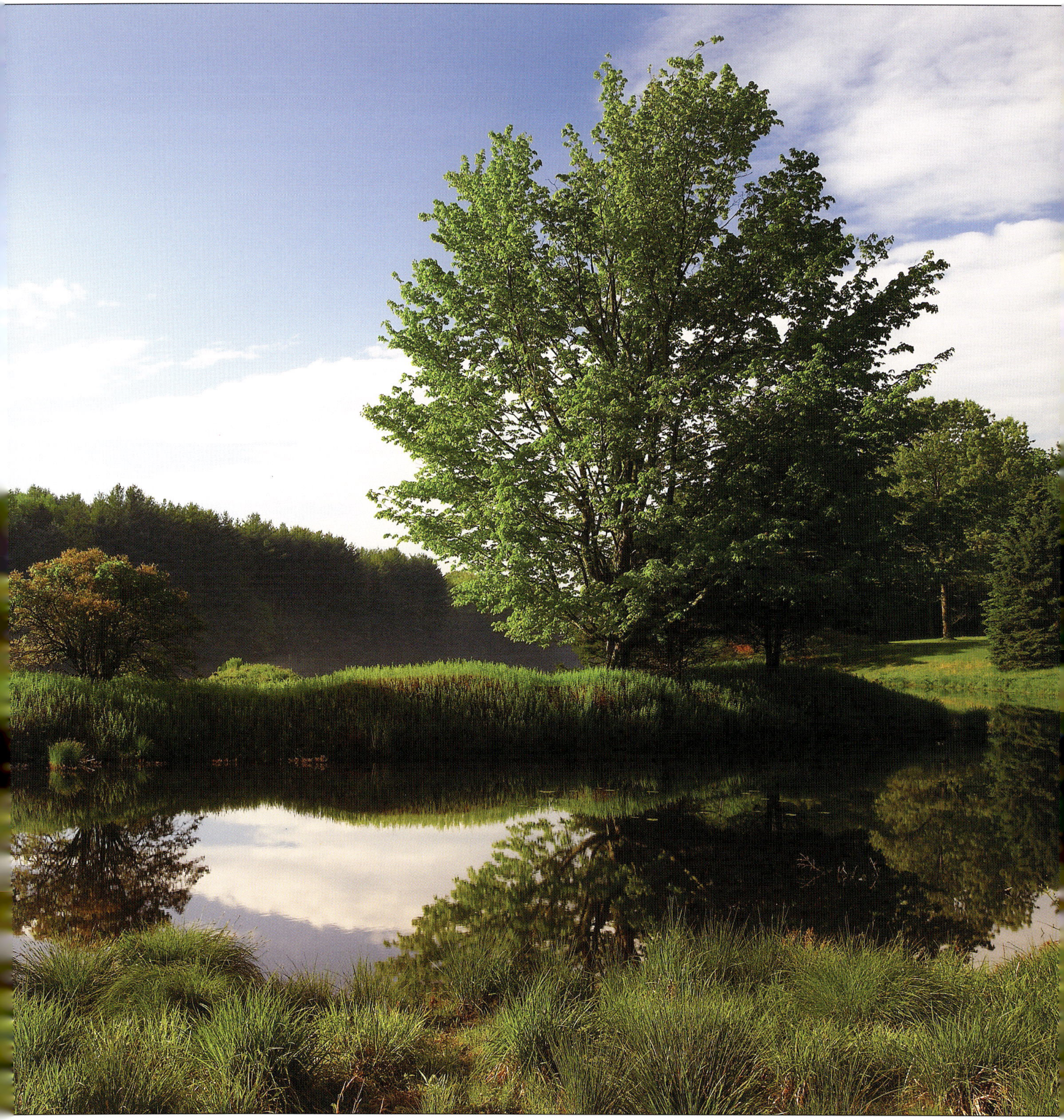

Web References

Adobe's Color Management User-to-User Forum: www.adobeforums.com

Chromaholics.com: www.chromaholics.com

Chromix.com: www.chromix.com

The International Color Consortium: www.color.org

International Standards Organization: www.iso.org *(look for ISO 3664)*

The Luminous Landscape: www.luminous-landscape.com

OpenRAW: www.openraw.org

Photoshop News: www.photoshopnews.com

Photoworkshop.com: www.photoworkshop.com

RawWorkflow.com: www.rawworkflow.com

Real World Color Management: www.colorremedies.com/realworldcolor/index.html

Rob Galbraith: www.robgalbraith.com

SWOP: www.swop.org *(for information on the SWOP publishing specification)*

X-Rite Color Services: www.graphintel.com

Index

OTHER BOOKS FROM

Amherst Media®

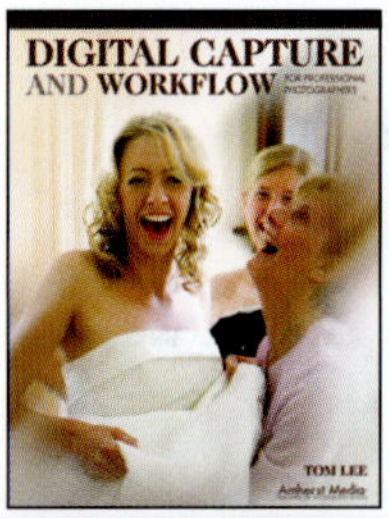

DIGITAL CAPTURE AND WORKFLOW

FOR PROFESSIONAL PHOTOGRAPHERS

Tom Lee

Cut your image-processing time by fine-tuning your workflow. Includes tips for working with Photoshop and Adobe Bridge, plus framing, matting, and more. $34.95 list, 8½x11, 128p, 150 color images, index, order no. 1835.

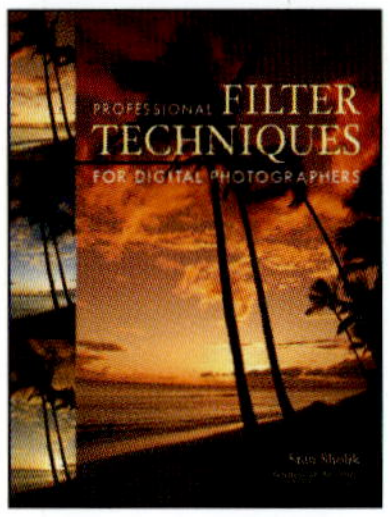

PROFESSIONAL FILTER TECHNIQUES

FOR DIGITAL PHOTOGRAPHERS

Stan Sholik

Select the best filter options for your photographic style and discover how their use will affect your images. $34.95 list, 8½x11, 128p, 150 color images, index, order no. 1831.

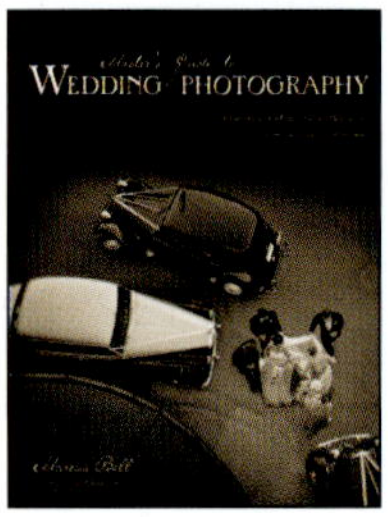

MASTER'S GUIDE TO WEDDING PHOTOGRAPHY

CAPTURING UNFORGETTABLE MOMENTS AND LASTING IMPRESSIONS

Marcus Bell

Learn to capture the unique energy and mood of each wedding and build a lifelong client relationship. $34.95 list, 8½x11, 128p, 200 color photos, index, order no. 1832.

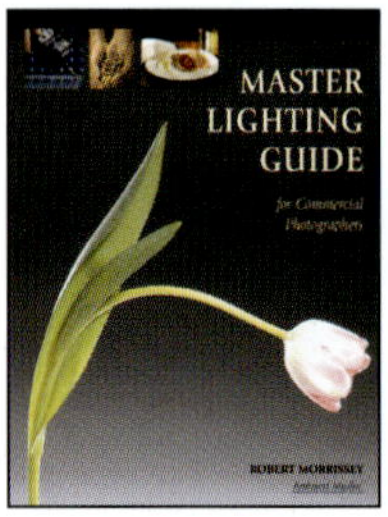

MASTER LIGHTING GUIDE

FOR COMMERCIAL PHOTOGRAPHERS

Robert Morrissey

Learn to use the tools and techniques the pros rely upon to land corporate clients. Includes diagrams, images, and text for a failsafe approach to creating shots that sell. $34.95 list, 8½x11, 128p, 110 color photos, 125 diagrams, index, order no. 1833.

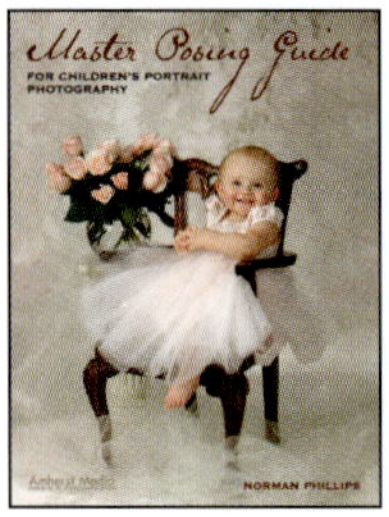

MASTER POSING GUIDE

FOR CHILDREN'S PORTRAIT PHOTOGRAPHY

Norman Phillips

Create perfect portraits of infants, tots, kids, and teens. Includes techniques for standing, sitting, and floor poses for boys and girls, individuals, and groups. $34.95 list, 8½x11, 128p, 305 color images, order no. 1826.

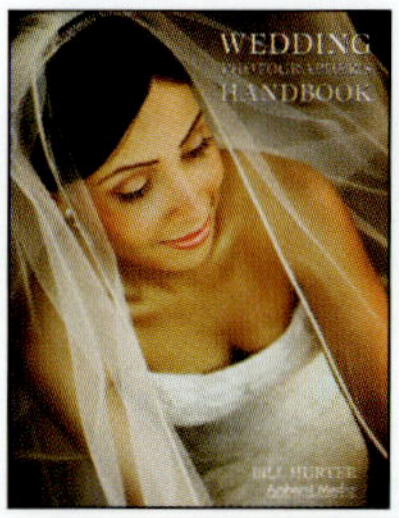

WEDDING PHOTOGRAPHER'S HANDBOOK

Bill Hurter

Learn to produce images with unprecedented technical proficiency and superb, unbridled artistry. Includes images and insights from top industry pros. $34.95 list, 8½x11, 128p, 180 color photos, 10 screen shots, index, order no. 1827.

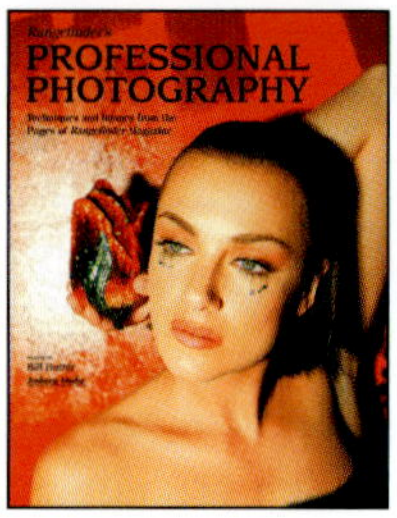

RANGEFINDER'S PROFESSIONAL PHOTOGRAPHY

edited by Bill Hurter

Editor Bill Hurter shares over one hundred "recipes" from *Rangefinder's* popular cookbook series, showing you how to shoot, pose, light, and edit fabulous images. $34.95 list, 8½x11, 128p, 150 color photos, index, order no. 1828.

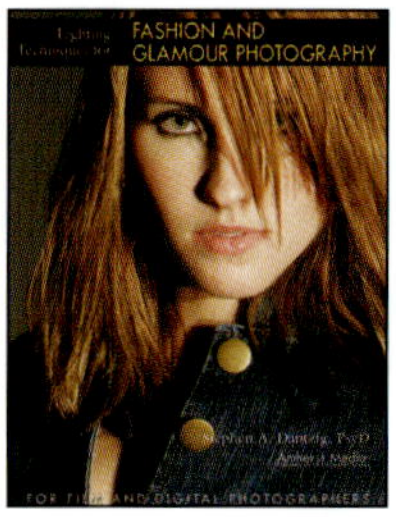

LIGHTING TECHNIQUES FOR FASHION AND GLAMOUR PHOTOGRAPHY

Stephen A. Dantzig, PsyD.

In fashion and glamour photography, light is the key to producing images with impact. With these techniques, you'll be primed for success! $29.95 list, 8½x11, 128p, over 200 color images, index, order no. 1795.

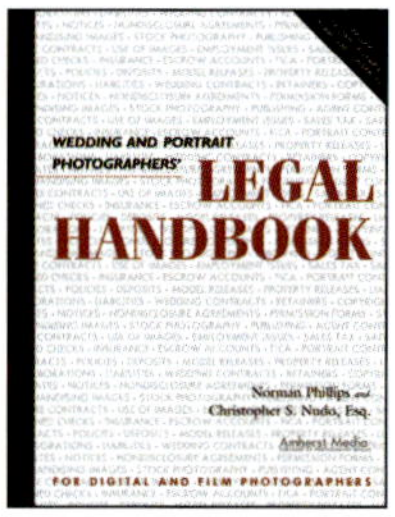

WEDDING AND PORTRAIT PHOTOGRAPHERS' LEGAL HANDBOOK

N. Phillips and C. Nudo, Esq.

Don't leave yourself exposed! Sample forms and practical discussions help you protect yourself and your business. $29.95 list, 8½x11, 128p, 25 sample forms, index, order no. 1796.

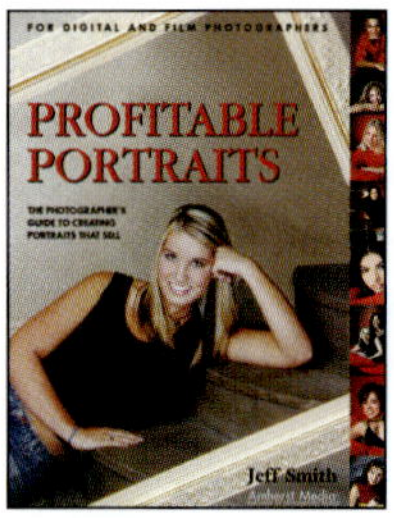

PROFITABLE PORTRAITS

THE PHOTOGRAPHER'S GUIDE TO CREATING PORTRAITS THAT SELL

Jeff Smith

Learn how to design images that are precisely tailored to your clients' tastes—portraits that will practically sell themselves! $29.95 list, 8½x11, 128p, 100 color photos, index, order no. 1797.

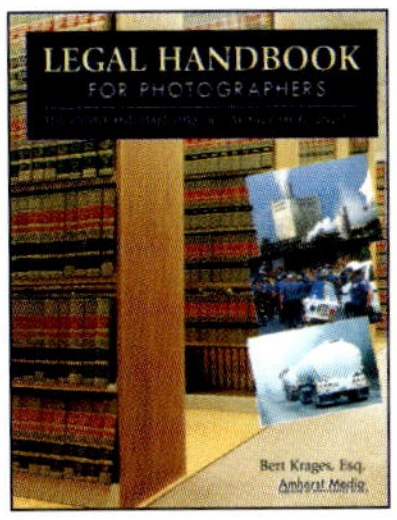

LEGAL HANDBOOK FOR PHOTOGRAPHERS, 2nd Ed.

Bert P. Krages, Esq.

Learn what you can and cannot photograph, how to handle conflicts should they arise, how to protect your rights to your images in the digital age, and more. $34.95 list, 8½x11, 128p, 80 b&w photos, index, order no. 1829.

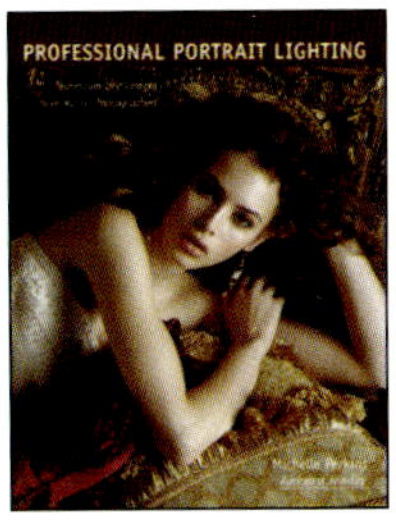

PROFESSIONAL PORTRAIT LIGHTING

TECHNIQUES AND IMAGES FROM MASTER PHOTOGRAPHERS

Michelle Perkins

Get a behind-the-scenes look at the lighting techniques employed by the world's top portrait photographers. $34.95 list, 8½x11, 128p, 200 color photos, index, order no. 2000.

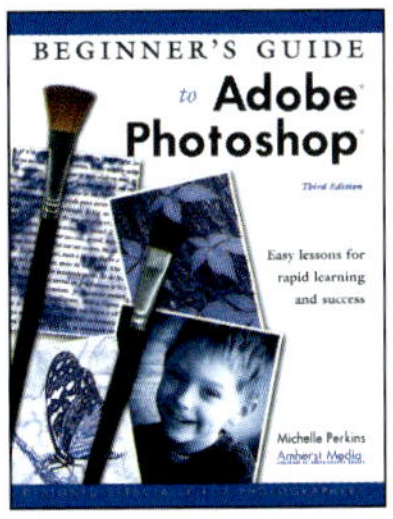

BEGINNER'S GUIDE TO ADOBE® PHOTOSHOP®, 3rd Ed.

Michelle Perkins

Enhance your photos, create original artwork, or add unique effects to any image. Topics are presented in short, easy-to-digest sections that will boost confidence and ensure outstanding images. $34.95 list, 8½x11, 128p, 80 color images, 120 screen shots, order no. 1823.

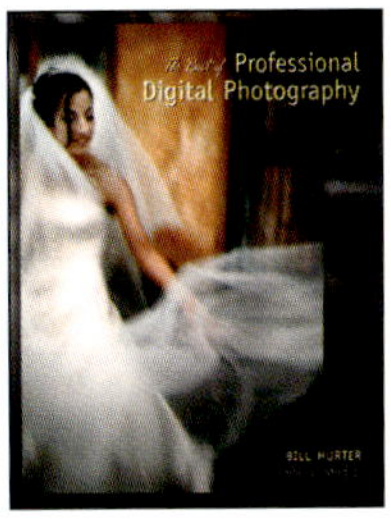

THE BEST OF PROFESSIONAL DIGITAL PHOTOGRAPHY

Bill Hurter

Digital imaging has a stronghold on the photographic industry. This book spotlights the methods that world-renowned photographers use to create their standout images. $34.95 list, 8½x11, 128p, 180 color photos, 20 screen shots, index, order no. 1824.

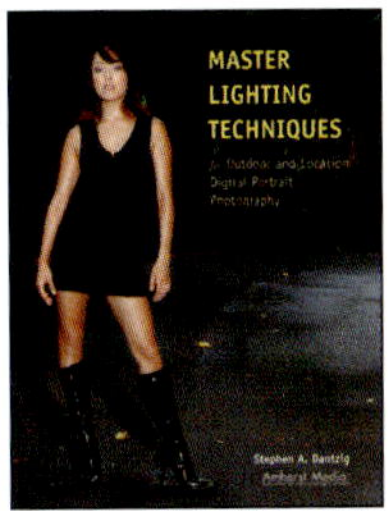

MASTER LIGHTING TECHNIQUES

FOR OUTDOOR AND LOCATION DIGITAL PORTRAIT PHOTOGRAPHY

Stephen A. Dantzig

Use natural light alone or with flash fill, barebulb, and strobes to shoot perfect portraits all day long. $34.95 list, 8½x11, 128p, 175 color photos, diagrams, index, order no. 1821.

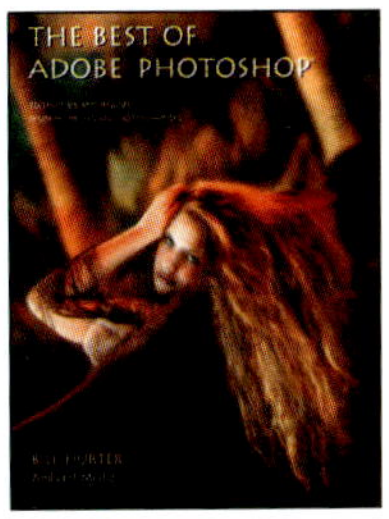

THE BEST OF ADOBE® PHOTOSHOP®

Bill Hurter

Rangefinder editor Bill Hurter calls on the industry's top photographers to share their strategies for using Photoshop to intensify and sculpt their images. No matter your specialty, you'll find inspiration here. $34.95 list, 8½x11, 128p, 170 color photos, 10 screen shots, index, order no. 1818.

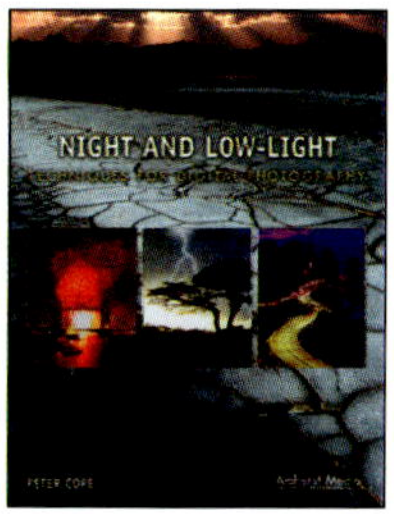

NIGHT AND LOW-LIGHT TECHNIQUES FOR DIGITAL PHOTOGRAPHY

Peter Cope

With even simple point-and-shoot digital cameras, you can create dazzling nighttime photos. Get started quickly with this step-by-step guide. $34.95 list, 8½x11, 128p, 100 color photos, index, order no. 1814.

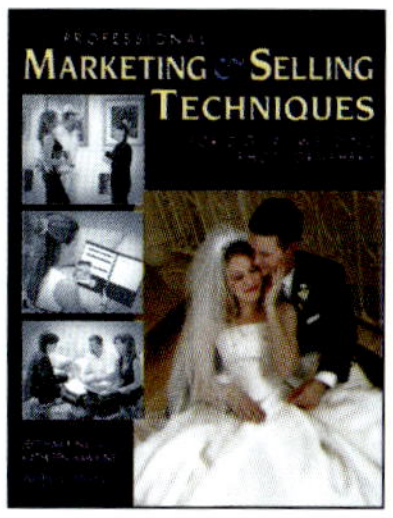

PROFESSIONAL MARKETING & SELLING TECHNIQUES

FOR DIGITAL WEDDING PHOTOGRAPHERS, SECOND EDITION

Jeff Hawkins and Kathleen Hawkins

Taking great photos isn't enough to ensure success! Become a master marketer and salesperson with these easy techniques. $34.95 list, 8½x11, 128p, 150 color photos, index, order no. 1815.

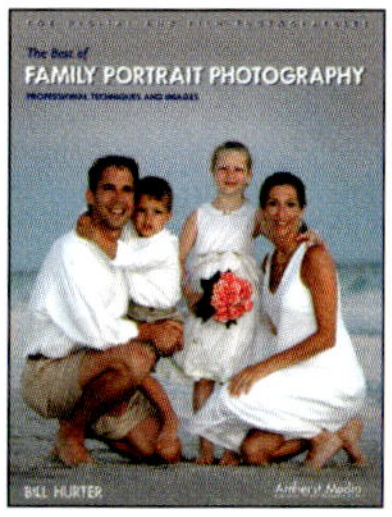

THE BEST OF FAMILY PORTRAIT PHOTOGRAPHY

Bill Hurter

Acclaimed photographers reveal the secrets behind their most successful family portraits. Packed with award-winning images and helpful techniques, this book will speed you on your way to success. $34.95 list, 8½x11, 128p, 150 color photos, index, order no. 1812.

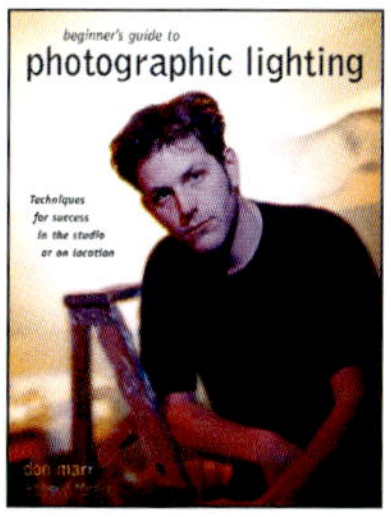

BEGINNER'S GUIDE TO PHOTOGRAPHIC LIGHTING

Don Marr

Learn how to create high-impact photographs of any subject with Marr's simple techniques. From edgy and dynamic to subdued and natural, this book will show you how to get the myriad effects you're after. $29.95 list, 8½x11, 128p, 150 color photos, index, order no. 1785.

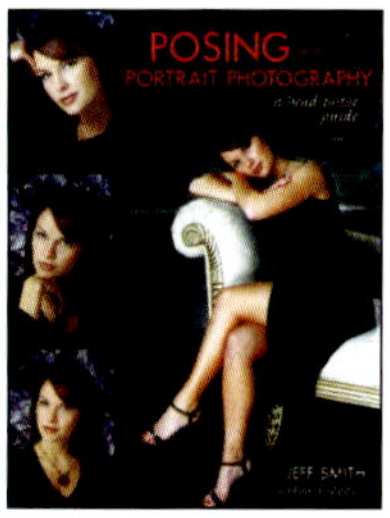

POSING FOR PORTRAIT PHOTOGRAPHY

A HEAD-TO-TOE GUIDE

Jeff Smith

Author Jeff Smith teaches you dozens of surefire techniques for fine-tuning every aspect of your subject's pose for the most flattering results. $29.95 list, 8½x11, 128p, 150 color photos, index, order no. 1786.

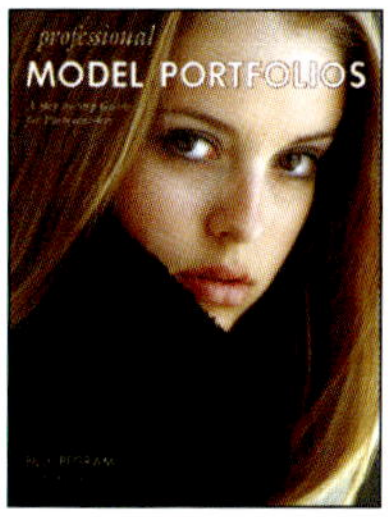

PROFESSIONAL MODEL PORTFOLIOS

A STEP-BY-STEP GUIDE FOR PHOTOGRAPHERS

Billy Pegram

Learn how to create dazzling portfolios that will get your clients noticed—and hired! Includes tips for lighting, posing, and much more. $29.95 list, 8½x11, 128p, 100 color images, index, order no. 1789.